Business Writing and Communication

Strategies and Applications

Harry M. Brown

Karen K. Reid

Midwestern State University

D. VAN NOSTRAND COMPANY
New York   Cincinnati   Toronto   London   Melbourne

D. Van Nostrand Company Regional Offices:
New York   Cincinnati

D. Van Nostrand Company International Offices:
London   Toronto   Melbourne

Copyright © 1979 by Litton Educational Publishing, Inc.
Library of Congress Catalog Card Number: 78-62190
ISBN: 0-442-20942-8

Published by D. Van Nostrand Company
135 West 50th Street, New York, N. Y. 10020

10 9 8 7 6 5 4 3 2 1

Preface

Business Writing and Communication: Strategies and Applications is designed to meet the needs of the basic business communication course. The book is equally suitable for employee development programs in industry or as a reference for anyone interested in communicating more effectively in business. Good business writing means shaping a message that evokes the desired response from the reader. What is it that makes a letter or memo most effective in eliciting this response? What strategies, style, and characteristics will best influence the reader? *Business Writing and Communication* answers these questions and stresses the development of a close relationship between the writer and reader.

The three most important qualities of business correspondence are clarity, appeal, and conciseness. The plan of this book is based on the development of these qualities, covering individual topics such as precision of information; forcefulness in writing; writing strategies; reader's interest and point of view; effective tone, tact, and wording; and proper attitude and psychological framework.

Specialized types of communication drawn from actual business situations are illustrated and analyzed. Included are guidelines, techniques, and models for adjustment claims, inquiries, credit checks, recommendations, collections, orders, confirmations, refusals, goodwill messages, announcements, congratulations, requests, replies, conciliations, and job applications. Problems and exercises in each unit require the student to write "on-the-job" letters. Strategies for oral communication are also provided. The Appendix is replete with checklists and glossaries of helpful information such as spacing, word division, spelling, punctuation, usage, abbreviation, forms of address, business terms, and model letters.

The structure of the book is flexible; the sections are complete in themselves and are not interdependent.

An Instructor's Manual is available which contains lecture suggestions and answers to questions in Part I.

We would like to extend our thanks to Stephanie Yaworski, Bowling Green State University; Kenneth Manko, DeKalb Community College; John Penrose, the University of Texas at Austin; and Elsie McClelland, the University of Indiana of Pennsylvania, for their valuable criticism in the preparation of the manuscript.

Contents

Part 1

The Basic Principles: Clarity and Character

1 The Double Message: The Total Message

The Effective Business Letter
Planning the Letter

THE EFFECTIVE BUSINESS LETTER

The business letter may be defined as a written message that tries to influence its reader to take some action or adopt some attitude desired by the writer. That is, the writer tries to get his or her reader to agree with the message of the letter. This attempt at agreement should always be part of the letter, whether the goal is immediate and tangible, such as the collecting of a bill, or whether it is an intangible attitude like goodwill. Any letter is judged by how successfully it gains agreement from the reader. The successful sales message gets its reader to agree that a product or service is worth buying. The effective collection letter convinces the debtor that payment of the bill is the wisest policy. The convincing application letter makes the prospective employer agree that the applicant is highly desirable for the job.

But what makes a business communication effective? How do you get the reader to agree with your message? The first thing you must remember is that a written business communication has a double message. Its reader gets meaning from *what* is said and from how it is said. The primary message is the information, the factual material presented. The secondary message is the manner in which the letter delivers the message.

The combination of the two messages is the *total message*, which is like a face-to-face conversation. A person's tone of voice, way of speaking, the urgency or calmness of his voice, the frown or smile on his face, the glint in his eye, all tell something beyond what words say. Sometimes the secondary message reinforces the words; sometimes it contradicts. A severe contradiction can cancel the verbal message, and the manner becomes the primary message. "I hear what you are (or mean), not what you say."

These two messages are called the *informative message* and the *character message*. Why is it important to keep these two messages in mind? Because with the business letter we are trying to evoke a certain response from the reader. We must make sure that both the clarity of the letter (*what* the letter says) and the character (*how* the letter says it) help to bring about that response. Since a business letter is written for a specific purpose, its message cannot be neutral. It will work either for you or against you. Give attention to clarity and character, and you can make them work for you.

Let's see how clarity and character work, or fail to work, in a letter.

Clarity

Assume that you are a customer service correspondent in the home office of Auto General, Inc. Recently you have had several complaints from customers (managers of retail auto parts stores) that checks due them for exchange parts (brake shoes and generators, for example) and returned merchandise are slow in reaching them. They say your competitors are much faster. You alert your supervisor, and he decides that each district office of Auto General should prepare its own refund checks so that customers will get them sooner. He writes the following memo to the district managers telling them about the new procedures.

To: All District Managers   Date: April 17, 1978

From: B. D. Collins

Subject: Refunds

Effective May 1 and thereafter issue all checks for any amount written out to customers for exchange parts and for returned merchandise from your office directly to the customer without having to go through the home office.

We feel that this plan and procedure will not only help to improve customer relations substantially but will also close the gap on one of the important areas where our company compares unfavorably with other companies in its contacts with customers.

However, you may or may not find in your previous or committed routine that this is feasible. This new practice may be too time-consuming. Comment on same at the bottom of this memo and return it to me. Please do this by return mail, as we hope to effectuate this new procedure immediately. Thank you for your cooperation.

You can easily see that the message is garbled. It is clumsy, wordy, and hard to read. The managers will finally be able to figure it out, after "crawling" through "underbrush" and "deadwood."

See how you like a revised version—direct, brief, essential, and cordial.

```
To:  All District Managers        Date: April 17, 1978

From:  B. D. Collins

Subject:  Refunds


     Beginning May 1, please send all checks for
exchange parts and returned merchandise to customers
directly from your office.  This procedure should
speed up the process and get rid of the complaints
we've had from some of our customers.

     The idea should work; let's give it a try.
Let me know if you run into any problems.
```

In another message clarity fails, and the recipient can do nothing. The writer neglected to give the address of the new warehouse. More communication is necessary.

```
        S P R I N G   A P P L I A N C E   C O .
        Colorado Springs, Colorado 80901



                                      March 20, 1978


        The Yale Manufacturing Co.
        3120 Railway Street
        New Haven, Connecticut 06510

        Gentlemen:

            This is to confirm the telephone order I placed this
        afternoon for the following:

            3 Alaskan King refrigerators, model 250K

            These refrigerators are to be delivered in three weeks.
        But please deliver them not to our main store as usual,
        but to the new warehouse.

                                      Sincerely,

                                      Ralph Keating

                                      Ralph Keating
```

Character

Information can be complete and clear in a business letter, and the message will still fail because it lacks *character*. The following letter is clear enough: the company is sending the latest catalog. But how dull! The recipient is likely to lay the catalog aside without making a purchase.

```
Dear Mr. Taylor:

    With reference to yours of recent date would
state that we are enclosing herewith our latest
sales prospectus.  Should the need arise for any
of our parts, we will be very glad to fill your
order for same.

                    Very truly yours,
```

With a little thought and concern for the reader, the writer could have added positive character to the informative message.

```
Dear Mr. Taylor:

    Here is the latest catalogue of United parts
and equipment, as you requested.  Please note that
you, as a new customer, will receive a 10% discount
on your first order.  Whenever you do wish to place
an order, you can count on our usual promptness at
filling it.

                    Sincerely,
```

It is reader directed. Besides using the other-directed pronouns "you" and "your" five times (against only one use of the self-centered pronouns "I" and "we"), the letter points out two direct benefits to the reader—discount and prompt delivery. The reader is likely to feel warm toward the company and its products.

Again, in the following letter the informative message is clear enough, but the tone is insulting. There probably will be no more business from that customer.

```
Dear Mrs. Walters:

    Because you delayed so long in your response,
Model GSF is out of stock.  If you are interested,
we have some similar models on hand.

                    Yours truly,
```

The accusation "you delayed" and the discourteous indifference of the last sentence will likely cause Mrs. Walters to crumple the letter and throw it into the wastebasket. Some reader interest and a positive alternative could add the tone that might produce a sale and a satisfied customer.

```
Dear Mrs. Walters:

    If I had known your needs before May 20, I
could have shipped Model GSF immediately.  However,
the spring sale drained our stock.

    The Model GSK, a similar instrument, is in stock,
and you could have it at the same price as the GSF.
It normally sells for $10.00 more.  We will ship it
as soon as you give us the word.

                    Sincerely,
```

This letter is successful. It works for the company because its total message is positive.

PLANNING THE BUSINESS LETTER

How do you achieve the positive total message that has both clarity and character? As we have been demonstrating, a successful business letter is the result of careful thought and of concern for the reader. Before beginning to write, the writer must ask two questions:

1. What are my objectives?
2. How can I best accomplish my objectives?

Defining Objectives

Just what are you trying to accomplish in this letter? It is fairly easy to list the general purposes for which all business letters are written.

1. To supply information
2. To get action
3. To build goodwill

We usually think of business letters by types, such as collection, adjustment, order, claim, credit, and sales. But one or more of the three purposes—information, action, goodwill—will form the framework. A response to an inquiry is mostly informative. A collection letter wants mostly action. A response to a complaint wants mostly goodwill. A refusal of credit wants to furnish information and also to build goodwill. Goodwill is almost always present.

But beyond these general purposes and letter types, you must determine exactly what your objectives are in each particular letter. Do you want to apologize? Do you want to say "no"? Do you want to explain a blunder? Do you want to make the customer happy? Do you want to offer an alternate purchase plan or piece of merchandise? Clarify your specific objectives, and jot them down in the order in which you want to deal with them. Then you can deal with them—effectively.

Look at the following two letters, written for the same situation. Which message shows careful planning? Which writer figures out exactly what he or she wanted to accomplish?

```
Dear Sir:

We cannot fill your order of February 10 for 12
dozen men's shirts to retail at $5.50 because we
are no longer manufacturing them.  We have gone
into the production of more expensive shirts for
men.  In the event that you need any of these, we
will be glad to serve you.

                    Yours truly,
```

Dear Mr. Turner:

We regret that we cannot fill your order of February
10 for 12 dozen men's shirts to retail at $5.50.

We have found that men are demanding a shirt that will
wear longer and look better than those that can be
made to sell at $5.50.

In order to meet this demand, we have designed "The
Esquire," a genuine broadcloth, preshrunk shirt to
sell at $8.50. These shirts will give you, the
dealer, a larger margin of profit; they will enable
you to take advantage of our national advertising
campaign which features "The Esquire"; they will
help to convince your customers that your store
carries quality merchandise.

The enclosed post card lists the wholesale prices
for "The Esquire." If you will sign and mail it
today, a supply of these high-quality shirts will
reach you within a week to bring you added profit
and satisfied customers.

                                    Sincerely yours,

The first writer does not show the slightest sign that he thought about what his letter ought to do. He is just answering a letter, getting a job off his back. A routine, thoughtless person—he stops with the refusal of the order.

The second writer has thought out what she wants her letter to do. She wants to refuse an order for $5.50 shirts (she has to), but she has clarified several of her objectives:

1. To keep the customer's goodwill
2. To explain reasonably why the order can't be filled
3. To sell higher priced shirts
4. To make it easy for the customer to reorder the higher priced shirts

After determining those objectives, the writer can then go ahead and consider the next step: How to accomplish those objectives and produce an effective letter.

Accomplishing the Objectives

What will make your letter most effective in getting your reader to do what you want him or her to do? What techniques, devices, styles, and characteristics will most influence your reader? As you can see, the real answer leads to the reader. You can gain your objective only through him or her. So we must look at those basic qualities that make a business letter successful—its clarity and its character. They make up the total message and determine what the reader will do about your letter. What makes a letter clear? What gives it an appealing character?

Clarity is a product of three things—precise format, precise information, and precise wording. *Character* is more complex. It is a product of five qualities or techniques: the three precisions of clarity, effective words and sentence structure, the you attitude, tone, and specialized technique. Let's define the five qualities briefly to see what is ahead for us.

1. *Precision*—the care with details that produces clarity (format, information, and wording) influences the reader's attitude.
2. *Effective words and sentences*—the total selection of words and phrases and how they are put together.
3. *The you attitude*—the reader's point of view. It emphasizes his interests, motives, and benefits.
4. *Tone*—the quality that, like the warmth of the sun, can't be seen but certainly can be felt—a product of tact, sincerity, and positiveness.
5. *Specialized techniques*—methods adapted for a particular purpose and kind of letter. Thus a bad-news letter like a refusal of credit uses a technique different from that of a good-news letter like an announcement of a promotion.

The principles and applications of precision, effectiveness of word and sentence, the you attitude, and tone are examined in the early chapters of this book. Chapter 2 deals with format. Chapter 3 discusses precision of information. Chapters 4 and 5 present techniques for precise and forceful words and sentences. Chapter 6 describes the you attitude. The three qualities of tone—tact, sincerity, and positiveness—are handled in Chapter 7. These qualities of precision, effective wording, the you attitude, and proper tone are essential to all kinds of letters. The later chapters of the book consider specific kinds of communication with specialized techniques for each.

EXERCISES

1. Rewrite the following statements to make them clear. Be direct, brief, natural, and friendly.

   a. It is apparent and obvious, therefore, that sound knowledge of letter composition and cultivation of the accurate thinking by which it must be accompanied should constitute an exceedingly worthwhile achievement.

b. Verification that functional requirements of products are satisfied at minimal cost is established by design value reviews prior to final engineering release.

c. It has been found that a number of business decisions are capable of easier resolution as a consequence of advance cost estimates.

d. There are those among the top management groups who would inject more incentive into pay practices by gearing increases to differences in performance.

e. The two most important considerations in determining the global communications system or systems that will be most appropriate for a given organization are speed and cost.

f. We are making this analysis for the purpose of providing a basis for improving the sales picture in the months to come.

g. I have your letter of August 9 before me and am happy to tell you that we will be able to completely outfit you in the uniforms you want in the colors and sizes you requested in your letter.

h. Do you think it would be possible for you to engage the King's Room for our use as the meeting place of our task force on July 8?

i. It is the consensus of opinion of the Labor Personnel Relations Board that work stoppages would decrease impressively and substantially if the equipment were kept in constant and complete repair and working order.

j. District supervisors held a meeting for the purpose of discussing the distribution of sales territories in the various geographical areas.

2. Mr. Holloway, a furniture dealer and longtime customer, has ordered a red maple coffee table that can't be delivered because the line—Colliers—has been discontinued. He was sent this blunt, clear note.

```
        Dear Mr. Holloway:

        We can't fill your order and are
        therefore cancelling it.  Sorry.

                        Sincerely,
```

But the writer violated the principle of character. Mr. Holloway is entitled to better treatment. At the very least, he deserves to be told "why." The writer has also passed up the opportunity to keep the customer's goodwill and thus keep the customer. Rewrite the letter. Objectives should be clear:

a. Cancel the order (but courteously).
b. Keep Mr. Holloway's goodwill.

    c. Provide an explanation.

    d. Offer Mr. Holloway a reasonable alternative. (He does want a coffee table.)

3. The following memo is hard to read. Rewrite it to make it clear. You may have to change words and reorganize the ideas. But make the message clear.

To: All personnel   Date: May 19, 1978

From: Emily Hoggard

Subject: Interoffice mail

Interoffice envelopes are provided to all departments by the mail room. If you have a shortage of these envelopes, they can be obtained from Miss Tillich.

Because of the excessive cost of using envelopes designed for purposes other than interoffice mail (letter envelopes, etc.), it is requested that interoffice envelopes be used whenever practical.

---

4. Assume that you are the assistant vice-president of Arrow, Inc., a large manufacturer of sporting goods. Write a brief memorandum (under 150 words) to your staff (the department heads, junior executives, and clerical help) stressing the importance of the communications they write. It has been brought to your attention that some badly written messages have been sent out lately. You want to keep the memo brief and general to avoid sounding like a preacher, but you want to get the message across. Observe the principles of the "double message."

5. You have gone to work for Valley View Resort Hotel in High Ridge, Colorado, as a customer-relations expert. The manager has asked you to prepare a promotion letter to be sent in early January to each guest of the previous summer at Valley View. Your idea objectives are:

    a. To thank the guests for patronizing Valley View and to make resort facilities available to them.

    b. To mention the new facilities that the resort will be able to offer next summer—sauna baths, a tennis pro and a golf pro, color television in every room, and a delicious Sunday brunch—with no increase in rates.

    c. To state that the hotel looks forward to serving the guest next summer.

6. What is wrong with the following letter? List what the objectives should be in such a letter. What principles of character have been violated? What is likely to be the reader's total reaction to the letter?

Dear Mr. Watson:

Your claim for reimbursement under the terms of our insurance contract has been rejected. Here's why:

As stated in your policy, Section III., item 4, the policy holder is under obligation to report to police when articles are stolen from their automobiles. Also, they should file claims within five days. This you have not done. We trust that you can understand why you are not being reimbursed for the CB radio you say was "lifted" from your automobile.

Sincerely,

J.B. Benton
Claims Consultant

---

7. Point out the qualities in this letter that make it effective.

Dear Dr. Alexander:

Yes, I am pleased to accept your invitation to speak at your Careers Day program on March 18. Since the talk will be illustrated with slides, I will bring my projector. Could you please arrange to have a screen in the room? The entire presentation will take about half an hour. As you suggested, we will meet in room 20 of the Student Union at 1:30 on March 18.

Sincerely yours,

Jane Bennett
Jane Bennett

---

2 The Format: No Margin for Error

Basic Formats
Essential Parts
Special Features
Other Marks of Physical Precision
Format of a Memorandum

Physical appearance is important. Tests have shown that a well dressed, clean-cut stranger gets better treatment than a poorly dressed, sloppy person does. In an experiment the investigator dressed well, asked strangers for directions, and almost always received courteous, helpful treatment. Then, poorly dressed and unkempt, he again asked people for directions and almost always received curt, suspicious treatment.

People react the same way to the appearance of a business letter. They will judge you and your message by the physical appearance of the letter. A peculiar-looking letter suggests something peculiar about the writer. A sloppy letter—one with smudges, erasures, cross-outs, and errors—is like the unkempt stranger, not to be given serious consideration.

A neat, attractive format contributes to the positive character of your message. Such a format indicates that the company is well managed, does work of high quality, and cares about the sensitivities of its readers. Attractive, proper appearance is effective communication. Effective communication is good business. This chapter gives a rundown of the essentials of appropriate letter style and format.

BASIC FORMATS

Business letters usually have one of the following styles.

Blocked or Modified Block

The blocked form is the form most frequently used. The paragraphs are not indented. Date, complimentary close, and signature begin near the center of the page. All other parts—the inside address, the salutation, the body, and any notations—are blocked flush with the left margin. (See Figure 2-1.)

Semiblocked

Semiblocked form is the same as blocked style except that the paragraphs are indented. It is a popular style. (See Figure 2-2.)

Full Blocked

Full blocked form starts all parts of the letter (except letterhead) flush with the left margin. This is a fast style to type because there is less carriage movement. (See Figure 2-3.)

Simplified

In the simplified style recommended by the Administrative Management Society, the salutation and the complimentary close are eliminated. A subject line is used, but the word "subject" is omitted, and the subject line is typed in capitals. Suggested as a time-saver, the simplified style has not caught on because it sacrifices the personalized touch. (See Figure 2-4.)

Hanging Indentation

This style is not used for routine business correspondence. It is a distinctive style for sales or advertising letters in which you want to emphasize the first words of each paragraph.

The first line of each paragraph begins flush with the left margin. The other lines are indented five spaces. (See Figure 2-5.)

Novelty is allowed with this format. For instance, instead of the inside address you may use a sales blurb that takes the same form as the inside address.

```
        Furniture Bargains
        Are Great Now
        At The Home Market
```

N A T I O N A L   I N D U S T R I E S ,   I N C .

3800 East Elm Street   Des Moines, Iowa 50328

May 10, 1978

Mr. Ralph Cannon, Sales Manager
Tri-State Farm Equipment
  Company, Inc.
278 River Drive
Shreveport, Louisiana 71104

Dear Mr. Thompson:

This letter is in blocked form, the most frequently used in
business. All parts except the date, complimentary close,
and signature begin at the left margin. These last three
elements begin about the center of the page.

Besides the blocked form, this letter illustrates several
other features common to many letters. Because this letter
uses mixed punctuation, the only end-of-line punctuation
is the colon after the salutation and the comma after the
complimentary inside address, except after an abbreviation;
for instance, "Inc." Internal punctuation is used, such as
the comma after the city and between Cannon and his title.

In the inside address an unusually long title or company
name (as shown here) may occupy two lines; the part carried
to the second line is indented two spaces. In the signature
block, the signer's title may be typed on the line below his
name; or it can be split and typed on two lines.

The term "Enclosures 2" in the reference section shows that
two additional items are being enclosed in the envelope. It
could have been abbreviated "Encl. 2." The notation "cc"
indicates that a carbon copy is being sent to Mr. Terry Bell.

                              Sincerely,

                              Morton Weller

                              Morton Weller, Manager
                              Credit Department

MW:mb
Enclosures 2
cc: Mr. Terry Bell

Figure 2-1 Blocked letter (standard spacings and mixed punctuation)

B E L L I N G H A M   F U R N I T U R E   C O .
3947 N·Street N.W.
Washington, D.C. 20012

November 14, 1978

Credit Department
General Range, Inc.
302 Trimble Street
Lansing, Michigan 48921

Attention: Mr. Samuels

Gentlemen:

The semiblocked form is the same as the blocked except
that the paragraphs are indented five or more spaces.

This model letter illustrates other features common to
many letters.

The attention line here is at the left margin, two lines
below the inside address, and underlined. It need not be
underlined, and in semiblocked form it could be indented with
the paragraphs. It could also have been centered and typed
in all capital letters without underscoring. If you wanted
Mr. Samuels' name in the salutation, you would type his first
name (or two initials) and his surname above Credit Department.
Then you would omit the attention line and use "Dear Mr.
Samuels" in the salutation.

An enclosure notation is usually abbreviated "Encl." and
the specific item may be indicated--"Check."

Very truly yours,

William Hemphill

William Hemphill
Purchasing Agent

WH:hb
Encl.--Check

Figure 2-2 Semi-blocked

THE VAN HEUSEN COMPANY · 190 MADISON AVENUE · NEW YORK, NEW YORK   10016

Mr. Benjamin Crandell
President
Commercial Analysts, Inc.
1297 North Avenue
Plainfield, New Jersey 02001

Dear Mr. Crandell

In this full blocked letter, all parts begin at the left margin.
You gain speed through less carriage movement.

This letter also illustrates other features of standard letters.
Open punctuation is used here; many firms prefer open punctuation
with full blocked form. Punctuation after the salutation, the
complimentary close, and abbreviations such as that for "Enclosure"
are omitted.

If the letter writer used a "we" point of view instead of "I"
in the letter, as here, the writer's company name is usually
typed in.

Other accepted forms of reference initials could, of course,
be used with this letter style. Also the "Registered Mail"
or other special services (such as special delivery) notations
could be typed in full capitals two lines below the date instead
of under the reference initials.

Sincerely yours

THE VAN HEUSEN COMPANY

Jean Mitler

Jean Mitler, Manager
Advertising Department

JM/mh
Enclosure

Registered mail

Figure 2-3 Full blocked

M I D W E S T   D E V E L O P M E N T   C O M P A N Y

85 St. Joseph Street * Sioux Falls, South Dakota 57101

February 27, 1978

Miss Angie Turner
River Real Estate
246 Polymer Circle
Billings, Montana 59107

FORMAT FOR SIMPLIFIED LETTER

The simplified letter form, Miss Turner, has been recommended
by the Administrative Management Society as a time saver in
typing business letters. The format saves about 19 key strokes.
Here are its features:

1. Full blocked form.

2. Open punctuation.

3. Omission of salutation and complimentary close, but to
    personalize, the reader's name is used at least in the
    first sentence.

4. Subject line in all capitals and omits the word "subject."

5. Signer's name and business title typed in all capitals.

6. Typist's initials and other references typed below signer's
    name.

The simplified form does save time, Miss Turner, but it has not
caught on very well.

Timothy Davis

TIMOTHY DAVIS--PERSONNEL DIRECTOR

bh
Enc 3
Messrs. Mike Jones, Carl Worley

Figure 2-4 Simplified

BILLINGS OUTFITTERS
_____ 2800 TEDFORD STREET
                    /_____ DAYTON, OHIO 45409
                                       /_____

                        June 20, 1978

Mr. Thomas Harding
270 Oak Lane
Dayton, Ohio 45409

Dear Mr. Harding:

The hanging indentation letter is used in sales and
    promotion letters. It is usually not suitable
    for routine business correspondence.

The first line of each paragraph begins flush left
    and the other lines are indented five spaces.
    The value of the format is to make key items
    stand out and still give the tone of a
    personalized letter.

Complimentary close and signature begin about the
    center as in the blocked form. Reference
    notations also follow the blocked form, placed
    even with the left margin. You may use either
    mixed or open punctuation.

                        Cordially yours,

                        John Billings

                        John Billings
                        General Manager

JB/tr

Figure 2-5 Hanging Indentation

ESSENTIAL PARTS

The standard business letter has seven parts.

1. Heading (or letterhead and date)
2. Inside address
3. Salutation
4. Body
5. Complimentary close
6. Signature
7. Identification line

The letter in Figure 2-1 illustrates these seven parts.

Heading

The heading is usually the company letterhead, showing name and address. The date is placed at least two spaces below the letterhead.

   If a printed letterhead is not available, the complete address and date (but not the name of the company) are typed in the upper right-hand part of the letter sheet, with at least an inch margin at the top and to the right.

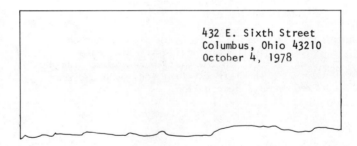

Inside Address

The inside address includes the name and address of the firm or individual to whom the letter is addressed. It is placed at the left-hand side of the sheet, at least two spaces below the heading. The inside address must occupy at least three lines. If the individual or firm has no street address, type the city and state on separate lines. The exact position of the inside address depends on the length of the letter and the size of the sheet. The margins of the letter are adjusted, according to the length of the letter, to give a picture frame effect. Here is an example of spacing for the inside address, date, and letterhead.

```
///////////////////////////////////////////
/////////////// LETTERHEAD //////////////
///////////////////////////////////////////


                                    //// DATE ////


Modern Interiors, Inc.
5 West 38 Street
Cincinnati, Ohio 45221
```

No matter what style is used in typing a business letter, such words as "Mr.," "Mrs.," "Miss," "Ms.," "Dr.," "Dean," and "General" must always appear before the name. When the person addressed has an official title, this should appear after the name, either next to it or on the following line. Such titles are gestures of ordinary courtesy and are justifiably expected.

The movement to end discrimination against and among women has caused some people to address all women as "Ms." If you have reason to believe that your reader will be pleased by that form of address, use it. At the same time, remember that some women can be offended if the conventional titles of "Miss" and "Mrs." are not used, believing that "Ms." is a cheap, token substitute for genuine feelings and actions of equality.

Here are examples of the proper forms of inside address:

an individual	Mr. Frank Strong 2980 Longview Road Fond du Lac, Wisconsin 54935
several individuals	Messrs. John Ellis and Fred Wilson 340 Bayou Street Monroe, Louisiana 71201 Dr. and Mrs. Bruce Aikens 983 Seventh Avenue Springfield, Illinois 62702

an individual	Mr. George Russell, Director
with a title	Public Relations
	Warmer-Thompkins Company
	210 Tracy Avenue
	Spokane, Washington 99202
	Mrs. Ann Meadows
	Director of Public Relations
	Marine Supplies, Inc.
	830 Shore Drive
	San Diego, California 92115
	Dr. Harold Bowes
	Industrial Research Laboratories
	317 Central Avenue
	New Brunswick, New Jersey 08901
a section or a	Customer Service Department
department	National Chemical Corp.
within a	372 Western Lane
company	Davenport, Iowa 52803
	Personnel Director
	Comstock Milling Co.
	378 Hill Boulevard
	Raleigh, North Carolina 27602
an entire	Comstock Milling Co.
organization	378 Hill Boulevard
	Raleigh, North Carolina 27602

PUNCTUATION AND ABBREVIATIONS FOR INSIDE ADDRESS AND HEADING

1. *Streets.* Numbered streets up to ten or that take only one word are either spelled out or written as figures. Numbered streets beyond ten requiring two words or more are written as figures.
    2801 Fifth Street
    392 30 Street
    392 Thirtieth Street
    392 32 Street

2. *Dates.* Write date in standard form.

    March 20, 1975

    Avoid the bureaucratic form of date writing (20 March 1975) and stay away from all number forms (3-20-75, 3/20/75).

3. *Number indicators.* Do not use "st," "nd," "d," "rd," or "th" with figures used for numbered streets or for the days of the month.

    1918 22 Street

    May 3, 1976

4. *Separating comma.* Be sure to put a comma between the city and state and between the day of the month and the year.

    Chicago, Illinois

    June 18, 1977

5. *Abbreviations.* Use abbreviations sparingly. A good rule to follow is "When in doubt, spell it out."

    Abbreviations are appropriate for the following titles: Mr., Mrs., Ms., Messrs. (as for a law firm of Messrs. White, Green, and Black). Other common abbreviations are: Jr., Sr., Mt. (Mount), St. (Saint), Inc. (Incorporated), Ltd. (Limited), D. C. (District of Columbia); compound directions, NW. or NW or N. W. (Northwest); and the professional degree symbols such as B. B. A., Ph. D., M. D., C. P. A. The title Dr. (Doctor) is usually abbreviated, especially when the first name or the initials are used with the surname.

    The following words should be spelled out whenever possible: president, superintendent, honorable, reverend, professor, building, company, association, department; as well as street, boulevard, avenue, east, west, north, south. City names and generally state names should also be spelled out. The names of businesses may be abbreviated when their own letterheads contain the abbreviation (James T. Drew Co.).

    Names of states and possessions may be abbreviated if space is lacking, but District of Columbia is usually abbreviated. Include the zip code in all addresses.

    You may use the two-letter abbreviations authorized by the U. S. Postal Service, expecially on the envelope. But many letter writers prefer the more dignified tone of the spelled-out state for the letter itself.

Salutation

The salutation is placed two spaces below the inside address, flush with the left margin. The first and last words and every noun are capitalized. A colon follows the salutation in business letters unless open punctuation is used.

```
/////////////////////
/// INSIDE ADDRESS ///
/////////////////////

Dear Mrs. Henson:
```

Common forms of salutation

named individual	Dear Mr. (Miss, Mrs., Ms.) Adams: Dear Bill:
individual's name unknown	Dear Sir: Dear Madam:
company or association	Gentlemen:
organization consisting entirely of women	Ladies:
feminine company, like Arlene Terell, Inc., that consists of both men and women	Gentlemen:
box number, which gives no name	Gentlemen:

Body

The body is the most important part of the letter, since it does convey the central message. The style and content of the body will be discussed throughout this book. Here we can point out a few features about the physical precision of the body.

Single space the lines within a paragraph; double space between paragraphs. Allow enough room at the bottom for the signature block and some blank space. If the letter won't fit neatly onto one page, use a second page. Make sure the second page contains at least the last three lines of the letter's body; a second page bearing nothing but a signature block looks silly. For a second page (and a third, if necessary), use plain stationery without a letterhead. Second and third pages take a one-line heading—addressee's name, the page number, and the date—or a three-line block at the left margin. With both styles begin about one inch from the top. Allow three lines before continuing the body of the letter.

```
Mr. Thomas C. Titler      - 2 -    May 9, 1978
```

```
Mr. Thomas C. Titler
Page 2
May 9, 1978
```

Complimentary Close

Place the complimentary close two spaces below the body of the letter. The closing goes at the right-hand side of the sheet, except in the full block style and the simplified style, in which the close appears at the left-hand margin. The complimentary close is omitted when the simplified style is used. Only the first word of the complimentary closing is capitalized. A comma is placed at the end, except when open punctuation is used.

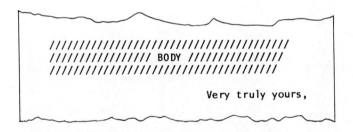

Here are the more commonly used forms of complimentary closing:

Sincerely,	Respectfully,	(Entirely Personal)
Sincerely yours,	Respectfully yours,	Yours,
Yours sincerely,	Yours truly,	Your friend,
Very sincerely,	Yours very truly,	
Cordially,	Very truly yours,	
Cordially yours,		

Assertive lead-ins, like the following, are no longer acceptable. Avoid such closings. They sound stilted, artificial, and obsolete.

> Expecting an early reply, I am,
> Hoping to hear from you soon, I remain,
> Thanking you in advance, I remain,
> I am, obediently yours,
> I remain, your humble servant,

Signature

Place the signature directly below the complimentary close. It must be handwritten in ink and legible. No punctuation follows the signature. Titles or degrees, such as Mr., Rev., M. D., and Ph. D., are not used with the signature in business letters. However, Mrs., Miss, or Ms. may be used.

The name of the person who is signing the letter is typed about four spaces below the complimentary close. If the simplified style is used, the complimentary close is omitted, and the signature line is typed four spaces below the body. An official title, if used, is placed directly below the typewritten name or on the same line with the name.

Sincerely yours,

Paul Miller

Paul Miller

When a letter is sent on letterhead stationery, the signature block indicates who in the company has written the letter and what his or her position is. On the Peerless Office Supplies letterhead, signature blocks might read

Respectfully yours,

Timothy Akers

Timothy Akers
Credit Manager

Yours truly,

Ed Goodman

Ed Goodman, Director
Market Research Department

If the Peerless letterhead also read "Market Research Department," Ed Goodman's signature block would read simply

Yours truly,

Ed Goodman

Ed Goodman, Director

If the pronoun "we" is used instead of "I," the name of the firm appears before the writer's signature. The firm's name is typed in capital letters two spaces below the complimentary close, with the writer's name four spaces below the company name.

Sincerely yours,

PEERLESS OFFICE SUPPLIES

Timothy Akers

Timothy Akers
Credit Manager

Though a man doesn't call himself "Mr." in the signature block, a woman should indicate her marital status so that a respondent can address her correctly.

Sincerely,   Sincerely,

Betty Short   *Celia Clemens*

(Miss) Betty Short   (Mrs.) Celia Clemens

Some women prefer to write the title in parentheses after their name instead of before—Betty Short(Miss) and Celia Clemens(Mrs.). This form emphasizes the name rather than the status.

The abbreviation "Ms." may be used instead of "Miss" and "Mrs." when the woman has not indicated either a status or a preference.

When a secretary signs his or her employer's name to a dictated letter, his or her own initials are placed directly below the handwritten signature.

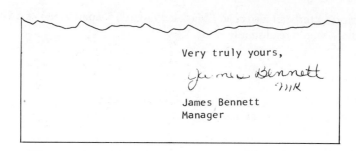

When a secretary signs a letter in his or her own name, he or she indicates this as follows:

Because a signature makes a letter official and gives it a look of completeness, any letter in which the signature is omitted or rubber-stamped seems to say either, "I, the writer, care little about this communication," or "This letter is just part of my everyday routine." However unintentional these intimations might be, they can ruin a reaction-evoking communication. Always sign a business letter by hand.

Identification Line

The identification line is made up of the initials of the person who dictated the letter and those of the secretary or typist. The initials may be all capital letters, all small letters, or capitalized letters for the dictator's initials and small letters for those of the secretary or typist. The identification line is usually typed two spaces below the signature, flush with the left-hand margin. The two sets are separated by a colon or a slash.

//SIGNATURE//

HM:vc

Here are other common forms for identification lines:

> hem/vc
> HEM:vc
> HEM:VC
> H.E. Miller:vc
> H.E. Miller:VC

SPECIAL FEATURES

Besides the essential parts, a business letter may have one or more of eight notations or references. These special features are:

1. Personal notation
2. Reference line
3. Attention line
4. Subject line
5. Enclosure notation
6. Carbon copy distribution notation
7. Mailing notation
8. Postscript

Personal Notation

If your letter is confidential and you want it read by a particular person only, use the word "personal" or "confidential" to indicate your wish. This notation should appear four spaces above the inside address in the letter, as well as on the envelope.

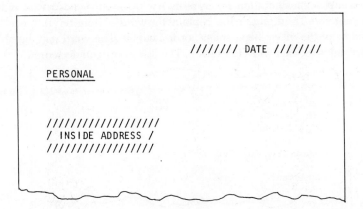

Reference Line

A reference line can refer to a bill, an order, a code, or a letter. It is typed four spaces below the date line.

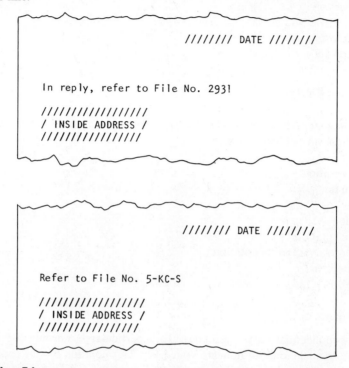

Attention Line

If you want a business letter directed to the attention of a particular individual in a firm, use an attention line. This line is placed a double space below the inside address and a double space above the salutation. It may be flush with the left-hand margin, indented five spaces, or centered. The attention line contains the word "Attention" followed by a colon and the name of the office, department, or individual. The word may be abbreviated (Attn) or typed in all caps (ATTENTION). The line may be underscored.

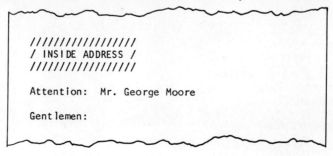

Although the letter above is directed to an individual, a plural salutation is required because the letter is addressed to the firm.

An attention line is never used when the inside address contains a person's name. It is useful when the writer does not know the name of an individual but wants his message to go to a particular title, such as Sales or Personnel manager. It is also useful when the writer knows only the last name of an individual and thus cannot use the first name on the first line of the inside address.

Subject Line

The subject line saves time and confusion. It indicates the subject matter of the letter and makes it unnecessary to devote the first paragraph to giving this information. This line is generally centered on the same line as the salutation or two spaces below. If the full block style is used, type the subject line flush with the left-hand margin, two spaces below the salutation. Place a colon after the word "Subject," and use initial capital letters for all important words. Avoid "re" or "in re"; they are outdated. Underscore for quick attention.

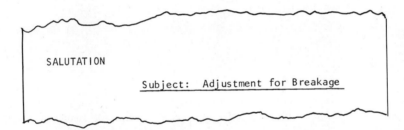

```
SALUTATION

              Subject:  Adjustment for Breakage
```

If the simplified style is used, the subject line is typed in capital letters, but "Subject:" is deleted.

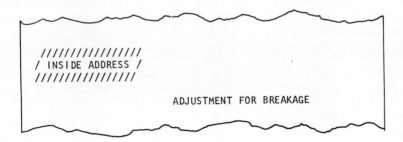

```
/////////////////
/ INSIDE ADDRESS /
/////////////////

              ADJUSTMENT FOR BREAKAGE
```

Enclosure Notation

When a letter has an enclosure, the notation to that effect is typed one or two spaces below the identification line, flush with the left-hand margin. Use either the entire word

"Enclosure," or its abbreviation, "Enc." or "Encl." If a letter has more than one enclosure, the number should be stated.

HEM:vc
Enclosure

HEM:vc
2 Encls.

Carbon Copy Distribution Notation

This notation states that a carbon copy of the letter is being sent to another person. It is typed one or two spaces below the identification line and enclosure line, flush with the left-hand margin. Either the words "Copy to" or the abbreviation "cc" (carbon copy) may be used.

HEM:vc
Enclosure

Copy to Mr. Harold Piper

HEM:vc
Enc.
cc: Mr. H. Piper

If you do not want the addressee to know that other people are getting a copy of the letter, you can type "bcc" (blind carbon copy) and the recipients' names on the carbon copies only.

HEM:vc
Enc.
bcc: Mr. Gregory Hutson

Mailing Notation

This notation states the method of mailing: whether a letter is to be sent registered, certified, special delivery, or another way. The mailing notation is usually typed two spaces below the identification, enclosure, and carbon copy block. It serves as a record to indicate that the letter was sent by other than regular mail.

HEM:vc

Registered

HEM:vc
2 Encls.

Special Delivery

Postscript

The postscript (P.S.) is used in business letters, not in the original sense as an after-thought or an omitted idea, but as a special device to emphasize or personalize. If a reader thought a postscript really represented something the writer forgot to say in the body of the letter, he or she might react skeptically toward the apparent poor planning. If something important was omitted from the body of the letter, rewrite the letter. The postscript is placed at least two spaces below all other notations.

Writers of sales letters often withhold one last convincing argument for emphatic inclusion in a postscript. Some executives, to add a personal touch to their typewritten letters, occasionally add a postscript in pen and ink, as shown here:

```
. . . to see you at the Annual Sales Meeting at the

Hillside Plaza on January 10.

                    Sincerely,

                    Butch Slaughter

                    Butch Slaughter
                    Sales Manager


P.S. I understand the special
entertainment is great.
                    BS
```

The abbreviation P.S. is the accepted form, but the use of the notation itself is entirely optional. When the notation is used, however, the initials of the person who dictated appear below the postscript or name.

```
    JAC:cr

    //////////////////////////////////////////////
    /////////////////// POSTSCRIPT ///////////////////
    //////////////////////////

                    JAC
```

All the parts of a business letter are illustrated in Figure 2-6. The proper spacing for the parts of the letter is illustrated in Figures 2-7 and 2-8.

1. *Heading*	457 Plains Highways North Platte, Nebraska 69101 February 14, 1979
2. *Date*	
3. *Personal notation*	PERSONAL
4. *Reference line*	Refer to File No. 2931
5. *Inside address*	Solar Power, Inc. 276 Mesa Place La Cruces, New Mexico 88001
6. *Attention line*	Attention: Miss Mary Morley
7. *Salutation*	Gentlemen:
8. *Subject line*	Subject: The Parts of a Business Letter
9. *Body*	You are reading a letter containing all the parts of a business letter. The attention line follows the inside address. Because it is really a part of the address, it should also be placed on the envelope. The subject line follows the salutation. It is considered part of the body of the letter.
10. *Complimentary close*	Cordially, RESEARCH ASSOCIATES, INC.
11. *Signature*	*Nelson Baker* Nelson Baker Vice President
12. *Identification line*	NB:rc
13. *Enclosure*	Encl.
14. *Carbon copies*	cc: Jason Conerly
15. *Mailing notation*	Registered
16. *Postscript*	P.S. The postscript should never be used as an afterthought. It may be used, however, to emphasize or to personalize.

Figure 2-6 Parts of a Business Letter

Heading
    2-line space, at least
Date
    2-line space, at least

Inside address
    2-line space
Salutation
    2-line space

Body
    2-line space

Complimentary close
    4-line space
Signature
    2-line space

Identification

```
                     RESEARCH ASSOCIATES, INC.

        457 Plains Highway          North Platte, Nebraska 69101

                          February 14, 1979


     Solar Power, Inc.
     276 Mesa Place
     La Cruces, New Mexico 88001

     Gentlemen:

     You are reading a letter containing the basic parts of
     a standard business letter.  The spacing indicated as 2
     means double-space, or the spacing you get when you hit
     the 2-space key on the typewriter.  It is the same as
     one blank line.

     The space shown between the heading and the date is
     shown as two, but it could be increased to three or more
     depending upon the length of the letters.  The principle
     holds for the space between the date and the inside
     address.  Space could also be increased to five after
     the complimentary close to allow for a broader
     signature.

     All other parts should always be separated as indicated--
     by a double space, or one blank line.

                              Cordially,

                              Nelson Baker

                              Nelson Baker
                              Vice President


     NB:rc
```

Figure 2-7 Spacing for basic parts of a business letter

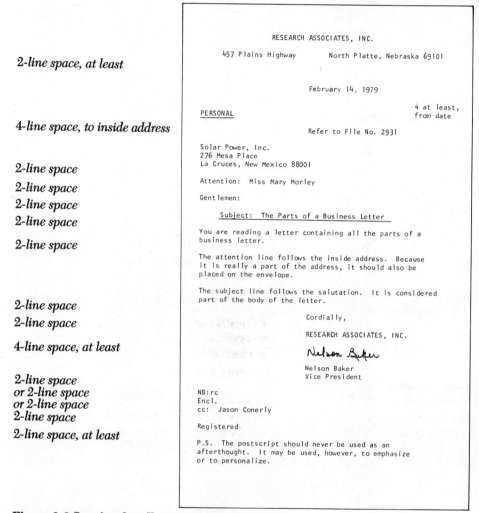

2-line space, at least

4-line space, to inside address

2-line space
2-line space
2-line space
2-line space

2-line space

2-line space
2-line space

4-line space, at least

2-line space
or 2-line space
or 2-line space
2-line space

2-line space, at least

Figure 2-8 Spacing for all parts of a business letter

OTHER MARKS OF PHYSICAL PRECISION

Stationery

The stationery generally used for business letters is 8½-by-11-inch, twenty-weight, plain white bond. For special purposes, however, different sizes, weights, or colors can be used. Short, informal communications are often typed on smaller letterhead stationery. Carbon copies are done on lightweight paper to lower costs and to allow the typist to obtain more copies from a single typing.

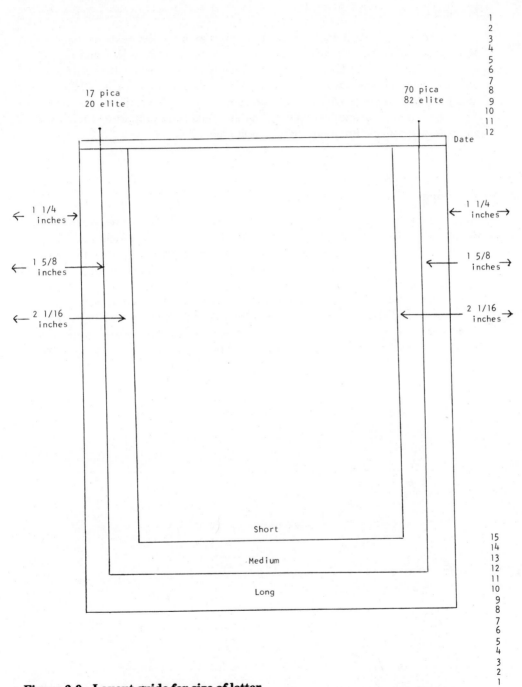

Figure 2-9 Layout guide for size of letter

Margins

Margins contribute substantially to the visual impression a letter makes upon its reader. Margins should create the effect of a well-framed picture. Both left- and right-hand margins should be at least 1¼ inches wide, preferably more. A letter with a relatively brief body can have margins as wide as 2½ inches. The right-hand margin should be made as nearly regular as possible, without too many splits of multisyllabic words. The amount of white space at the top and bottom of the letter should be in proportion to the vertical margins, giving a "picture frame" effect, as in Figure 2-9.

Envelope

The envelope should look like the ones in Figures 2-10 and 2-11. The recipient's address is centered on the front side of the envelope or placed in the lower right quarter of the envelope. The return address is usually placed in the upper left-hand corner, though some companies use the glue flap on the other side. Most companies imprint their names and addresses attractively, not only for the benefit of the post office in case of return but also to make a handsome first impression upon the recipient. Attention lines and personal notations (discussed earlier) are repeated on the face of the envelope left of the address. There is only one correct place for the stamp—the upper right-hand corner. Type-of-mail notations ("Special Delivery," "Certified," or "Registered Mail") are usually placed about ½ inch below the stamp.

People react even to the way a letter is folded—so fold carefully. For insertion into a regular business envelope, the 8½-by-11-inch letter is folded horizontally into thirds, typed side inward. For a smaller envelope the same letter is folded horizontally in half, then vertically into thirds.

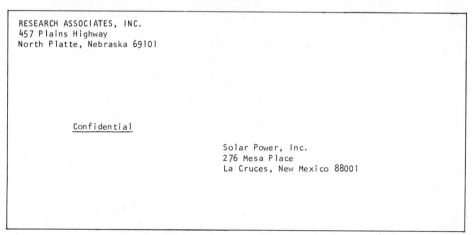

Figure 2-10   Well-addressed business envelopes

RESEARCH ASSOCIATES, INC.
457 Plains Highway
North Platte, Nebraska 69101

                                        Solar Power, Inc.
                                        276 Mesa Place
                                        La Cruces, New Mexico 88001

RESEARCH ASSOCIATES, INC.
457 Plains Highway
North Platte, Nebraska 69101

        Attention: Mary Morley

                                        Solar Power, Inc.
                                        276 Mesa Place
                                        La Cruces, New Mexico 88001

RESEARCH ASSOC.ATES, INC.
457 Plains Highway
North Platte, Nebraska 69101

                                                        SPECIAL DELIVERY

                                        Solar Power, Inc.
                                        276 Mesa Place
                                        La Cruces, New Mexico 88001

Figure 2-11   Well-addressed business envelopes

    If you are in a locality where the post office uses a machine to read addresses, you can get better mail service by following certain guidelines. Because machines such as the Optical Character Reader (OCR) are programmed to scan a specific area on all envelopes, the address must be located entirely within a specific read zone. A safe area is the lower right quarter section of the envelope, with the last line of the address more than ½ inch from the bottom. The OCR can read envelopes with dimensions ranging from a minimum of 3 by 4 ¼ inches to a maximum of 5 ¾ by 11 ½ inches. The address should be clearly imprinted on a light background and should be parallel with the bottom edge of the envelope. In addition, follow these guidelines:

1.   The format should be single-spaced and blocked, not indented.

       Correct   *Incorrect*
       Miss Marla Tellman   Miss Marla Tellman
       281 Main Street   281 Main Street
       Columbus, OH 43210   Columbus, OH 43210

2.   City, state, and zip code must be put in that sequence on the bottom line.

       Correct   *Incorrect*
       Johnson Smith and Co.   Johnson Smith and Co.
       3701 Hill Road   3701 Hill Road
       Norfolk, VA 23502   Norfolk, VA
                                          23502

3.   Street name or box number should be on the line immediately above the city, state, and zip code.

       Correct
       Mr. Roger Cole
       2819 Shore Drive
       Key West, FL 33040

       Mr. Roger Cole
       P. O. Box 887
       Key West, FL 33040

4.   Number of an apartment, suite, room, or other unit should be placed immediately after the street address—on the same line.

       Correct   *Incorrect*
       Mr. Roger Cole   Mr. Roger Cole
       2819 Shore Drive, Apt 27   2819 Shore Drive
       Key West, Fl 33040   Apt 27
                                     Key West, FL 33040

5. Notations other than addresses, such as "Please forward," "Confidential, " and account numbers, should be typed either fully outside the read zone or fully inside the read zone on any line above the second line from the bottom. See Figure 2-12 for sample envelope.

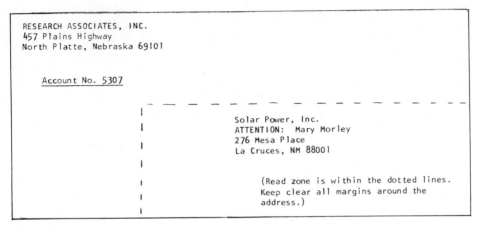

Figure 2-12   Envelope addressed for machine scanner

Continuing Sheet

Most business letters rarely exceed one page. If a letter requires more than one page, use a continuing sheet of the same color, weight, and quality as the letterhead. A letterhead must never be used for the continuing sheet. Each page of a letter beyond the first page should be numbered consecutively. The name of the addressee, the page number, and the date of the letter should appear at the top of each continuing sheet.

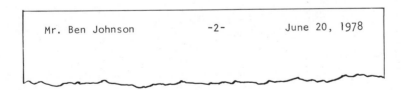

Spacing and Punctuation

The inside address of a letter is usually single spaced. The body of the letter should also be single spaced, with double spacing between the paragraphs. If, however, the letter is very short and the paragraphs are indented, the body of the letter may be double spaced to improve the appearance of the letter. (See Figure 2-13.)

JENSON ORNAMENTAL, INC.

2938 Circle Road   Buffalo, New York 14205

November 20, 1978

Miss Alyce Watts
3214 Parmer Avenue
Cleveland, Ohio 44106

Dear Miss Watts:

    Your order for 3 dozen picture frames, size
12" x 16", catalog No. 2843, was shipped today.

    We appreciate receiving Watts Decorator Shop
as a new account. Thank you for your initial
order, and we look forward to a pleasant business
relationship.

                         Sincerely,

                         Martin Wadsworth

                         Martin Wadsworth
                         Manager

MW:bs

Figure 2-13 The Double-Spaced Letter

A letter may be punctuated in *closed, open,* or *mixed* style. *Closed punctuation* requires punctuation marks after the date line, each line of the inside address, the complimentary closing, and each line of the signature. *Open punctuation* does not require any punctuation marks at the end of a line unless it is necessary to abbreviate a word at the end of a line. *Mixed punctuation,* the preferred style today, is a modification of open punctuation. It requires a colon after the salutation and a comma after the complimentary closing. *Closed punctuation* is practically outdated. In all punctuation styles a comma is put between city and state and between the day of month and year.

Mixed Punctuation	*Open Punctuation*	*Closed Punctuation*
June 20, 1977	June 20, 1977	June 20, 1977.
Mr. Henry Swift 280 Oak Street Kent, Ohio 44240	Mr. Henry Swift 280 Oak Street Kent, Ohio 44240	Mr. Henry Swift, 280 Oak Street, Kent, Ohio 44240.
Dear Mr. Swift:	Dear Mr. Swift	Dear Mr. Swift:
Sincerely yours,	Sincerely yours	Sincerely yours,
Tim Rogers Credit Manager	Tim Rogers Credit Manager	Tim Rogers, Credit Manager.

Correct Typing and Use of English

The physical preparation of your letter must be precise. Sloppy typing, obvious erasures, cross outs, strikeovers, inky smudges, and mistakes in the basic mechanics of the language—bad grammar, misspellings, poor punctuation—will ruin a communication.

A smudge or sloppy erasure will make the reader think you are sloppy. A misspelling or incorreit use of English will make the reader question your sophistication and intelligence. A punctuation error can actually blur the meaning. The question, "Did you call, Mr. Watson?" is changed entirely if the comma is accidentally left out. Follow these guidelines in preparing a letter.

1. Proofread carefully.
2. If you make an error, start over, unless time does not permit.
3. If you must erase, erase neatly.
4. Never cross out or strike over.
5. Unless you're absolutely sure, check the dictionary or handbook for spelling and usage. Most errors are not made with difficult words like "plenipotentiary," but with the common words people think they know how to spell, such as "receive," "existence," and "occurred."

FORMAT OF A MEMORANDUM

The stationery on which memos are written contains printed headings that eliminate the need for formal inside addresses, salutations, and closings. Although memorandum forms differ, most of them contain at least four headings: TO, FROM, SUBJECT, and DATE. Other headings are added to speed delivery or establish identification: DEPARTMENT, LOCATION (branch office, for example), FLOOR, TELEPHONE EXTENSION, ROOM, or FILE NUMBER. (See Figures 2-14 and 2-15.)

" To" LINE.   The addressee is not usually given a courtesy title such as "Mr.," "Miss," or "Dr." (It is common, however, to use "Mr." when addressing a person of much higher rank than the writer.) The job title (Vice President, Operations) may be used in very formal circumstances. If there is no provision in the form for "department," this may be indicated alongside the addressee's name; for example, "Walter Smith, Personnel Relations." Such an identification may be very important in a large company.

When the memorandum is addressed to several people, the "To" line may appear as follows:

TO: Publications Committee

TO: See below. (The names or initials of the individuals addressed are listed at the end of the memorandum, thus: Distribution HMB, LRB, RJH, RMS, RTR, CIG.)

COPY NOTATION.   The name of the person receiving a copy of the memorandum may be placed below the addressee's name but is more often at the bottom left margin. If several people are to receive copies, the notation is placed at the bottom of the memorandum:

cc: Willard Sell   Paul Taylor
     Betty Kurtz   Carl Router

Sometimes you may wish to indicate that distribution is made to a whole group instead of named individuals.

cc: Accounting Department

"FROM" LINE.   Neither a courtesy title nor a job title is given to the writer of the memorandum. However, when the memorandum form does not provide for an identification of the department from which the message is sent, the writer should include this information beside or below his or her name; for example, FROM: *Fran House, Customer Relations*. This is especially important when the writer is a new employee in a large company or an employee who is not likely to be widely known in the firm.

"DEPARTMENT" LINE.   The department from which the memorandum comes and to which it goes is usually taken for granted. If there is a chance, however, that the memo may be misdirected, it is wise to identify the department. (See Figure 2-15.)

"SUBJECT" LINE.   Stating the subject of the memorandum lets the reader know at a glance what the memo is about. The wording should be as short as possible but long enough to tell the reader what you're going to talk about in the memorandum.

> SUBJECT: Request for Leave of Absence
>
> SUBJECT: Overpayment to White Stores
>
> SUBJECT: ANALYSIS OF BRANCH MARKETS (may be all in capitals)

BODY.   The body of the memorandum, like the body of a letter, is usually single spaced, with paragraphs blocked. If the message is very short, double spacing may be appropriate.

SIGNATURE.   Many memorandum writers feel that their name on the "From" line makes a signature unnecessary, either typewritten or handwritten. If you choose to personalize your memos, either initial or sign them. The best place for a signature is at the bottom of the memo, although some people like to sign or initial below their typewritten name on the "From" line.

```
                                          General Auto Supplies
                        M E M O R A N D U M



  To:  Terry Secrist                    Date:  May 18, 1978

          cc:  Ben Collins
               Frank Burroughs
               T.S. Powers

  From:  James Turner

  Subject:  New Office Typewriters


     ///////////////////////////////////////////////////////
     //////////////////////////////////////////////////////
     /////////////////////////////////////////
```

Figure 2-14   Standard Memorandum Form

```
            I N T E R O F F I C E    M E M O R A N D U M


    To  Richard Burley                    From  Ted Bingham


    Dept.  Market Research                Dept.  Executive


    Subject  Profits and Southmoor  Branch    Date  May 10, 1978



    I have finished studying the Southmoor Branch sales figures for
    the 1st quarter and see they are about $255,000 under projections.
    That is the third straight quarter that Southmoor has fallen short.

    Will you prepare a new analysis of the Southmoor market potential?
    I know you did one--and a good one too--three years ago before
    Southmoor opened.  But maybe some factors have changed and we
    need to look into them.

    Ben Tebbins is working up a report from the sales and promotion
    angle.  He'll finish about June 15.  If you could be ready then,
    we'll get together and see if we can solve the Southmoor problem.



    TB:ac
    cc:  Ben Tebbins

                                           T B
```

Figure 2-15 Standard Memorandum

Although the memorandum format is simpler and less formal than that of a letter, it must be just as physically precise, for its recipient is likely to react against shoddy format. A memo *is*, in fact, a letter; it just doesn't travel as far.

Memoranda are usually sent through interoffice mail in special envelopes. In the absence of a special envelope a plain white business envelope indicating the recipient's name and department will do.

EXERCISES

1. Write the proper headings for the following—without letterheads.

    a. 4 August 1971
        728 W. 8th St.
        Pullman, Wash. 99163

    b. Mr. Joseph Turpin
        1312 Cajan Ave.
        New Orleans, La. 52345
        Sept. 3rd, 1978

2. Write the correct inside address.

    a. Mr. William Betson, M. D.
        2619-20 Avenue N. E.
        Columbus
        Ohio 43210

    b. Professor Lynn Johnson, Ph. D.
        School of Economics
        University of Indiana
        BLOOMINGTON 47401

    c. Timmons Carpet Co.
        2809 Lansing Ave.
        Detroit

3. Write a correct signature block, identification line, and enclosure notation.

    a. (open punctuation)

                            Yours Truly,
                            Pacific Loan assn.,
                            Mr. Ronald Jones
                            President

        R. A. J./T. E. D.
        INCLOSURE

    b. (mixed punctuation)

                            Sincerely Yours,
                            Credit Manager

        Gerald E. Burton

    c. (mixed punctuation)

                            Respectfully yours
                            BENSON & SMITH, INC.
                            Ralph Stubb
                            Prod. Mgr.

4. Write correct inside address, salutation, and complimentary close. Use mixed punctuation.

   a. Veterans Adm.
      Detroit, Mich. 23456

      Attention: Dr. Lucy Bauer

      Dear Dr. Lucy Bauer

                                      Respectively yours.

   b. Dr. Jay Ellis
      618 Wrigley Bldg.
      Chicago 14, Ill. 34567

      Dear Jay,

                                      Sincerely yours

   c. Milton Payne
      17,672 3rd St., N. E.,
      New York City 11111

      Dear Sir:--

                                      Yours

   d. Carol Penner
      218 Atlas Bldg.
      Des Moines, Ia. 22222

      Dear Miss Carol Penner

                                      Yours truly

   e. Atlantic Company, Inc
      Purchasing Department
      Phila, Penna., 19144

      Dear Miss Kinder

                                      Your faithful friend

                                      Elco & Co.

      Incl.   George Pendell
      gp:AK   Personnell Mgr.

5. Correct the language and mechanics of this letter, and write it in blocked form. Write it in full blocked form.

```
                                        June, 12th '78

The Universal Electronics Corpor.
1448 South Aveneue
Plainfeild,  07001  New Jers.


Attention, (Mr.) Lynn Reilly,



My Dear Mr. Reilly;

We wish to extend our congradulations to you on you're recent
promotion into the Vice presidency of one of the most successful
and most friendliest companies with who we do business.  Knowing
what a honor this is for you, our staff recieved the news with
much pleasure.



Respectively Yours

Mr. John Moore
Sales Representive
```

6. Write the following material in a letter with suitable format.

Subject: Committee Assignments for the Spring Season. Mrs. Holder, 18 Twiller Lane, Boston, Massachusetts. The enclosed list is the final draft of our committee assignments for the Spring Culture Series Program. I am delighted that you agreed to serve as finance chairman. The four men and women selected to serve on your committee are well known to you, I'm sure, for their willingness to assist the association in any way they can. Will you arrange with each of them for an organizational meeting? Please let me know when your meeting time is arranged. I'll make every attempt to attend and will be glad to help you in any way possible. Cordially BOSTON ASSOCIATION Wm. J. Proxmire, President
WJP:DO
Enclosure

7. As assistant to sales manager William Weller of the Bayou Marine Supply Co. (289 Canal Street, New Orleans, Louisiana), you receive the following note. Prepare these announcements for mailing. Use the physical format you think looks best.

My secretary didn't send out 3 announcement letters to our shareholder's meeting. She's went home sick so could you please get them out for me. They should read as follows—"We are pleased to announce that Bayou Marine Supplie's 15th annual shareholder's meeting will be held on Friday March 2C, at that Hillside Plaza in Lands End."

Send them to Thomas Bird, 218 Meadow Lane, New Orleans; 1st Federal Reserve Bank (make that attention of Mabel ~~Timkins~~ Timkins) 392C Shore Drive, Jackson, Miss; and Timothy Dicer President of Gulf Products, Inc., 2931 Alamo Blvd, Houston, Tex. (zip # 77CC4.)

Better send the last one special delivery.

Thanks—
WW

3

The Information:
Exact and
Exactly Enough

Inaccurate Data
Omissions
Irrelevancies
Ambiguities
Contradictions

The format of your letter—its design and shape—may be perfect. But if you have flaws in the information in your letter, the letter will fail. Your factual message must be exact and clear. The reader must get all the necessary information and grasp it clearly. Several flaws can get in the way of factual precision. Especially beware of these five demons: inaccurate data, omission of important information, irrelevancies, ambiguities, and contradictions.

INACCURATE DATA

Absolute accuracy is essential for written messages. It is not enough to feel sure of your facts. You must check every fact, every figure, every word. You must proofread carefully, check information, and confirm figures and dates.

Errors may be expensive. One wrong digit can make a difference of thousands of dollars (for example, $55,000 instead of $85,000). Even a small error in a few cents can be annoying to customers and undermine goodwill. Any wrong figure, as in a price or an account number, must be corrected—at great expense of time, money, and jangled emotions.

Day-date mix-ups can also lead to confusion. For example, the announcement of a certain sales meeting read, "Will be held on Friday, October 12, 10 A.M." Phones rang all morning and important jobs were put off because people were confused. The correction finally came through: "Sorry, the date is *Thursday*, October 12, same time, same place."

Frequently a garbled or mistaken word produces embarrassment as well as impeding the direct message. For instance, consider the embarrassment caused by the letter sent to all company employees, and to the police force and city employees inviting them to hear a talk given by "Lieutenant James Hood, a defective on the police force." A follow-up letter sent to ease the blunder didn't help much! "The event has past, and we are all friends." Did you spot the misspelled word?

Consider what prospective customers thought of this little blunder in a sales letter from a drapery and carpet firm:

Nothing can change the appearance of your living room quite so much as an undraped widow.

A more serious blunder is to write a letter basing decisions or opinions on inaccurate or insufficient information. Costly time, effort, and goodwill can be lost. The memos in Figures 3–1 and 3–2 illustrate how failure to use accurate data can bring about a lot of disturbance. The names of company and people have been changed; otherwise, the memos are intact as actually sent. Tom Boone wrote his suspicious memo without gathering efact information, and he made somewhat of a fool of himself. Not only did he get Randall's witty, sarcastic reply, but he must have suspected what the gossip was about him—especially among those to whom Randall sent carbon copies.

Consider how much total time and effort was wasted in this need to "generate documents." Consider also the bad feelings that must have existed for at least a little while between Randall and Boone. If Boone had spent just 30 seconds on the phone, he could have gathered enough exact information to prevent the costly blunder.

OMISSIONS

The clarity and force of the message diminishes if anything the reader needs to know is left out. To check for full information, it is helpful to use the "five W's and an H." Ask yourself "who, what, when, where, why, and how?" Frequently you also need to ask "how many?" and "how much?" You may not need to answer all these in any one letter, but you will usually use most of them, and they provide an excellent check against omissions. The letter is a one-time thing—get everything necessary in it. The following request omits three essential pieces of information.

Please send a few copies of your pamphlet to our new downtown store.

What are the omissions? They are "what?" "how many?" and "where?" The receiver of the letter cannot really act until receiving the exact title of the pamphlet, the exact number of copies, and the exact address of the downtown store. (If the store is new, its address may not be readily available.)

MORRIS Communications and
Information Handling

To James Randall	From Tom Boone	Date April 14, 1978 Data Communications Division Correspondence

SUBJECT: Removal of Lease Deck Equipment from the Factory

Recently a Recommendation was floated by Product Management covering
write-off of missing off-rent Lease Deck equipment. Included in the
Recommendation was a paragraph or two covering reasons for disappearance
of equipment; however, recently I have discovered a reason which was
not put forth in the Recommendation.

Last week you were observed removing a Morris 1000 from the front door
of the factory and loading same into the trunk of a visitor's car.
Subsequent investigation revealed that the S/N of the equipment was
21200 and that it was being given to City of Dallas as a demo
replacement for a unit already in their possession. The unit to be
replaced, however, was not returned at the time of pickup of the
replacement, nor has it been returned to date to my knowledge.
Further investigation revealed that you removed the unit from the
storeroom area by having it assigned to an "R" job. This is of
course a refurb job. The unit was not actually removed for refurb
purposes as explained above. Now we have a unit charged to an R job
which is in fact in a customer's hands. If we took a physical today
and you were no longer with us, we would be missing one terminal since
no one but you knew where the terminal ultimately was sent. The only
paperwork available charges it to an "R" job. In addition, we have
another terminal which should be returned, but only you know about
this fact. No shipper has been cut to my knowledge to cover return
of the replaced unit.

Our existing procedures state that a unit may not be shipped to a
customer or prospective customer without a shipper issued by Order
Entry. Also, equipment is to be shipped by Factory personnel through
shipping dock and not delivered at the front door by Product Managers.
I seriously question what authority you have to violate the existing
Company Procedures in this matter. I also wonder how much of our
missing equipment is due to Product Managers removing equipment without
proper paperwork.

I have made Ted Burford aware of the method used to remove the 1000
from the factory and he has advised me that it will not happen again
unless existing Procedures are revised.

I would also appreciate your following up on the City of Dallas for
the return of the replaced unit and, in fact, I feel you should have
Order Entry cut a shipper to cover the return.

Willis Vaughn will be in touch with you in the next few days regarding
the return of this unit.

cc: R. Wallace
     W. Vaughn

Figure 3-1

```
                MORRIS      M      Communications and
                                   Information Handling


    ┌─────────────────────┬───────────────────────┬──────────────────────────────┐
    │ To                  │ From                  │ Date                         │
    │    Tom Boone        │    James Randall      │ April 19, 1978               │
    │                     │                       │ Data Communications          │
    │                     │               JR      │ Division Correspondence      │
    └─────────────────────┴───────────────────────┴──────────────────────────────┘
```

SUBJECT: Your Memo of April 14 on Removal of Lease Deck Equipment

I would like to commend you for your amazing detective work in uncovering
the facts in this case--considering that you did not talk to me and,
according to your memo, I was the only one who knew what was going on.

There was a demo order issued for a 1030-11 terminal for the City of
Dallas. This was done through the normal channels, with all the proper
paperwork. Upon installation, there was an interface problem, and the
customer requested a model 1040-11. It was agreed the best thing to do
was physically swap the terminals, then Order Entry would notify Lease
Deck Accounting of the serial number swap against the existing demo
order. Messrs. Goldman, Brinker, Rollins, Myers, and Gerber were aware
of this and the location of the terminal.

The Division is already choking on excess paperwork, including your
memo and this one; but since you have caught me in my underhanded
scheme to deprive the system of the necessary paperwork upon which it
thrives, we will comply.

By copy of this memo, I am instructing Marketing to issue a demo EOF
for a model 1040-11, S/N 21200. Order Entry will then issue a Manufacturing
Work Order. The MID checking the terminal out of inventory already
exists--Order Entry will then issue a "paperwork only" shipper. Field
Engineering should then fill out an EIR.

Marketing must also generate a cancellation of order 21954-10, model
1030-11, S/N 10495. Order Entry will then issue a return shipper for
this terminal and Field Engineering a removal EIR.

This assumes that the customer does not purchase one of the terminals
in the meantime, and further complicate the paperwork. Should this
happen, however, I am sure you have procedures to cover it, since
we are in business to sell terminals, as well as generate documents.

cc: H. Goldman
     M. Brinker
     N. Rollins
     W. Vaughn
     R. Wallace

Figure 3-2

Likewise, the information in the following sentence is so spotty that action is impossible.

High-Guard Doors can be installed on any normal-sized garage.

Just what does "normal-sized" mean? Give the dimensions in feet and inches or in meters and centimeters.

A serious fault is to omit an idea necessary to connect two other ideas.

Our company is moving out of this building to Crestline Highway, and I am planning to buy a Pontiac.

The writer omitted a "why"—the idea needed to connect moving and buying a car. He probably meant something like this:

Our company is moving out of this building to Crestline Highway, and since there's no bus service from my house to Crestline Highway, I'm going to need a car to get to work. I'm thinking of buying a Pontiac.

IRRELEVANCIES

Have enough information in your communication, but only enough. A sentence is typically a single, unified statement. Don't allow irrelevant elements to weaken the thought flow.

Computers, *whose memory capacity has been increasing rapidly in recent years,* would have had a major influence on the economic recovery of the 1930s if they had existed sooner.

The idea of increasing memory capacity has nothing to do with the point of the sentence. It just makes us juggle conflicting references to the 1930s and the 1970s. The sentence should be shortened and rearranged to bring out the straightforward, precise information.

If computers had been available in time, they would have had a major influence on the economic recovery of the 1930s.

Here is another message that gives us information we do not need to know.

The customer, who wore a conservative blue suit, never did get around to saying what kind of tennis racket he wanted.

Although the detail of the blue suit may help us visualize the customer, it has nothing to do with the essential message about the tennis racket.

AMBIGUITIES

A word or statement is ambiguous if it can be interpreted in more than one way. For clarity, every word, phrase, or sentence in a business communication should have only one possible meaning. Chapter 4 gives extensive help on precise use of words, and Chapter 5 helps develop skills in writing clear, direct sentences. Here we can introduce some common causes of ambiguity: careless pronouns, misplaced modifiers, words with more than one meaning, and vague words with little or no meaning.

Careless Pronouns

A pronoun must clearly refer to one definite noun, not two:

> The saleswoman, Sarah Hampstead, told the complaining customer that the fault was *hers*.

Just which woman does "hers" refer to? Whose fault was it? Ambiguity can easily be cleared up, according to which meaning is intended.

> The salesclerk admitted her fault to the complaining customer.

> The salesclerk accused the complaining customer of being at fault.

Misplaced Modifiers

A modifier tries to modify the closest possible term. If the modifier is placed incorrectly, we shake our heads in confusion—or, sometimes, in humor.

LUDICROUS: She wore a jade ring on her right hand, which she had bought in Hong Kong.

PRECISE: On her right hand she wore a jade ring which she had bought in Hong Kong.

UNCLEAR: The new shipping clerk almost worked for ten hours.

CLEAR: The new shipping clerk worked for almost ten hours.

Words with Multiple Meanings

When a word can have more than one meaning in a given context, build a clearer set of words around it. In the following piece of sales advice, we are left in doubt as to whether "low" means "not loud" or "vulgar."

> Low conversation annoys most customers.

A better context is needed, as in the examples below.

Vulgar conversation annoys most customers.

Most customers are annoyed if you don't speak loudly enough.

Vague Words

Some lazy writers use broad, general words that convey little or no meaning because it takes sharp mental work to pin down the specific information. Yet only the specific really communicates information. Avoid terms like "everywhere," "nobody," "lots of," "in this matter," and "etc." Give precise information instead.

VAGUE: You can find B & I Variety Stores *everywhere* in St. Louis.

DEFINITE: You can find B & I Variety Stores at seven convenient locations in St. Louis. The one closest to you, Mrs. Thompson, is at . . .

The following excerpt from a sales letter gives us an almost meaningless comparison:

The new Copy Mate 620 makes copies a lot faster than the older 310.

Until we know how many copies per minute (or equivalent) for each machine, we cannot sensibly decide to purchase the new 620.

CONTRADICTIONS

One of the worst lapses in thinking is that of contradiction—making one statement and then following it by another that denies the first.

A hurricane hit the Gulf Coast that day, but in St. Petersburg, Florida, the weather was calm.

This note is a contradiction because St. Petersburg is on the Gulf Coast. More careful wording would have given clear information.

A hurricane hit *most* of the Gulf Coast that day, although in St. Petersburg, Florida, the weather was calm.

Again, in the following examples, the writer is not saying what he thinks he is saying.

We do not advocate strikes, but we feel striking is the only way for hospital nurses to get their rights.

If you "feel striking is the only way," then you *do* advocate.

Most errors in factual precision come not from ignorance of the information, but from not taking the mental care to select and arrange the words that say exactly what you mean.

EXERCISES

1. Check these sentences for misspelled or mistaken words or figures.

   a. Be sure to write down the name and phone number of every perpective buyer.
   b. The bad news did not effect her optimism.
   c. The Certificate of Deposit will automaticly be renewed unless you give instructions to the contrary.
   d. We are shipping you ½ dozen (6) green Sportsman jackets, size 38, at $11.25 each. Please send your check for $76.50.

2. The following sentences lack factual precision because essential information has been omitted or irrelevant information has been included. Rewrite the sentences to include appropriate detail and to remove irrelevancies.

   a. Parker's is down Main Street, past the post office.
   b. Send us everything you have on your accident, Mrs. Jones, and we will expedite your claim immediately.
   c. Thank you for the request for the pamphlet.
   d. Hillside Resort has long been known as the complete convention center for business and professional groups such as yours. Whatever your preference in the way of sports, Hillside has it. There's golf, tennis, swimming, water skiing, horseback riding, volleyball—you name it. And the big news is that it won't be long before we'll have winter sports, too. (Just what makes winter sports big news? How long is "long"?)
   e. Your instructions were to ship 300 catalogs to Pittsburgh, 250 to Cleveland, and 430 to Columbus. I want to see what is happening to our shipments.
   f. The Scott Company employs 250 men and 150 women; therefore Scott discriminates against women.
   g. Wichita Falls, which was named from the waterfall five miles up the Wichita River, is the center of a large oil industry.
   h. Also enclosed in our letter are two well-known customers of ours.
   i. Mae has earned her promotion through hard work, and she graduated from Briarcliff in 1973.

3. Rewrite these sentences, clearing up ambiguities, vagueness, and contradictions.

   a. It was twenty minutes before three, maybe less.
   b. Billings told Tillman that he should write a follow-up letter.
   c. DAILY COFFEE SHOP HOURS
      Breakfast — 7:30 – 9:30
      Lunch — 12:00 – 2:30
      —Closed Mondays—
   d. Nobody uses Vesper's Nature Lotion anymore.

    e.   One cannot praise Turner too highly for his sales efforts.

    f.   Add the cleaner to the water when it reaches 185 degrees.

    g.   She almost typed 25 letters after lunch.

    h.   Bursting suddenly, three men were killed by the gas tank.

    i.   Your dog will not shrink from being washed with Doggy Foam.

    j.   All pamphlets from suppliers should be sent to the head buyer.

4   The Words

Precise
Alive
Direct

Individual words are the ultimate building blocks of the business letter. One word is worth a thousand pictures, if it is the right word. If it's the wrong word, it's worth a lost customer. The effective writer must carefully select and place each word so that it is precise, alive, and direct. People do not read very long that which is sloppy, confused, dull, or hard.

PRECISE

The first principle of your message is to be accurate. It is not enough for your information to be accurate. You must convey that information to the reader. If your words are inaccurate, you will fail.

Choosing precise words has two major problems. First, the relationships between words and their meanings is not one-to-one. Many words have more than one meaning, and your meaning can be expressed by more than one word or set of words. Second, words have two kinds of meaning—the dictionary meaning (or denotation) and the emotional or suggestive meaning (or connotation).

Denotation—The Precise Definition

The denotation of a word is its basic dictionary definition and identifies an idea, an object, or a quality. It is the word's core of meaning and is the first you must consider.

The basic dictionary denotation of "mother" is "female parent." "War" is "a major armed conflict between nations or between organized parties within a state." To the extent that a word refers to the same thing for all people concerned, the meaning is denotative. Some words, such as magnesium, diatom, parallax, and diesel, have only one denotative meaning with no other suggestive force or shade of meaning. But most words have different shades of meaning that different people associate with the word because of their particular experience with it.

Connotation—The Precise Tone

The connotation of a word is the suggestions, associations, and emotional responses of the word. Connotations are somewhat different for everyone. But many words have fairly standardized connotations. Thus, "mother" usually means more than the dictionary's denotation of "female parent." The word often connotes emotional warmth, security, and comfort. "War" would have different emotional meanings for one who has been maimed by war, for a family who have fled for shelter when the bombs fell, for one who is getting wealthy because of war. The connotation of a word may not only indicate a special shade of meaning different from a near synonym (such as "drunk" or "plastered") but also suggest attitudes, such as approval or disapproval, ludicrous or serious.

> That poor shipping clerk needs somebody to *mother* him. (Approval: to care for, give affection, comfort, and security)

> Janet is spoiled because the boss has been *mothering* her. (Disapproval: overprotecting, catering to)

The adjectives "thin," "skinny," and "slender" all have the same denotation in referring to below average weight for one's height. But you may please a customer if you call her slender, displease her if you call her *skinny*.

In using words with exact meaning, you must check both the denotation and the connotation. Ask yourself two questions about the word.

1. *Does the word have the meaning you give it?*   Check the various definitions in the dictionary to see if the word has the meaning you are trying to give it. Are you confusing it with another word? For instance the word "infer" is occasionally misused as if it had the same meaning as "imply."

   INCORRECT: He *inferred* by his smile that he had made a big sale.
   EXACT: He *implied* by his smile that he had made a big sale.
   EXACT: I *inferred* from his smile that he had made a big sale.

2. *Is the meaning of the word the meaning you want?*   Check both the dictionary and your knowledge of human experience to see if the word has the proper shade of meaning to express your thought. Do you want to suggest approval or disapproval?

   INEXACT: It certainly was an exhilarating experience to hear the president's after-dinner *spiel* about the future of the company.

EXACT: It certainly was an exhilarating experience to hear the president's after-dinner speech about the future of the company.

Here are some examples of words commonly confused in meaning.

all ready, already	"All ready" means entirely ready; "Already" means previously.
amount, number	Whenever you count the units, use "number." "Amount" refers to bulk, weight, or sums.
anxious, eager	"Anxious" implies worry, whereas "eager" conveys keen desire.
effect, affect	As a noun "effect" means result, condition or influence. "Affect" is not often used as a noun. Both words are verbs—to "effect" is to bring about, to "affect" is to influence.
fewer, less	If you can count the items, use "fewer"; "less" refers to amount or quantity.
personal, personnel	"Personal" relates to an individual; "personnel" refers to a group of people employed in the same work.
please, kindly	As a rule, use "please." "Kindly" means "in a kind manner." If you say, "kindly tell me," you are really asking someone to tell you something in a kind way.
principal, principle	"Principal" means "chief" or "main." Whenever you can substitute "rule," use "principle." In all other instances use "principal."
we, I	"We" means the organization; "I" refers to the individual.
which, that, who	"That" refers to persons or things; "who" to people; "which" only to things.

Part of the connotation of a word is the emotional tones it evokes. Besides its core idea, the word can suggest approval or disapproval, disgust or delight, dullness or alertness. Select the word or near synonym which suggests the desired emotional tone. For example, the following words have the same denotation, "never giving up in the face of difficulty": "persevering," "persistent," "obstinate," "stubborn," "pigheaded." If you want to describe Sam Cobbler, you will affect your reader's attitude according to whether you call Cobbler *persistent* or *pigheaded*. Likewise the tone is different if a person is designated as an "intellectual" or an "egghead," a "politician" or a "statesman," a "traveling salesman" or a "field representative." Select your words for the meaning (dictionary and emotional) you want. Bertrand Russell humorously illustrated the emotional meanings of words on a BBC radio program when he gave the following "conjugation" of an "irregular verb."

> I am firm.
> You are obstinate.
> He is a pigheaded fool.

Here are some others along the same line:

TABLE OF CONJUGATIONS

I am beautiful.
You have fairly good features.
She isn't bad-looking if you like that type.

I am rightfully indignant.
You are annoyed.
He is stirring up a lot of fuss over nothing.

I don't dance very well.
You ought to consider taking lessons.
He has the grace of a dilapidated camel.

I believe in being frank.
You sometimes speak too bluntly.
He has as much tact as a moronic jackass.

I collect rare, old objects of art.
You lucked into a thing or two that's worth
   looking at.
She has a flair for surrounding herself with
   bric-a-brac.

I am portly.
You are a trifle overweight.
He is a fat slob.

I am rather imaginative.
You are an escapist.
She ought to see a psychiatrist.

Of course I use a little makeup.
You really overdo it a little.
She is a painted clown.

I'm just an old-fashioned girl.
You're somewhat conservative.
She is living in the Dark Ages.

I am careful.
You are fussy.

He is a picky, old man.

Another humorous way to illustrate words that show approval and disapproval is to compile what we could call "The Handbook of Duplicity." We pick one term to describe our friends and another to describe our enemies—although the core of meaning of both terms is the same.

THE HANDBOOK OF DUPLICITY

For Enemies

damned lie
bum
male chauvinist pig

For Friends

white lie
homeless unemployed
forceful man

THE HANDBOOK OF DUPLICITY (continued)

dog eat dog	free enterprise
freeloader	houseguest
pig	guardian of public safety
fuzz	guardian of public safety
goof-off	student working below capacity
brat	clever, active child
copping out through drugs	expanding one's consciousness
brainwashed	enlightened
flunk out	separate from college
dead drunk	unwinding
crackpot	original thinker
fanatic	person of conviction
loafer	temporarily unemployed
retreat	strategic withdrawal
prostitute	lady friend
garbage collector	sanitation engineer
communism	government of the people
shyster	lawyer
tyrant	father
alienated	doing your own thing
copping out	getting out of the rat race
lazy bums	poor and needy

ALIVE

For your message to be alive, your words must be *concrete* and *specific* rather than abstract and general, and they must be *fresh* rather than worn-out.

Concrete and Specific

Concrete words refer to things you can perceive through the five senses. They describe things that are tangible, things that you can point to—"typewriter," "desk," "truck." *Abstract* words are conceptual. They refer only generally to ideas in the mind—an abstraction of concrete things—such as "writing instrument" (for "typewriter") or "delivery vehicle" (for "truck").

A *general term* names a class or a group and stands for broad characteristics of things. A *specific* term names a member of a group and stands for more precise, definite things or characteristics. "Typewriter" is general; "IBM Selectric" is specific. "Vehicle" is general; "1977 Chevrolet ½ ton pickup" is more specific.

Using too many abstract and general terms makes writing vague and dull. You must use abstract words to state ideas of significance, but pin them down to tangible experience by using specific and concrete words.

Vague, general	*Concrete, specific*
The new shipping clerk is a dedicated worker.	The new shipping clerk, Ted Alexander, worked two hours overtime without pay to get the Jenkins Corporation order off on schedule.
These tires provide the driver with miles of worry-free driving.	These Goodrich radial tires provide the driver with a 45,000-mile guarantee against blowouts.
Please send your check for the full amount soon.	Please send your check for $348.66 on or before October 15.
A quick start	A three-second start.
Our company has won several prizes.	Jettison, Inc., has won first prize in four regional contests within the past three years.
This machine reproduces sales letters fast.	The IBM Model 1600 Jet types 2,000 personalized 125-word sales promotion letters in one hour.

A troublesome kind of general word is the *relative* word or *opinion word,* which probably has meanings different for the writer than it has for the reader. For instance, how expensive is expensive? An $8000-a-year man and a $75,000-a-year woman will have different opinions. How fast is fast? It's different if you're traveling by foot than by jet. If you ask the distributor to ship the goods fast, he may think you want them in two months for Christmas, when you really want them in two weeks for your special fall sale.

The following list suggests the kinds of words that can lead to vague, imprecise communication:

a few	more	slow
a small number	most	small
high	nice	soon
large	quick	tall
low	several	very
many	short	

Strategic Generalization

In some situations, of course, it is strategic to use general expressions. Although sometimes you may not have definite facts or figures, you need to get off your basic message. At other times you may want to be diplomatic, so you may use *strategic generalizations.* For instance, instead of writing, "We have sent you three notices about your delinquent account," you may strategically write to a prompt-paying customer, "We have sent you *several* reminders of this overdue payment." Or specific facts might be important, as in *"Many* people were waiting at the front door at opening time." Again, strategic generalization is preferred in some cases (as in refusing credit) when specific reasons might anger the potential customer.

Fresh

Use fresh expressions, not trite expressions. A trite expression is also called a *cliché* or a *stereotyped expression.* It is one that has become worn out through overuse, such as "straight from the shoulder," "burn the midnight oil," "last but not least."

Individual words themselves do not become trite. Words like "buy," "sell," "eat," "wise," "pay," "nose" can constantly be fresh. It is the phrase, perhaps once vivid and fresh, that has become commonplace and meaningless through overuse and lack of original thought. Consider the following sentence:

Bill Toler earns his *bread and butter* by the sweat of his *brow.*

We are not convinced of the genuineness of Bill Toler's industry or difficulty. Because of trite thinking the wording is trite and the experience is empty. The following simple sentence, although not worthy of Shakespearean tragedy, evokes our sympathy for Toler.

Bill Toler works 48 hours a week at hard labor in a machine shop.

You can hardly avoid trite expressions entirely. But you can do two things. First, you can do your own authentic, original thinking and use the best words to describe your actual thoughts. And second, you can become aware of current clichés and try to avoid them.

Here are a few examples of trite expressions. There are thousands more. For a fuller list, see the "Checklist of Clichés" in Appendix.

a long felt need	drastic action	nick of time
abreast of the times	financially embarrassed	slowly but surely
better late than never	heartfelt thanks	to the bitter end
bring order out of chaos	last but not least	venture a suggestion
doomed to disappointment	needless to say	white as snow

DIRECT

Good business writing should usually be natural, simple, and straightforward. The reader is likely to doubt your sincerity if you use pretentious, artificial diction. Such writing tends to emphasize words rather than ideas, usually not even interesting words, but vague, fuzzy, and abstract words. There are four main kinds of indirect diction that get in the way of effective communication: *hackneyed phrases, jargon, exaggeration,* and *incorrect idiom.* There is one kind of indirect diction that is desirable in effective communication—the *calculated euphemism.*

Hackneyed Phrases

Hackneyed phrases are outdated expressions, still carried over from the distant past. Phrases like "enclosed herewith," "yours of the 10th received," and "thanking you in advance, I remain" should have been totally abandoned long ago. Such relics, though, persist in letter writing apparently because young writers in their greenness pick up their style from older writers who have not kept pace with the times.

```
     My dear Sir:

     Yours of the 10th received and contents duly
     noted.  In reply would state that as per
     agreement the undersigned agrees to perform
     indicated services in accordance with prior
     instructions.

     Thanking you for past favors, I remain,

                              Yours truly,
```

Contrast the following note written in plain, straightforward English.

```
     Dear Ed,

     I was pleased to have your letter and to
     know that we've reached an agreement.  You
     can count on our living up to our part of
     the bargain.

     Thank you for giving us this chance to work
     with you.

                         Sincerely,
```

Check the following "horse-and-buggy" expressions to see how they are improved by using modern, straightforward language.

We wish to advise that. . . .
(It's obvious that you *wish* to say what you're about to say. Don't say *advise* if you mean *inform*. It is best to delete this phrase if you ever catch yourself using it and just express the idea you wish to express.)

We beg to acknowledge. . .
(Begging has no place in a business letter. Just write "thank you for . . . .")

We are in receipt of . . .
(The phrase sounds too pompous. Just write "we have received . . ." or "thank you for. . . .")

I have your recent letter at hand . . .
(To say you have received something conveys a sense of action; to simply have it is static. The phrase "at hand" is superfluous; omit it. Once again, the expressions "we have received . . ." and "thank you for . . ." are simpler and much better.)

As per your report . . .
(Write more naturally "according to your report. . . .")

Permit me to say that . . .
(Permission is irrelevant. Simply say what you want to say.)

Yours of the 12th . . .
(Be specific. Write "your memorandum of June 12 . . . .")

and contents duly noted . . .
(This is a superfluous phrase. If you're answering a communication, obviously you have noted it.)

Re your claim . . .
(This is stiff and legalistic. Write instead "about your claim . . ." or "regarding your claim . . .")

Pursuant to . . .
(This too sounds stiff and legalistic. You probably mean "according to . . .," "complying with . . .," or "following upon . . .")

In reference to said contract . . .
(Using said as an adjective is also quite stiff.)

Attached herewith . . . , attached please find . . . , enclosed herein . . . , please find enclosed . . .
(These are stuffy ways of saying "we have attached . . ." or "enclosed is . . . .")

Anticipating your favor, I remain . . . ; awaiting your reply, we are . . . ; trusting we shall receive your favor, I am . . .

(These "-ing" endings have been old-fashioned for years. Get rid of the opening participle—"anticipating," "awaiting," "trusting"—and rewrite the closing as a self-contained sentence: "We look forward to hearing from you soon. Sincerely, . . .")

In due course. . .
(This is a vague and stuffy way of saying a specific time, such as "within three weeks . . .")

Under separate cover . . .
(Just write "separately," and if you can, add the mode of dispatch—"by air mail," "by parcel post.")

Allow me to express . . .
(This is another high-flown and superfluous opening. Just say whatever you wish to say.)

In response to same . . .
(This is another carry-over from legal documents—which for the most part are hideously written—into business letters. You are better off using the pronoun "it" or the appropriate noun: "In response to it . . . ," "in response to your recent inquiry . . . .")

Jargon

Jargon, in its best sense, is the technical or specialized vocabulary of a particular group, profession, or trade, such as legal jargon, educational jargon, medical jargon, real estate jargon, musicians' jargon. Such use of language is shoptalk and is quite appropriate if both reader and writer understand the terminology. But often specialists—insurance agents, lawyers, advertising executives, engineers, government bureaucrats, to list a few—forget that the outsider doesn't share their specialized language. Then we have cloud formations and private language.

For instance, somebody outside the real estate appraisal field might not understand such terms as "the residual techniques," "economic life, " and "unit-in-place factors." Government bureaucrats may use the term "units of nutritional intake," but most readers would better understand the more direct word "food."

Jargon at its worst uses long, abstract words, elaborately constructed sentences, circumlocution, and technical language for its own sake.

The cure for most jargon is clear, direct thought and simple, straightforward language.

JARGON: It is my considered opinion that by examining Turner's thought processes, we shall be in a position to determine the real validity of his hypotheses and conclusions concerning the Hillsdale project.

NATURAL: I think we should examine Turner's theories about the Hillsdale project to see how valid they are.

If clear communication were not so important, the use of jargon could be considered ludicrous. We could construct a "jargon-making machine" to humorously illustrate the point that jargon just does not communicate sincere, serious ideas. The machine is made up of three columns of selected jargon words:

JARGON-MAKING MACHINE: CHECKLIST

Input A	Input B	Base
0. operational	0. input	0. concept
1. compatible	1. incremental	1. feedback
2. optional	2. reciprocal	2. capability
3. systematized	3. organizational	3. projection
4. finalized	4. interface	4. options
5. functional	5. policy	5. rationale
6. total	6. logistical	6. mobility
7. parallel	7. relevant	7. flexibility
8. responsive	8. digital	8. programming
9. synchronized	9. monitored	9. contingency

What you do as a letter writer to spare yourself the work of thinking up jargon is to chose a three-digit number. Then choose the corresponding word from each column. For example number 892 gives you "responsive monitored capability." Number 168 produces "compatible logistical programming." These phrases can be dropped into your business letters at random to give them a tone of authoritative knowledge. Your reader won't have the slightest idea what you are talking about—and, of course, he won't ask you.

Exaggeration

Exaggerated expressions get in the way of direct communication. One kind of exaggeration makes use of extreme descriptions like "fabulous," "fantastic," "marvelous," "wonderful," and "miraculous." Another kind of exaggeration shows up in those intensifiers or superlatives that cover the universe like "very," "best," "must," "latest," "largest," "least," and "highest."

Such terms are obviously emotional, subjective, and inaccurate and so obscure or evade the basic information. The reader is disgruntled at the distortion or lack of information and also questions the writer's sincerity.

EXAGGERATED: This fantastic machine sells for $180.

DIRECT: This machine sells for $180.

From other information given, the reader can draw his or her own conclusions as to the quality of the machine.

EXAGGERATED: The Full-Scan camera is *positively* the *best* money can buy, and our stores give the *largest* discount available *anywhere.*

DIRECT: The Full-Scan Camera comes complete with high quality and low price. Compare.

It is a strain on communication to make the reader believe that the writer has such complete information and sound judgment about this and all other cameras.

Incorrect Idiom

Idioms are special word groups which have a total meaning not obviously suggested by the parts. The following idioms are ridiculous or nonsensical if analyzed literally:

board a train
look up an old friend
catch his eye
takes after her boss
strike a bargain

Prepositions especially get attached to certain words and natural usage demands accustomed combinations. We say "full of joy" not "full with joy," and "filled with joy" not "filled of joy." Likewise, you say "I differ *from* him" if you mean "unalike," and you say "I differ *with* him" if you mean "disagree."

Here are some examples of base words with their proper prepositions.

authority on (a subject)
authority over (a subordinate)
desirous of (doing something)
interest in
preparatory to
variance with (another)
vary from, in, with

The Calculated Euphemism

Sometimes a business letter shouldn't be direct. The writer has to express an unpleasant idea, but doesn't want harsh words to produce a negative attitude toward the reader or the central message. The writer can ease around negative reactions by using euphemisms.

A euphemism is a word or phrase used instead of another word or phrase in order to avoid (or at least soften) a negative connotation. The substitute word is rarely as precise or as expressive as the original, but it is preferable because the reader understands it without reacting adversely to it. Instead of "die," you might use the less offensive term "pass on." Instead of "graveyard," you would use "memorial park." Through the process of euphemism, "toilets" become "rest rooms" or "powder rooms," "syphilis" becomes a "social disease," "old people" become "senior citizens," and "garbage" becomes "refuse."

As a business writer, you should become sensitive to the techniques of euphemism and to the need for it. You will have to, occasionally, search hard for euphemisms to avoid displeasing terms. A partial list of the hundreds of euphemisms presently in use appears in this checklist:

EUPHEMISMS: CHECKLIST

The Unpleasant Term	The Euphemism
toilet bowl	commode
toilet (room)	rest room, men's room, ladies' room
garbage	refuse
servants	household staff
social blunder	indiscretion, *faux pas*
false teeth	dentures
women's underwear	lingerie
bad breath	halitosis
to urinate or defecate	to void
to spit	to expectorate
to arrest	to detain
to spy	to do intelligence work
indoctrination	education, pacification
propaganda	information
blockade	quarantine
death blow	*coup de grace*
elderly people, old people	senior citizens
neurotic	sensitive, high strung
psychopathic	disturbed
homosexual	gay
a dying patient	a terminal patient
to die	to expire, pass on
corpse	body, remains
undertaker	mortician, funeral director, grief therapist
tombstone	monument

cemetery	memorial park
retarded child	special child
cheap	inexpensive
to steal	to lift
a lie	a fabrication
to kill (for punishment)	to execute
to kill (for mercy, an animal)	to put to sleep
to kill (for mercy, a person)	euthanasia
to disembowel	to eviscerate
beheaded	decapitated
rape	criminal assault
foul smell	odor
payments	premiums

EXERCISES

1. Use each of the following words in a sentence to indicate the correct meaning.

   a. advise — inform
   b. enervate — invigorate
   c. practical — practicable
   d. disinterested — uninterested
   e. immigrant — emigrant
   f. receipt — recipe
   g. climactic — climatic
   h. acquiesce — consent
   i. acknowledge — admit
   j. opaque — translucent

2. Explain the differences in meaning among the following groups of words.

   a. outdo, surpass, excel, transcend, exceed
   b. fat, plump, obese, heavy, stout
   c. minimize, belittle, disparage, deprecate
   d. drunk, inebriated, plastered, intoxicated, stoned, potted
   e. dead, defunct, expired, deceased
   f. persistent, strong-willed, firm, stubborn, obstinate, pigheaded
   g. renown, fame, notoriety
   h. house, home, residence, dwelling, domicile, pad

3. Evaluate the word "old-fashioned" in the following sentences to see what meanings it has besides its denotation of referring to past time.

a. The dress she was wearing was rather old-fashioned.
b. He is decorating his living room in old-fashioned American.
c. That idea is a little old-fashioned, isn't it ?
d. I'm just a simple, old-fashioned girl.
e. I believe in the old-fashioned philosophy of no work, no eat.
f. Stop in for some old-fashioned cooking.

4. Make a list of more specific words for the following general terms. For instance, for "say," you could list "mumble," "mutter," "whisper," "shout," "yell," "state," "utter," "drawl."

a. vehicle   f. bad
b. building   g. entertainment
c. goods   h. person
d. walk   i. landscaping
e. good   j. land

5. Rewrite the following sentences, making general words more specific.

a. A man was looking into the store window.
b. I did a lot of things during my vacation.
c. Several aspects of the room made it unattractive.
d. The injury that our best saleswoman had suffered was serious enough to keep her out for quite a while.
e. After eating, we had some really good entertainment.
f. One member of the group was irresponsible about some of his duties.
g. During the last part of the project, we encountered several difficulties.
h. Many items around the place needed to be repaired before the people could move in.
i. It's an interesting machine.
j. The actions of the people represented both a test of skill and an effort to gain prestige for the cause.

6. The following sentences lack vitality because of clichés. Rewrite them in fresh language.

a. The manual is being sent under separate cover. Will you kindly acknowledge receipt of same?
b. According to our records, the project is to be completed in the near future.
c. Tilden is a borderline candidate for regional manager, but where there's a will there's a way.
d. Mrs. Jones fought tooth and nail to get the new school bill passed.
e. Mrs. Jenkins really burned the midnight oil; for seven straight days last week she worked until the wee small hours.
f. I told Mayford what we needed, and it was no sooner said than done.

g. He was up at the crack of dawn every morning because the early bird always gets the worm.

h. Making ends meet is rough sledding in this day and age.

i. For all intents and purposes, people who really care about their jobs are as scarce as hen's teeth.

j. While some of the salesclerks were stealing to their heart's content, Mary Adams remained as honest as the day is long.

7. Here is a short reply letter written in horse-and-buggy language. Rewrite the letter, making it direct and natural.

```
Dear Mrs. Barleyby:

Yours of the 18th received and contents
duly noted.  Enclosed herewith please
find one copy of "The New Antiques" as
per your request.

Thanking you for the opportunity to
provide you with same, I remain,

                    Yours truly,

                    Timothy Custer

                    Timothy Custer
                    Customer Service
                    Manager
```

8. Eliminate jargon and hackneyed phrases from the following sentences, and write them in simple, straightforward diction.

a. We may find it necessary to communicate with him tomorrow relative to the change in plans and ascertain what alternate arrangement he may consider feasible.

b. The last rays of the sun were sinking behind the western horizon, when I returned wearily to my domicile after my futile attempts to peddle my wares.

c. They did not find it practicable to make the journey to our place of business because of the inclement weather conditions.

d. They were holding an intense verbal contention as to whether canines or felines are the most desirable members of the animal kingdom.

e. We must be cognizant of the fact that although a substantial segment of the population occupies areas comprising numerous agricultural units, yet this same segment suffers a deficiency in units of nutritional intake.

9. These sentences use exaggerated terms. Tone them down, making them direct and believable.

    a. We are positive that you will agree that this is a fantastic price for such a camera.

    b. It's a marvelous time of the year to paint your house.

    c. This vacuum sweeper is the most efficient on the market.

    d. The fabulous increase in sales is attributed to the superb advertising campaign.

    e. Supersell Outlets give the largest discount available anywhere.

10. Correct the unidiomatic use of prepositions.

    a. We were quite desirous to arrive before the store closed.

    b. Ever since Mrs. Buxton became angry at me, she has refused to buy here.

    c. He would not admit to making the mistake, and his supervisor would not absolve him of the responsibility.

    d. The usual customer seems oblivious to the feelings of the salesclerk.

    e. His aims were identical to mine.

    f. Your aims are different than mine.

    g. The jury acquitted him from the the crime of arson.

    h. Three stenographers refuse to conform with the rule against smoking.

    i. Everybody complied to his request to talk softly.

    j. I am incompatible to his theories of let the buyer beware.

11. List several euphemisms for each of the following.

    a. fire (as *The boss fired him.*)

    b. dumb (not intelligent)

    c. failure (as *His attempt ended in failure.*)

    d. insane

    e. Pay your bill.

5   The Sentence: Clear and Forceful

Brevity and Directness
Consistency and Connection
Emphasis

The effect of your message is largely determined by the way you put words together into sentences to express your thoughts. If your letter is to be clear and forceful, you must go beyond mere correct grammar, though your grammar must be correct for both clarity and force. Your style can follow all the rules of spelling, punctuation, and good usage, and still be cumbersome and weak.

Several kinds of construction commonly creep into the arrangement of sentences and impede the effectiveness of the message. This chapter will identify some bad sentence habits and point out ways to eliminate them. The aim is to make your sentences effective in three areas:

1. Brevity and directness in wording
2. Consistency and connection between parts
3. Emphasis on important ideas

BREVITY AND DIRECTNESS

Without being curt, what you write should be brief and direct. Use only the words you need, and put them in the snappiest order. Your idea should move like an arrow to the target, not lumber like a mud turtle through the underbrush. Every word should contribute to the meaning or to the character of the message. Unnecessary words make your writing flabby and cloudy. The reader finds it too hard to get what you mean and tends to throw the letter away.

Wordiness does not mean using a lot of words. It means using more words than you need. In short, state your idea to the point in the fewest words possible. Here are some guides to being brief and direct.

Repeat for Emphasis Only

Avoid using words whose meanings are clearly implied by other words. Such wordiness is called *redundancy*. Don't say the same thing over and over and over—as I have just done with "over"—except for emphasis. Here are some examples of redundancy:

WORDY: Many of our customers like long, fictional literature. Reading novels is a real pleasure to them.

CONCISE: Many of our customers like reading novels.

WORDY: The contract shall be considered a valid contract if the terms of said contract are not made retroactive to the date on which the contract is signed.

CONCISE: The contract shall be considered valid if its terms are not made retroactive to the date of signing.

Beware of a pair of terms joined by "and" when one of the terms adds no meaning. Here are some examples:

Whatever *help* and *assistance* you need. . .
You are to *go through* the invoices and *separate* them into three piles. (You surely have to "go through" the invoices in order to "separate" them.)
The *worth* and *value* of this merchandise. . .
Jake's *capacity* to *understand* and his *ability* to *explain*. . . (If he can "explain," he certainly is able to "understand".)

Avoid double statements in which one term obviously implies the other. Here are some examples:

advance *forward*	visible *to the eye*
tall *in height*	*the month of* August
a *true* fact	his *personal* opinion
red *in color*	*a pair of* twins
when *first* begun	permanently disabled *for life*
surrounded *on all sides*	to combine *together*
consensus *of opinion*	a *complete* monopoly
modern youth *of today*	*absolutely* essential
audible *to the ear*	the *basic* fundamentals

Shorten Clauses and Phrases

When you can, eliminate constructions with "who," "whom," and "that," and reduce prepositional phrases to a key word or two.

WORDY: John Collins, who has been my friend all of my life, wants to work in the dispatching office with me.

CONCISE: John Collins, my lifelong friend, wants to work in the dispatching office with me.

WORDY: The tool which we use in this situation . . .

DIRECT: The tool used in this situation . . .

WORDY: Most of the new styles in this day and age pass quickly.

CONCISE: Most new styles pass quickly.

Check the following examples of common phrases and clauses against their one-word equivalents:

BREVITY: CHECKLIST

in this day and age	today
during the time that	while
a large number of	many
a small number of	few
in the same way	similarly
at an early date	soon
in the near future	soon
at the present time	now (or presently)
due to the fact that	because
most of the time	usually
leaving out of consideration	disregarding
without making any noise	noiselessly
as a result of	consequently
there is no doubt that	doubtlessly
it cannot be denied that	undeniably

The "to" Form of the Verb

Use the "to" form of the verb for a direct route as illustrated in the following example.

INDIRECT: He was here for the purpose of painting a sign.

DIRECT: He was here to paint a sign.

INDIRECT: In order that enough time be allowed . . .

DIRECT: To allow enough time . . .

Eliminate Unnecessary Articles

If you can use a plural subject instead of a singular subject for general statements, you can eliminate articles (*a, an, the*).

SINGULAR: A happy customer means a repeat sale.

PLURAL: Happy customers mean repeat sales.

Eliminate Indirectness

Cut out the phrases "it is" and "there is." Direct statements are more effective.

INDIRECT: It was on the first day of the sale that she bought the dress.

DIRECT: She bought the dress on the first day of the sale.

INDIRECT: There are two trucks that should be replaced.

DIRECT: Two trucks should be replaced.

Avoid Clusters of General Words

Use specific verbs, nouns, and modifiers instead of combinations of general adjectives and adverbs. "Run quickly" means "speed" or "rush." "Turned red with embarrassment" means "blush." "A person under twenty-one" is a "minor." "A worker in the factory" is a "factory worker." "Extremely tired" is "weary" or "fatigued."

Combine nouns and verbs into one verb. "To give advice" means "advise." "Became the owner of" means "bought" or "acquired."

Combine Short Sentences

A series of short sentences may use a wordy repetition of subjects and verbs. Combine series of short sentences into one reduced, direct sentence.

COMPOUND: There's a 4:30 plane leaving for Los Angeles on Friday. I'd better be on it if I'm to address the sales meeting.

REDUCED: If I'm to address the sales meeting Friday, I'd better be on the 4:30 plane to Los Angeles.

WORDY SERIES: He typed four letters in the morning. Then after lunch he filed invoices. Then he treated himself to a coffee break.

DIRECT: After typing four letters in the morning and filing invoices after lunch, he treated himself to a coffee break.

Avoid Multiple Hedging

Hedging on a statement causes wordiness and indirectness. A careful writer will not make an absolute statement unless he or she is sure of its validity. He or she will use phrases like "probably," "usually," "it is said that," and "he seems to be." The evasive and unsure writer, however, may hedge more than is necessary. Most evasions produce wordiness. For example, the following sentence contains three hedges.

I *believe* that market research *seems* to indicate that X-Shine will *probably* go over big.

Such multiple hedging suggests that the writer is unsure of himself. To evade making a direct assertion, he is unnecessarily wordy. One hedge would have been enough.

I *believe* that market research indicates that X-Shine will go over big.

Market research indicates that X-Shine *probably* will go over big.

CONSISTENCY AND CONNECTION

Your message will be vague, dull, and maybe even exasperating if the parts of your sentences are not consistent and clearly connected. If your thoughts do not move smoothly and neatly, your reader may not have the time, interest, and energy to labor to get your message. Awkwardness has many causes. Four of the common ones are examined here—fuzzy pronouns and pointers, dangling modifiers, shifts in perspective, and wrenched parallelism.

Fuzzy Pronouns and Pointers

The *customer* told *Sally* that *she* was still confused.

It is risky to use personal pronouns like "he," "she," and "they" and pointer words like "that," "this," "which," "the former," and "as mentioned above." These words take their meaning only from other words nearby, and if the connection is not perfectly clear, the communication fails.

PRONOUNS.   Make sure your pronouns point definitely to a noun word. The noun word that a pronoun points to is called an *antecedent* or *referent*. Check these five kinds construction for fuzzy pronouns:

1. *Two Possible Antecedents.*   If the pronoun can point to two nouns, change the sentence to leave one clear connection.

   FUZZY: James told his supervisor that he had made an error.

   CLEAR: James told his supervisor, "You have made an error."

   CLEAR: James admitted to his supervisor that he had made an error.

   CLEAR: James accused his supervisor of making an error.

2. *Almost Noun.*   The word referred to should be the exact form of the noun for which the pronoun is a substitute. Modifiers, possessives, and implied nouns are fuzzy.

   FUZZY: Before the repairman could tend to the rabbit cages, some of them ran away.

   CLEAR: Before the repairman could repair the rabbit cages, some of the rabbits ran away.

3. *Group of Words as Referent.*   The pronouns "which," "that," "this," and "it" are often used fuzzily to refer to a whole idea or group of words. Give them a single noun word or compound word to refer to.

   FUZZY: Jones refused to join the office raffle, which was considered as disloyalty to the company.

   CLEAR: Jones's refusal to join the office raffle was considered as disloyalty to the company.

   FUZZY: Mrs. Thompson protested about the new rule, but it didn't change anything.

   CLEAR: Mrs. Thompson protested about the new rule, but her protest didn't change anything.

4. *Far-off Nouns.*   If the word referred to is too far back in the sentence or paragraph, repeat the noun or rewrite the sentence.

   FUZZY: One waitress chased the flies off the counter and then sat down at the table with the other waitresses, but they came back immediately.

   CLEAR: One waitress chased the flies off the counter and then sat down at the table with the other waitresses, but the flies came back immediately.

5. *Personal Pronouns in a General Sense.*   The pronouns "you," "they," and "it" are usually fuzzy and illogical when they stand for people or things in general rather than for a specific noun word.

FUZZY: At Bay Harbor Resort they treat newcomers courteously.

CLEAR: At Bay Harbor Resort the staff treat newcomers courteously.

CLEAR: At Bay Harbor Resort the residents treat newcomers courteously.

FUZZY: I like courses in economics because they teach you the ideological basis for business.

CLEAR: I like courses in economics because they teach a person (or *me*) the ideological basis for business.

OTHER POINTERS.   To save words or sometimes because of laziness, writers may point the reader's attention backward on the page with expressions like these:

the aforementioned	the former
as mentioned above	the latter
the above listed	respectively

For example, a company memo might come through like this:

Parking permits for employees and volunteers are distributed by the Personnel and the Customer Service Departments *respectively*.

The pointer *respectively* is a device for connecting items in the sentence. The trouble, however, is that the reader must jump to the beginning of the sentence to get the meaning clear. And anything that makes the reader stop, stumble, and scramble back through the message to figure out the meaning is a flaw to be removed. The pointer is easily avoided by separate constructions and clear pronoun reference:

Parking permits for employees are distributed by the Personnel Department, those for volunteers, by the Customer Service Department.

Pointers can save a few words, but they should not be used at the expense of a clear connection between parts of the sentence.

Dangling Modifiers

Coming in by plane, the *smog* . . .

A modifier will usually be connected to some word or words that it describes. A dangling modifier, as the term implies, is a modifier given nothing to modify. It just hangs there, disconnected. If the word it should logically modify is not even in the sentence, the part appears to be attached to a nearby word to which it is not logically connected. The reader usually figures out the meaning, but the writer can be left looking rather foolish.

Check the following disconnected meaning with its ludicrous effect.

While *walking* through the showroom, the dirty *windows.* . . . (Halfway through the sentence, the reader gets the image of dirty windows strolling along.)

By following these guidelines, *your ability* to please customers will improve. (Who's doing the following, *you* or your *ability?*)

He was tired and nervous, causing him to make mistakes. (Not ludicrous, just fuzzy.)

Danglers are easy enough to connect, in one of two ways:

1. Give the phrase its own subject and verb, and it won't need a close attachment.

    While *I walked* through the showroom the dirty windows . . .

2. Insert the right noun or pronoun to tie the phrase together.

    While walking through the showroom, *I* noticed the dirty windows.

The other dangling modifiers can be tightened up the same way.

By following these guidelines, *you* will improve your ability to please customers.
If *you follow* these guidelines, your ability to please customers will improve.
Because *he was* tired and nervous, he made mistakes.
His *tiredness* and *nervousness* caused him to make mistakes.

Shifts in Perspective

When a *person* first realizes his job is important, *they* . . .

When a *person* first realizes a job is important, *he* . . .

Once you have selected your perspective and the kind of construction you are going to use for your message, stick to the pattern—unless you have a very good reason to shift. Your reader is following the trail you have set. Don't throw him off. Here are some checkpoints for shifts to be avoided: person, subject or verb, command and statement, direct and indirect discourse, and tense.

PERSON.   Avoid shifts from third person ("he," "she," "one," "a person," "they") to second person ("you") and from singular ("a person," "he," "one," "she") to plural ("they").

SHIFT: *All personnel* can use Parking Lot C. *You* do not need a permit.

CONSISTENT: *All personnel* can use Parking Lot C. *They* do not need a permit.

CONSISTENT: As a Burns Electronics employee, *you* can use Parking Lot C. *You* do not need a permit.

SUBJECT OR VERB.   A shift from active verb form to passive verb form changes the subject. In a series keep two subjects either both acting or both being acted upon.

SHIFT: I discovered I was out of typing paper, so a quick trip to Supply had to be made.

CONSISTENT: I discovered I was out of typing paper, so I had to make a quick trip to Supply.

COMMAND AND STATEMENT.   Make sure that you consistently use either commands or statements. Don't use both in the same sentence.

SHIFT: First read the directions carefully, and then all the parts should be laid out in order of assembly.

CONSISTENT: First read the directions carefully, and then lay out all the parts in order of assembly.

CONSISTENT: First the directions should be read carefully, and then all parts should be laid out in order of assembly.

DIRECT AND INDIRECT DISCOURSE.   Watch especially for shifts between statement and question.

SHIFT: He asked me if I liked the suit and would I like to try it on.

CONSISTENT: He asked me if I liked the suit and if I would like to try it on.

CONSISTENT: He asked me, "Do you like the suit and would you like to try it on?"

TENSE.   Watch especially for shifts between past and present.

SHIFT: Clemens *is* not fair to Pittman in calling him incompetent. He *cited* only Pittman's failures but *ignored* his successes.

CONSISTENT: Clemens *was* not fair . . . *cited* . . . *ignored* . . .

Wrenched Parallelism

Some words link pairs or series of equal importance, though the ideas may be contrasts or alternatives. Examples of such words are *"and," "but," "or," "nor," "for," "than," "not only-but also," "both-and," "neither-nor," "either-or."* Use the same kind of word pattern to express equal or parallel ideas. For example, link word with word, phrase with phrase, clause with clause. Link noun with noun, adjective with adjective, "-ing" word with "-ing" word, etc.

    Betty likes *typing*
                 filing, and
                 taking coffee breaks.

    Betty likes *to type*
                 to file, and
                 to take coffee breaks.

The sign words of parallel structure, such as "and," may not always be used, but the parts should still take similar form.

of the people, by the people, for the people
I came, I saw, I conquered.

    Parallel structure makes both ideas clear and emphatic. A repeated pattern shows that two or three items are equal and should be grouped. Parallel structure also hits hard because the key words stand out.

WRENCHED: The sales pitch was long, dull, and didn't make any point.

PARALLEL: The sales pitch was long, dull, and pointless.

WRENCHED: I didn't know whether I should become a salesperson or to go into advertising.

PARALLEL: I didn't know whether to become a salesperson or an advertiser.

PARALLEL: I didn't know whether to go into sales work or advertising.

WRENCHED: The foreman was a perfectionist himself and who expected perfection in others.

PARALLEL: The foreman expected perfection in both himself and others.

EMPHASIS

Emphasis is the technique of giving each of your ideas its due weight and of making your ideas hit the reader hard. Emphasis is the result of many skills: (1) clear thinking about your ideas; (2) correct and clear sentence structure; (3) vivid and accurate word choice; and (4) careful use of pronouns and pointers, of perspective, of modifiers, and of parallel structure. Beyond these skills, emphasis is achieved by the following devices:

1. Key positions
2. Order of climax
3. The suspense sentence
4. Delayed subject
5. The strong active verb
6. Unusual word order
7. Repetition of key words
8. The short sentence

Key Positions

Last and first are, in that order, the most emphatic spots. End your sentence with the most important idea. Strongest in our minds is what we read last. Lead off with your next most important idea. Bury the minor, dull but necessary ideas in the middle.

WEAK ENDING:	Because of careless inspection of the fire extinguishing system, over 200 lives were lost, it was calculated.
EMPHATIC ENDING:	Because of careless inspection of the fire extinguishing system, over 200 lives, it was calculated, were lost.
WEAK BEGINNING:	In my opinion, apathetic salesmen are the cause of decreased sales.
EMPHATIC BEGINNING:	Apathetic salesmen are, in my opinion, the cause of decreased sales.

Order of Climax

Three or more items in a series should be arranged in emphatic order, with the most important item last.

The country's main concerns are hunger, sickness, and death.

While some items usually take a logical order, such as death over hunger, you may choose your own rising order of importance according to context and purpose. For instance, you may wish to stress food problems:

The country's main concerns are sickness, death, and, most immediately, hunger.

Final position is most emphatic. Make sure you put the items in the order of importance called for by your context.

ANTICLIMACTIC: The fire in the warehouse killed ten people, injured twenty people, and destroyed two rooms of furniture.

EMPHATIC: The fire in the warehouse destroyed rooms of furniture, injured twenty people, and killed ten people.

The Suspense Sentence

The *suspense sentence* withholds its main or completing idea until the very end. A *loose sentence* states the full idea early and then adds qualifiers and other details, often parenthetical. With a loose sentence a reader's attention can lag after he reads the main idea. But a suspense sentence creates suspense and demands attention, because to get the meaning, the reader cannot stop until the period.

LOOSE AND UNEMPHATIC: Maxwell resumed his description of the fire, after standing silently before the committee for a full minute with tears in his eyes.

SUSPENSEFUL AND EMPHATIC: After standing silently before the committee for a full minute with tears in his eyes, Maxwell resumed his description of the fire.

In effective writing most of your sentences should be loose sentences. Too much straining for suspense may give a false sense of melodrama. Here is a standard, loose, effective sentence with the central idea first, where it belongs:

The cashier stopped the flow of blood with a piece of cloth torn from the hem of her dress.

Delayed Subject

The subject or central idea is delayed in the suspense sentence simply by putting phrases in a certain order. Verbal devices like the expletives "it is" and "there is," "what" clauses, and general synonyms also hold suspense by pointing to the subject to come later. These introductory words are like warning signs to alert the reader: "Important idea just ahead."

STANDARD: An angry crowd was gathering at the cashier's window.

DELAYED: There was an angry crowd gathering at the cashier's window.

STANDARD: Mr. Fleming's curt memo hurt company morale the most.

DELAYED: What hurt company morale the most was Mr. Fleming's curt memo.

Strong Active Verb

Because the active voice expresses the direct action of the subject, it is more emphatic than the passive. As a rule, use the active voice. Use passive, by which the subject is acted upon, only when you can clearly justify it.

WEAK PASSIVE: Fifty dollars was received by each worker.

STRONG ACTIVE: Each worker received fifty dollars.

The active voice is obviously the more direct, concise, and emphatic way of expressing the idea. However, there are two special occasions when you should use the passive voice. The first is when the receiver of the action is more important than the doer:

STRONG PASSIVE: A thin line of black paint is put along the edge of the plate to indicate where the motion block is to be attached.

STRONG PASSIVE: The new showroom was finished in September.

STRONG PASSIVE: The Christmas window was decorated entirely in blue.

STRONG PASSIVE: Cynthia Studdard was arrested, tried, and convicted of the crime of burglary.

The second effective use of the passive is to deliberately deemphasize the normal action of the verb, perhaps to soften the impact of bad news. We can call this the *diplomatic passive*.

DIPLOMATIC PASSIVE: When your check is received . . . (Instead of "When you pay your bill . . .")

DIPLOMATIC PASSIVE: Smoking in the fitting room is prohibited. (Instead of "Don't smoke in the fitting room," or "The management prohibits smoking in the fitting room.")

Unusual Word Order

Any word gains emphasis when it varies from the expected word order. For clarity we usually write a direct line sentence—subject→verb→any necessary receiver of the action or identifying word. When a word is put in an unexpected place, it gains sudden attention.

NORMAL: We should never have begun such a risky project.

UNUSUAL: Such a risky project we should never have begun.

NORMAL: We could hardly expect prompt payment from a man of his credit rating.

UNUSUAL: Hardly could we expect prompt payment from a man of his credit rating.

NORMAL: The best bargains in town are waiting for you at Burton's day after day.

UNUSUAL: Waiting for you day after day at Burton's are the best bargains in town.

Unusual order must be used sparingly. As a violent means for gaining emphasis, it can easily become artificial and affected. We could well advise, "Sparingly must unusual word order be used."

Repetition of Key Words

Repeating sentence patterns to achieve consistency has been discussed under "Wrenched Parallelism." Key words can also be repeated to emphasize your most important points. Notice the double force of the key word "help" in these sentences:

> Don't merely ask your client how you can *help* him. Tell him precisely how you can *help* him.

In this passage, the key idea of "new" comes across emphatically.

> Everything in the showroom is *new*. The furnishings are *new*; the merchandise is *new*; even the price tags are *new*.

Repetition must be confined to key words or sentence patterns and must be carefully used to gain emphasis. Careless and needless repetition of words leads to dull, flat writing.

WORDY: When *one* studies the *customer, one* will find that the many gestures the *customer* makes will give *one* clues as to what the *customer* is thinking.

The Short Sentence

The typical straightforward sentence runs from 13 to 17 words. You don't need to be a word counter as you write letters, but you should know if your sentences tend to be too long, too short, or monotonously unvaried. If you find that your usual sentence is more than 13 to 17 words long, your style might be cumbersome. Compare the following original with its revision. They both contain the same number of words.

CUMBERSOME: I have carefully checked the personnel records of all our field employees and found only two that I think will be of interest to Mr. Dexter as he faces the difficult problem of selecting the right person for District Manager of the Springfield area.

STRAIGHTFORWARD: I have carefully checked the personnel records of all our field employees and found only two that are promising. Mr. Dexter faces a difficult problem in selecting the right personnel for District Manager of the Springfield area. I think these two will interest him.

The cumbersome first memo has one sentence of 43 words. The snappy second memo has three sentences of 19, 18, and 7 words each.

If, on the other hand, most of your sentences contain fewer than 13 words, your style may sound choppy and juvenile. Compare the following choppy original with the revision, which gains force by combining sentences.

CHOPPY: Martin called today. He said the Model 210s were shipped Friday. They should be here tomorrow. When they arrive, display them in the Elec Room. I'll prepare an ad. I'll let you know when it's ready.

EMPHATIC: Martin called today saying the Model 210s were shipped Friday and should be here tomorrow. When they arrive, display them in the Elec Room. I'll prepare an ad and call you when it's ready.

Variation in sentence length is as important as the average length. Some of your sentences should be short, some average, some long, with no regular pattern of variation. Look again at the revised memo above about Mr. Dexter's search for a district manager. It contains three sentences with an average length of 14.66 words. But note how they vary: 19, 18 (beyond the standard 17), and then a concise, emphatic 7.

Analyze the varied sentence lengths of the following section from a confidential memorandum. The writer wanted to be personal and genial, but forceful.

The Springfield territory, which you are about to take over, requires a shrewd mind, a facile imagination, and a capacity for downright hard work. Others have tackled it and failed. The last two people took on the job with the same confidence you show, only to become frustrated quite quickly with its problems. Both of them underestimated the demands of the territory. I am confident you will not.

There are five sentences averaging 13.6 words—a fine average. But note the variation: first a long sentence (24 words), then a short one (6 words), another long one (23 words), then a medium short one (9 words), and a final brief one (6 words) that hits like a fist. The ideas gain emphasis through variation of sentence length.

Paragraph Length

Besides the number of words in a sentence, it is important to check the number of sentences in a paragraph. Again, as with the sentence, a message is ineffective if it has too many short paragraphs or too many long paragraphs.

The average paragraph has from two to six sentences. This is not a law, but a guideline. In business letters the paragraph is mainly a device to make the message easy to read. If your paragraphs are over six sentences long, the reader will likely get tired, and his attention will lag. Express your ideas in sections easy to grasp. Break your thoughts into logical subdivisions.

If your paragraphs consistently contain fewer than two sentences, except in brief and simple messages, you might be missing some logical connections between your ideas. You may seem scatterbrained. Occasionally of course, a paragraph may contain only one sentence because only one sentence is necessary to develop the idea fully. Opening paragraphs and closing paragraphs often require only one sentence. Also, a one-sentence paragraph, like the sudden, brief sentence, can be very emphatic—if not overused. Compare the following two letters to see how effective paragraphing can make a letter easy to read.

Dear Mr. Pender:

We are happy to tell you, in reply to your letter of June 8, that our service department has found nothing seriously wrong with your Luminex Camera, Model 20. A few inexpensive repairs and adjustments are needed, mainly the replacement of one part of the shutter mechanism and readjustment of the timing. The camera seems to have been dropped or seriously jarred. Our guarantee covers "any defect of workmanship or materials within one year of normal use," but as you no doubt realize, it does not cover improper handling. If you will send us your check for $6.37, we will put your camera in first-class condition and renew our guarantee on workmanship and materials for another year. Just as soon as you sign and mail the enclosed, stamped, addressed post card, we'll return your camera as good as new--ready to catch that perfect moment in film ahead.

Sincerely yours,

```
Dear Mr. Pender:

We are happy to tell you, in reply to your letter of June 8, that
our service department has found nothing seriously wrong with your
Luminex Camera, Model 20.

A few inexpensive repairs and adjustments are needed, mainly the
replacement of one part of the shutter mechanism and readjustment
of the timing.  The camera appears to have been dropped or seriously
jarred.

Our guarantee covers "any defect of workmanship or materials within
one year of normal use," but, as you no doubt realize, it does not
cover improper handling.  If you will send us your check for $6.37,
we will put your camera in first-class condition and renew our
guarantee on workmanship and materials for another year.

Just as soon as you sign and mail the enclosed, stamped, addressed
post card, we'll return your camera as good as new--ready to catch
in film that perfect moment ahead.

                    Sincerely yours,
```

The revised paragraphs are all short, with one to two sentences, because the message is simple. The letter breaks into four parts to express the logical parts of the message (refusing a request for adjustment): (1) a positive opening, giving a cushion for the bad news to follow, (2) the reason for rejection, (3) the refusal itself and a positive alternative, and (4) a positive close with reader benefit.

EXERCISES

1. Make the following sentences more brief and direct.

    a. ~~In the event~~ *If* that you can attend the meeting, plan ~~in advance~~ to offer some concrete suggestions on how to reduce the ~~cost and~~ expense of overtime in the Purchasing Department.

    b. Please find enclosed herewith a copy of the report, which is 20 pages in length.

    c. In view of the ~~foregoing facts and~~ figures, it seems appropriate to suggest an entirely new customer-service policy.

d. You will note when you study the cost of stationery that the expenditure of stationery has gradually and steadily increased for 1974, 1975, 1976, and 1977.

e. I have your letter of August 5 and wish to say that we'll be glad to give you a refund for the radio you bought here last week.

f. Accountants, in studying business procedures and methods of accounting, have been able to classify the business for purposes of their study. They have classified these concerns on the basis of the differences and similarities in the accounting functions.

g. The mechanization of office records is not a particularly new innovation in the business world.

h. Are you sending the invitations out in the mail in plenty of time so that those who are being invited will have sufficient advance notice in which to respond?

i. The accountants in our department individually and collectively agree with the decision arrived at to cease and desist the practice of amortizing product-development costs over a five-year period.

j. Please be assured that we are now rechecking and reviewing all of our specifications as it is our earnest and most sincere desire to be certain and for sure that this machine gives you satisfaction and good service in every possible way in the future.

k. In addition, will you please permit me to state in this letter that we will welcome any suggestions or comments that you may have at any time if you think of any methods for the improvement of our service to our customers.

l. Mr. Folk gave a talk on the growing increase in the popularity of bonus compensation systems for personnel in management positions.

m. Permit me to take this opportunity to call your attention to the fact that we have brought your account up to date.

n. For your information we are attaching hereto a carbon copy of the letter sent to Mr. Ted Black under date of July 14.

o. It seems as though we might be unable to agree on some of the terms you are posing here.

2. Revise the following sentences to eliminate fuzzy pronouns, dangling modifiers, shifts in perspective, and wrenched parallelism.

Fuzzy Pronouns

a. Gibson told the foreman that he should take the day off.

b. Then a police car arrived, and they arrested the two shoplifters.

c. The park which belongs to the city extends over 50 acres and includes three ball diamonds, a fishing pond, and a small zoo. It is free to the public.

d. The customer kept interrupting, which annoyed the salesman.

e. The report showed that on the Lower East Side they are not very sanitary.

Dangling Modifiers

f. Working at top speed in the morning, fatigue may overtake you in the afternoon.

g. To function smoothly, you must oil the machine every hour.

h. I enjoyed his speech at the dinner, which was very forceful.

i. To be baked just right, you should heat the oven to 375° before placing the cake inside.

j. We borrowed a calculator from the sales department which works perfectly.

Shifts

k. Any executive should be considerate of the opinions of their employees.

l. She resealed the letter after its contents had been carefully read.

m. First, write a courteous reminder; then if there is no response, you should write an urgent request for payment.

n. Jameson is not fair in calling Miss Olson irresponsible. He mentioned only her weaknesses and overlooked her strengths.

o. All salespersonnel may pick up a new Sun-Ray Kit immediately. You need only show your ID card.

Wrenched Parallelism

p. The personnel manager is responsible for the selection of the right worker, providing appropriate orientation, and the worker's progress.

q. The shipping clerk made three resolutions: (1) to be on time, (2) following instructions carefully, and third, the reduction of waste.

r. The new secretary is good at taking dictation, filing, and ability to type reports.

s. We have three objectives in mind: to finish the job in the shortest time possible, absolute accuracy, and insure that appearance is attractive.

t. The stories in this magazine have three shortcomings:
    (1) they appeal only to a small group of teenagers;
    (2) too many picture illustrations are employed, and
    (3) Why must they all be about the bad things in life?

3. Rewrite the following sentences to make them more emphatic according to the principle indicated.

Key Position

a. The markets are in for a period of inactivity, if I can read the signs correctly.

b. On the other hand, the new additive will increase mileage by 20%, tests show.

c. As our lawyer sees it, the trial will be prejudiced against the company from the beginning.

d. Without a doubt, the computer has had a great effect on business.

Order of Climax

e. The news of Betty's winning the Customer Award made her want to shout for joy, to dance, and to laugh.

f. The dog, dragging its chain, raced through the showroom, scraping the paint on the cars, cracking a show window, and overturning a flowerpot.

g. The new credit manager, Jeb Campbell, was president of the Northwest State Bank, chariman of the hospital board, and a member of the Kiwanis Club.

Suspense Sentence

    h.   Joe finally sold the yacht after three feverish days of phone calls, house calls, and demonstrations.

    i.   Walter put the territory in the black after six months of brilliant, tireless work.

    j.   We will have a better economy only when both management and labor agree that each has a right to its fair share.

Delayed Subject

    k.   The sarcasm of the office supervisor made the typists nervous.

    l.   The job can be done in more than one way.

    m.   To observe a customer being nasty to a salesperson is never very pleasant.

    n.   Ineffective advertising seems to be the most serious weakness of the Eastland unit.

Strong Active

    o.   The window has been decorated for the Easter sale.

    p.   Your merchandise is being shipped this morning.

    q.   The letter was written by the new assistant to Mrs. Nelson.

    r.   Your cooperation will certainly be appreciated by us.

Diplomatic Passive

    s.   You are not entitled to a new catalog; your purchases last year were less than the required $85.00.

    t.   You have included much useless information in the report.

    u.   You did not launder the shirts according to the instructions inside the collar.

Unusual Word Order

    v.   Jack would never make such a quota in a hundred years.

    w.   You could certainly expect accurate work from a secretary with her sense of responsibility.

    x.   All the power of that once great industrial empire is gone.

    y.   We dare not risk such a dangerous lawsuit.

4.   Improve the emphasis of this message by varying the sentence length.

Dear Miss Duval:

The error in your May statement was our error. We admit it is ours. We are enclosing a corrected statement. Your records and ours now agree. Thank you. We appreciate your help.

              Sincerely,

5. Make the following sentence more emphatic by using repetition of the key word "studied."

When Ben Taber took over the Springfield territory, he studied as he had never done before—before work, during lunch hour, at night, and on weekends—until everything in the territory became one piece of knowledge with himself.

6. Improve the clarity and emphasis of this portion of a memo by breaking up the one long sentence.

Because more than one freight classification may apply to the same type of goods, the traffic manager can effect further savings by a careful auditing or checking of freight bills the company is called upon to pay, since these charges are complicated and involved, and errors are often made in computation as well as in classification.

7. The following one-paragraph letter would discourage the usual reader. Break it into shorter, easy-to-grasp, but meaningful paragraphs.

```
        Dear Mr. Kramer:

        Thank you for asking us about a type of pen for
        which you have received many recent requests.  We
        do not carry such pens.  However, I would suggest
        our new Prince pen with giant cartridge.  Although
        just recently introduced, it is a best seller and
        is increasing in popularity, judging from orders
        received.  Our Prince pen, because of the large
        capacity of the giant cartridge, requires infrequent
        replacement of the cartridge and has won acceptance
        of many conventional pen owners.  The variety of ink
        colors available and the low cost of replacement
        cartridges are additional desirable features.  A
        descriptive folder highlighting the many features
        of this pen is enclosed.  The price list appears on
        the last page.  We can make shipment within four
        work days from the date of your order.  Our district
        representative, Mr. Timothy Dwight will be in Canton
        on May 10.  He can show you our full line and supply
        any additional information regarding our products.
        He will call you in the morning and arrange to see
        you at your convenience.  Do let me know if we can
        be of further assistance.

                    Sincerely yours,

                    William Kerr

                    William Kerr
                    Regional Sales Manager
```

6

The You Attitude: Getting the Reader Involved

Emphasize The Pronoun "You"
Point Out Reader Benefit
Have Real Interest in Your Reader
Check Your Reader-Interest Index

With it generally recognized that every business communication is a sales message, much attention has been given to the psychology of selling, of hidden persuaders, of the correct attitude of the letter writer. Actually, of all the strategies of letter writing, one principle is uppermost. We can more readily persuade others to do what we want them to by demonstrating that it is to their advantage to do it. This point of view is known as the "you attitude." The technique is to adopt the reader's point of view. You write not in terms of "how much *we* would like to have your order," but of "when *you* order this merchandise, *you* will benefit by increased profit and utility." People must be shown not just that they should agree, but that it is to their advantage to agree. The first requirement, then, of a successful letter is that it should have the "you attitude." It should take the reader's point of view. Four special techniques may help you develop the you attitude.

EMPHASIZE "YOU" INSTEAD OF "I"

This includes, of course, the pronoun's relatives. "You," "your," and "yours" should predominate, not "I," "me," "my," "mine," "we," "our," and "ours."

Your reader is usually more concerned about himself than about you or the company you represent. He appreciates seeing his name instead of merely "Dear Sir" in the salutation of your letter, and he likes seeing his name again in the body of a long letter. He is likely to read your message when he sees the pronoun "you" rather than "I," "we," "us." Try to get your reader into the first paragraph; if possible, begin with "you" or "your." And keep your reader in the message until you finish.

The following department store letter contains 20 "we-our-us-I-my" pronouns and only three "you" and "your" pronouns (underlined).

THE HUB

228 Scott Street

Oxford, Ohio

45056

Executive offices

Mrs. Sarah Thompson
2390 Milford Road
Oxford, Ohio 45056

Dear Mrs. Thompson:

I wish to take this opportunity to express my appreciation for the account you recently opened with our store. We are pleased to offer a wide variety of products for the home or individual.

We want you to take full advantage of our store services, for we have the largest stock in the city. Also we make deliveries of our customers' purchases free of charge within thirty miles of our store.

We always like to receive visits from our customers, but we also fill orders by phone. Our Customer Service Department aims to fill every order within the same day we receive it.

When shopping at our downtown store, customers are invited to use the free customer parking privilege provided just across the street from us.

We welcome you to The Hub. If we can be of additional service in any manner, please call on us.

Yours very sincerely,

Joseph N. Prossman

Joseph N. Prossman, President

JNP:pg

In contrast, the following letter—rewritten for more "you attitude"—contains 19 "yous" and "yours" (underlined) and only two "we-our-us" pronouns (underlined):

```
Dear Mrs. Thompson:

Thank you for the account you recently opened at
The Hub.  Serving you with your needs for clothing
and home furnishings is a pleasure.

You will find 28 departments at The Hub, stocked
with a variety of quality items.  And courteous sales
clerks are here to assist you in selecting the
merchandise that best meets your requirements.

If you prefer to shop within the comfort of your home,
instead of coming to the store, you need only to
telephone 762-1349 and ask for "Personal Shopping
Service."  A Personal Shopper will gladly take your
order for any number of items, answer your questions
about brands and sizes available, and see that the
goods you order reach you by store delivery within a
few days.

When you shop at our store downtown, you are invited
to use the free customer parking privilege provided
just across the street.

You are always welcome at The Hub.  Please call on
us whenever you need additional service.

                                Sincerely,
```

The opposite of the you attitude is the "we attitude," in which the writer views every matter from his own (or his organization's) standpoint rather than from the reader's.

We Attitude	You Attitude
We allow two percent discount for cash payments.	You earn two percent discount when you pay cash.

We Attitude	*You Attitude*
I want to send my congratulations . . .	Congratulations to you on your . . .
We have enclosed a reply envelope.	Just mail your check in the enclosed envelope.
The Hub is proud to open a new store here.	The Hub will open a new store here to serve you.

POINT OUT READER BENEFIT

Proper use of the you attitude is not merely a matter of words and phrases using "you" many times. You must keep in mind the interests and desires of your reader and design your letter to appeal to his or her motives and interests.

Point out features related to the reader's advantage—specific things like pleasure, usefulness, profit, appearance, or prestige. Flip through the advertising pages of a magazine to see how effectively copywriters point out reader benefit.

It might be profit and security ("A small investment in tires now will bring you great economy and the secure knowledge that your family is safe on Firestones"). It might be pleasure ("You'll love Carros in the summer"). It might be personal achievement ("Have you ever wished you could read and learn faster?").

Most of us are trapped by ourselves and tend to write about *our* problems, *our* products, and *our* wishes. In letter writing it is an important principle to set oneself aside and assert one of the fundamentals of all communication—write for your reader.

In these two letters observe how one appeals to reader benefit and the other to writer (company) benefit, although both letters aim at the same result.

```
Dear Sir:

Enclosed is a questionnaire we are sending
to all our retail outlets in this region.
Will you please fill it out and return
it as soon as possible? It is necessary
for us to have an immediate reply because
we are delaying plans for this year's sales
meeting until we get replies.

                    Very truly yours,
```

Dear Mr. Plummer:

The enclosed questionnaire was designed to
give us information so that we can make
this year's sales meeting most useful to
you and your sales force.

Your opinions about past programs and our
tentative plans for this year will help us
to serve your needs. If you will fill
out and return the questionnaire as soon
as possible, we can let you and our other
dealers know promptly about the changes
recommended.

We will greatly appreciate your assistance
in this important phase of our training
program.

Sincerely yours,

Even a simple request gets better response when reader benefit is emphasized. For example, an insurance company that wanted to update its address files sent to one half of its policyholders a double postcard with this message:

Since we haven't written you in some time,

please help us bring our records up-to-date

by filling in and returning the other half

of this card.

The request is clear and courteous, and a response would be simple—checking or correcting an address. Yet only three percent of the cards came back.

To the other half of its policyholders, the company sent the same request—but rewritten to point out reader benefit:

```
So that dividend checks, premium notices, and

other messages of importance may reach you

promptly, please fill out and return the other

half of this card.
```

This request brought 90 percent of the cards back in a few days.

When you try to see a situation from your reader's point of view, you will find it easier to show that you are aware of and are doing something about his or her needs and interests. This concern for your reader should be in every letter.

HAVE REAL INTEREST IN YOUR READER

The you attitude is not achieved just by pronouns and by indicating reader benefits. It is a product of your real respect and consideration for the reader as a human being. There is a danger that an inexperienced letter writer will think of the you attitude as a pose or a gimmick that offers a shortcut to success. People are not so easily fooled.

In the term "you attitude," the emphasis should be placed on *attitude,* the reflection of our feelings, moods, or convictions. What are the attitudes that we ought ideally to reflect in our relations with others? Sincerity, truthfulness, and integrity should rank high on the list—and unless we use the you attitude sincerely and in good faith, we shall twist its intent and defeat its purpose. Readers of letters are quicker to detect insincerity than any other quality, and effective writers have learned that in good human relations they must avoid superficial cordiality and exaggerated claims. Properly used, the you attitude tells the reader in an honest, tactful, truthful manner the benefits he obtains from an action or attitude implicit in your letter.

You must feel and show genuine interest in your reader and a real desire to help. The following excerpts carry the you attitude beyond the bounds of reason, believability, and sincerity.

```
So that you may be able to buy Ace equipment at an

extremely low price and sell at a tremendous profit,

we now offer you the complete line at a 50 percent

price reduction.
```

```
We are extremely pleased to be able to help you,

Mrs. Cummings, and want you to know that your

satisfaction means more than anything to us.
```

Consider the following request and two different replies to see how the you attitude must come from a real desire to help. A prospective customer sent the following letter to Classic Crystal, Inc.:

```
                                    428 Line Avenue
                                    Akron, Ohio  44304
                                    October 12, 1978


        Classic Crystal, Inc.
        2480 Lincoln Boulevard
        Louisville, Kentucky  40103

        Gentlemen:

        I saw your advertisement in last month's
        Interiors magazine and would like you to
        send me that lovely crystal Starlight Tea
        Set with ½ dozen cups.  My check for
        $98.50 is enclosed.

                            Very truly yours,

                            Ana Harlow

                            (Mrs.) Ana Harlow
```

The ad to which Mrs. Harlow referred did run in last month's *Interiors* magazine, and it announced the Starlight Tea Set at $98.50. The ad also indicated that Starlight crystal is available at department and jewelry stores throughout the Midwest, but Mrs. Harlow evidently overlooked this last piece of copy. The Customer Relations Director gave the letter to a young staff member to answer. To inform Mrs. Harlow that the company does not fill consumer orders, he jotted down the following letter, subject to the approval of the Customer Relations Director.

```
Dear Mrs. Harlow:

We received your order for the Starlight Tea Set,
but unfortunately we cannot send them to you.
We manufacture these sets.  We do not sell them
to customers.  They are distributed by us to
wholesalers who sell them to retail stores.  Your
local store is where you should go.  A careful
reading of our recent ad would have prevented
your mistake, and eliminated the necessity of
our having to return your check.

                        Yours truly,
```

The Customer Relations Director, of course, did not allow this letter to be sent, for its tone is almost sure to alienate a customer. The letter lacks empathy in both its attitude and its explanation. A person with genuine interest in Mrs. Harlow would try to help her. He would help relieve her little bit of embarrassment at having made a mistake, and he would help her get the tea set.

The Customer Relations Director wrote the following letter, using a genuine you attitude.

```
Dear Mrs. Harlow:

We are glad to receive your order for the crystal Starlight
Tea Set, and compliment you on your taste in selecting
Starlight.

However, to give our users of crystal a wider selection
and faster service, we market Starlight through dealers
only.  You also save handling and shipping charges.  You
will be able to get your crystal Starlight Tea Set at
The Crystal Shop, located at 238 Main Street in Canton.
We are enclosing your check so that you may purchase
your tea set there.

Stop by The Crystal Shop for your Starlight Tea Set, and
also the opportunity to look at many other fine pieces
of Classic Crystal.

                    Sincerely yours,
```

CHECK YOUR READER-INTEREST INDEX

For a final check on your use of the you attitude, you may apply a "Reader-Interest Index." Although the you attitude is much more than simply a matter of using the pronoun "you," one way of evaluating the you attitude in a letter is by counting the number of first- and second-person references in the letter and calculating its Reader-Interest Index. When you have finished the first draft of a letter, count all the second-person references (pronouns, possessive adjectives, and proper nouns) and subtract from that the number of first-person references ("I," "we," "ours," "me," "the company"). The result is your Reader-Interest Index. The higher its positive value, the more likely it is that your letter possesses the you attitude. A negative index would tend to indicate more of a we attitude than a you attitude.

Count the pronouns in the two letters from The Hub earlier in this chapter on p. 101 and p. 102. The first letter has twenty "we-our-us-I-my" pronouns and only three "you's" and "your's." With a Reader-Interest Index of –17, the attitude and the letter need serious revision. In contrast, the second letter has 18 "you's" and "your's" to only two first-person pronouns. With a Reader-Interest Index of +16, the tone of the letter is likely to be very effective.

For further study of the techniques of reader interest, you might wish to read Rudolph Flesch's *How to Write, Speak, and Think More Effectively.* Flesch tells how to find the "Human Interest Score" of your writing, which is determined by your percent of personal words and personal sentences. Further, two of Flesch's 25 rules of effective writing deal directly with reader interest: "Put yourself in the reader's place," and "Don't hurt the reader's feelings."

The sales letter from American National Bank (Figure 6-1) may be analyzed as a summary of the you attitude. Though it is an institutional letter, it is genuinely personalized and conveys a strong interest in the reader. All four main features of the you attitude are expressed.

1. The you point of view dominates every paragraph.
2. Definite reader benefit is pointed out in the itemized list in paragraph 2.
3. The whole letter expresses interest in the reader—its tone is sincere and cordial, it avoids high pressure, it offers comfortable options, and it makes action easy.
4. The reader-interest index is +5 (11 "you's" to 6 "we's"), and all uses of "we" are merely natural ways of getting the identity and services of the institution to the reader.

The letter, through its effective use of the you attitude—the genuine benefits offered and the sincere desire to help the reader—is almost certain to draw new clients.

August 23, 1978

Mr. George McBroom
Box 359
Midwestern State University
Wichita Falls, Texas 76308

Dear Mr. McBroom:

You are a valued customer of American National Bank and
since you are a college student you are now one of a
select group. We have a new club at our bank--a College
Club--and it's just for you!

As a full time student, enrolled for twelve hours or more,
you may belong to the club for $1.00 per month and for that
amount you will be provided with the following:

* free personalized checks
* no minimum balance required
* allowance of 20 checks per month to be written
  at no additional charge--5¢ per check for each
  check over 20
* no charge for cashiers checks
* reduced rates on travelers checks
* reduced rental on safe deposit boxes--$1.50 per
  year off each box

Of course you have the option of continuing to use your regular
checking account. If you choose to convert to the new club plan,
come by the bank and sign the necessary papers, and we'll get it
set up for you.

We hope that our convenience, together with the club plan and a
friendly, willing attitude from our staff, will make banking
at American National Bank a pleasure for you.

Sincerely,

Pat Belote

Pat Belote

PB/eb

P.O. Box 4141 · 2732 Midwestern Parkway · Wichita Falls, Texas 76308 · Phone (817) 691-1221

Figure 6-1

EXERCISES

1. Rewrite these sentences to emphasize a you attitude instead of a we attitude.

    a. We are pleased to announce our new bank-by-mail service.
    b. To help us clear our records, please send us a duplicate copy of our invoice.
    c. This is just the kind of job I am looking for, since it offers me a chance to get practical experience in personnel work.
    d. We hope to have the pleasure of showing you what we think is the finest assortment of Italian boots in the city.
    e. We value your patronage, for satisfied customers are the foundation of our success.
    f. Since we have our own obligations to meet, we must ask your immediate attention to your past-due account.
    g. We do not send receipts because of the extra work involved for us; of course, you have your canceled checks anyway.
    h. Our pamphlet is designed to help its readers get the most out of raising beautiful roses.
    i. These sweaters fit well around the shoulders, as our ad shows.
    j. You should send us your dry cleaning because you will be helping us increase our business.

2. Rewrite the following sections of letters to emphasize the you attitude.

    a. This new camera is our greatest engineering triumph. We developed it in our own laboratories, and we are going to distribute it through our own exclusive dealers. You will know why we are so proud of this instrument when you see it demonstrated at your dealer's.
    b. We hope that you will send us the answers we ask for in this questionnaire because this information is of vital importance to us. We are deferring the whole plan of our new sales program pending the answers to these questionnaires. Since you can realize how important this matter is to us, won't you help us by sending your answer today?
    c. I especially hope that you will give favorable consideration to this application. I am very anxious to work for your company since it enjoys a reputation for treating its employees fairly and generously. In addition, I need employment badly because I incurred a debt of $2,200 in order to acquire my college education. I hope you will consider these facts when you examine my qualifications.
    d. In asking for an adjustment on the suit that you purchased from us, you seem to lose sight of the fact that if we granted such claims, we should be unable to stay in business very long. We purchase these garments from a wholesale clothing company, and we certainly do not expect them to grant such adjustments to us.
    e. We ask that you will soon send us your check for $120.50. After all, we have

bills of our own to meet, and we can pay them only by collecting our own bills. The first of the year is a time when our own obligations are especially heavy, and for that reason, we are urging you to send us your remittance.

3. Rewrite the following letters to show a cordial tone and a you attitude.

a.

> Dear Sir:
>
> This will acknowledge your letter of March 18 for 6 dozen No. 207 socket tool sets. Price of $4.40 quoted you last January has been advanced to $4.60. We are billing you at this price for 2 dozen which are going forward today.
>
> We have only a limited supply of these sets on hand, as manufacturer is behind on orders. Therefore must back order 4 dozen, as there are many orders to be filled ahead of yours.
>
> Trusting you will understand this situation, we remain,
>
> Yours truly,
>
> *John Fitzsimmons*
>
> John Fitzsimmons

b.

> Dear Madam:
>
> We wish to acknowledge receipt of your letter of April 10 enclosing order for a Summer Ease Lawn Set, Model 57, and check in the amount of $76.00. In reply we wish to advise that same has been shipped and should reach you without undue delay.
>
> Permit us to take this opportunity to enclose a recent brochure which describes our new line of products for outdoor living, and to call your attention to a special sale on barbecue grills to begin June 1.
>
> Yours very truly,
>
> *Charles Matson*
>
> Charles Matson

7 Tone: The Sound That Sells

Tact
Sincerity
Positiveness

A business letter is business, but not strictly. Don't forget that the reader of your letter, no matter how businesslike, is a human being. If you cut him, he'll bleed, whether he's a president or a sweeper. The reader of your letter will react not only to what you say and to the verbal power with which you say it but also to the *tone* your letter puts forth. If she doesn't like the tone, your letter will fail.

Achieving effective tone is a complex skill, but most of it grows out of your awareness of the reader as a human being. You must attempt to know him and to feel for him. Though the evidence may be meager, you must sharpen your sensitivity to the interests, attitudes, motives, and possible reactions of anyone you are writing to. For instance, if she is an engineer, you must write from an engineer's point of view. If your reader is a lawyer, a file clerk, a homemaker, then you must imagine them and write with their points of view in mind. Tone, like everything else in a business letter, is shaped for the reader. If tone is effective, it is a product of real respect and consideration for the reader as a human being. This attitude will be reflected in three features: *tact, sincerity*, and *positiveness*.

TACT

Tact is the proper way to handle people. It results from a balance between cordiality and practical wisdom. Cordiality is the warmth and friendship you show toward your reader. Practical wisdom is the sensitivity and discretion you show. When writing a letter or memo, you should carefully reckon your relationship to your reader and then make sure that your communication strikes the balance between cordiality and discretion appropriate to that relationship. The tone of a memo to a coworker in the next office will differ from the tone of a memo to the company president. But to succeed, both memos must achieve the appropriate balance between cordiality and practical wisdom that constitutes tact.

The ancient Greeks had a saying about balance: "Be bold, be bold, be bold . . . be not too bold." We could add a modern counterpart: "Be friendly, be friendly, be friendly . . . be not gushy." Though most errors in cordiality and discretion are accidental, they are harmful nevertheless.

Tact is ruined in a business letter if your reader feels that you are being abrupt, sarcastic, irritable, or suspicious of his motives. Your chances of a favorable response are also destroyed if he or she feels you have insulted, blamed, talked down to, or been overly familiar with or presumptuous toward him or her. The list of blunders in tact is long, but the following survey may help you avoid accidents.

Abruptness

Don't be too curt. Surely you shouldn't waste your reader's time by using more words than necessary, but if you are too brief, you may suggest unconcern for your reader. Abruptness can result from being too hasty or from trying too hard to be concise. In either case, the effect on the reader is a cold chill.

For instance, how do you think Mrs. Thompson's attitude changed after she received this abrupt letter? She had written a long and detailed letter to the Colorado Hills Resort telling how much she enjoyed her two-week summer stay.

```
Dear Mrs. Thompson:
        Thank you for your recent letter.  We are
always glad to hear from our guests.
                    Yours truly,


                    Colorado Hills Resort
```

The writer did not mean to offend Mrs. Thompson. But he was too abrupt. Her effort in writing a long letter demanded a more substantial and personal reply. Mrs. Thompson will probably not be back next summer.

Irritability

A whining and irritable tone indicates a petty person. Who wants to put up with him? Nobody likes peevishness, even in a letter. Here is a piece taken from an interoffice memo. Imagine how the readers liked it.

> How do you expect us to keep order around here if you don't put the folders back into the file *as you're supposed to?* You ought to know better!

The petty irritability of this excerpt will hardly arouse enthusiastic cooperation in the reader. Who needs it!

Sarcasm

Sarcasm usually works if you really want to hurt somebody. But seldom is a business letter helped by sarcasm, by trying to hurt. Sarcasm is that special kind of wit that says the opposite of what is meant. Its purpose is generally to ridicule. Sometimes sarcasm will be used to give expression to the writer's own ill feelings. At other times, sarcasm is used to prod people to better efforts. But most people respond very poorly to sarcasm, because it demeans them as human beings.

The following piece of sarcasm was written by a region manager to a staff of ten salespeople. The manager wanted to inform them emphatically that they had fallen short of the month's sales quota and to urge them to greater efforts.

```
        Congratulations, men.  I am proud to inform

    you that because of your dazzling and breath-taking

    efforts last month, we fell only $21,000 short of

    our sales quota.  Be sure to pick up your medals on

    the way out for the weekend.

                            P.F. Faulkland
                            District Manager
```

The sarcastic tone, rather than prodding the salespeople to extra effort, probably fired tempers, lowered the urge to work, and made a few effective salespeople say, "I don't have to work for that hyena."

Suspicion

Phrases like "If what you say is true," and "If, as you state," can make a letter writer seem suspicious of the writer's integrity. The phrases may be entirely harmless and tactful in a face-to-face conversation, where voice and facial expressions indicate tone and meaning. But such words in a letter or memo can flatly suggest that the writer doubts the reader's honesty. Consider the implications of this letter.

If the blender was defective when you bought it, as you claim, we will surely replace it with a new one. It does seem odd, however, that you waited so long to inform us . . .

The tone is a blunder in tact. The writer is doing what the customer wants—replacing the blender. But where is the practical wisdom? What does he expect to get from his accusation except ill will and a lost customer?

Accusation

Blaming your reader for some wrong or error is a sure way to destroy the effectiveness of a letter. Nobody wants to be accused or preached at. Your reader has either done wrong or hasn't. Either way, it's not your job to reprimand him or her—if at the same time you want a favorable reaction. Even a mildly accusing remark will turn the reader off.

You certainly ignored our request to return the sample within seven days.

The same idea could have been written more tactfully like this:

We had hoped that you would return the sample within the seven days specified.

A commanding tone is almost sure to create resistance. Generally it is better to suggest or to show the reader that he or she will benefit from your request.

COMMANDING: Please send payment immediately.

TACTFUL: To preserve your good credit rating, please send check by (date).

PREACHY: You ought to . . .

TACTFUL: Perhaps you could . . .

Intentional or not, a writer should avoid expressions that seem to accuse, instruct, or preach at the reader. The following list suggests some of the irritating expressions to be avoided. They are especially inflammatory when used with "you" and "yours."

IRRITATING EXPRESSIONS: CHECKLIST

contrary to what you say
delinquency (delinquent)
due to your questionable credit
   we are unable to
failed
failure
force
I'm sure you must realize
I do not agree with you
ignored
inexcusable
irresponsible
it is against our company policy
   to do so
lack of response
mistaken
obnoxious
obviously you overlooked
regrettably
simply nonsense
surely you don't expect
we are confused
we are surprised
we don't believe
we expect you to
we find it difficult to believe that

we must insist
we take issue
why have you ignored
why is it always
you are delinquent
you are probably ignorant of
   the fact that
you claim that
you did not tell us
you don't expect us
you failed to
you forgot to
you have to
you leave us no choice
you neglected to
you overlooked sending
you say
you should be aware
you should know
your apparent disregard of our previous
   request leaves us no alternative
your complaint
your failure to
your stubborn silence
your insinuation
your neglect

Superiority

A tone of superiority is sure to alienate a reader. No one likes being talked down to. It's all right for a company to believe its products are superior to those of other companies. It is all right for a person to have a certain assurance about his or her own abilities. But we must be careful not to wave those banners before others.

Note tactless talking down in these words used by a department store manager in a a customer.

   With a company as large and as reputable as ours, Mrs. Mellon, we seldom have cause to . . .

How much more courteous could he have been?

We try very hard, Mrs. Mellon, to live up to our reputation for . . .

The out-and-out braggart is equally offensive, almost inviting hostility and the rejection of the communication.

Our Beauty King Carpeting costs more than the competition because it's worth more than other carpeting.

A job applicant can often, unintentionally, seem to be boasting:

I possess a superior record.

The same remarks can be made tactful with only a little toning down.

Our Beauty King Carpeting does cost more than other carpeting, but we honestly believe it offers more value for the money.

I possess what my present employer has called a superior record.

Presumptuousness

It's risky to take the reader and the reader's wishes and decisions for granted. You may think you know what's best, and you may be eager to have a decision in your favor; but presumptuousness seldom works. Almost anyone is offended by a communication that presumes that he or she will do something before he's made up his mind.

Consider what reactions were provoked by the following excerpt from a letter used in a fund-raising campaign by a large nonprofit organization. It was sent to prospective donors to introduce a solicitor who would call upon them.

We do not ask for an immediate decision, but we do ask you to take a few minutes when he leaves to consider what our organization has meant and will continue to mean to your community. He will make arrangements to pick up your pledge card from you at a later time after you have had an opportunity to determine a gift appropriate to your circumstances. It will be an investment we know you will take satisfaction in having made . . .

The word "ask," even in the negative, presumes a favorable decision. The phrase "to determine a gift" leaves no choice, and the phrase "we know" has tones of superiority as well as presumptuousness. These hints of presumptuousness are enough to turn off a certain percentage of prospective donors.

A confident belief in the product never hurt a business letter, but a presumptuous tone is dangerous. One must not sound *too* sure, and one must not give the reader the feeling that he or she has no choice.

SINCERITY

A tactful attitude in a business letter is a great asset, but only if it is believed. The reader must feel that the expressed cordiality is genuine and not just a device for self-gain. Of course, the reader knows that the business is interested in gain. But the point can be made through a genuine consideration for the customer or attempted through an artificial interest.

To sound sincere in a written communication, you must be sincere. A false sincerity shows through.

Even though you may be genuinely sincere, you must watch for blunders in phrasing that can make you seem false. Especially watch for errors in *false humility, flattery,* and *exaggeration.*

False Humility

True humility is very much in order in business communication. Humility is the opposite of the blunder of superiority, discussed above as a violation of tact. Humility can arise only from a genuine sense of the worth of the other person.

But if your expression of humility is overdone, you risk sounding insincere. People do not believe, and do not like, letters that drip with humility.

```
Dear Mr. Jensen:

     We are so, so sorry for our foolish blunder
in handling the delivery of your furniture. Our
most sincere apologies.  Our delivery coordinator,
our driver, and I all wish to say we are extremely
sorry.

     We are also very appreciative for the opportunity
you have given us to serve your needs.  We shall
continue trying, to the limits of our ability, to
justify your faith in our efforts.

                    Most sincerely yours,


                    John Overdown
```

Apologies are very much in order, if warranted, and so are compliments. But John Overdown overdoes both and demeans his company in doing so. His humility is extreme. How could he possibly mean it?

Flattery

Sincere praise can contribute to the effective tone of a business letter, but "flattery will get you nowhere"—at least no where good. Flattery means insincere praise, and if the flattery is obvious, the reader is certain to spot the insincerity and turn the other way.

> We call upon you, Mrs. Turner, because only you can handle this difficult assignment for us.

> A man of your widely acknowledged talents, Mr. Barton, is just the man to head this project for us.

These assertions are such obvious flattery that they are sure to cast doubts on the writer's sincerity. Addressing the person by name within the letter is a useful way of emphasizing the you attitude. It praises the person by acknowledging his or her personal identity. We all tend to love to see or hear our own names.

But the obvious use of the name for purpose of flattery or overfamiliarity will show the insincerity behind the writer. The request for subscription renewal in Figure 7-1 shows its insincerity by the obvious appeal to the reader's name. The letter is written as if by the editor himself, a man of worldwide reputation, writing personally to the reader. Yet the letter is an insult to the reader's intelligence, for the reader sees the mass-printed signature and knows that thousands of copies of this letter are being mailed.

The falseness is evident in several ways. The special typeface of the address and the salutation indicates a machine heading for a mass-produced form letter—certainly inappropriate in a personalized letter. The use of the first name in the salutation shows a label-type greeting—again machine made. The omission of standard punctuation in address and salutation makes the machined format blatant. The use of the name of a company employee in the second paragraph, "Jeff Reece," again is an obvious attempt to link the reader personally with the company. But such overfamiliarity is false—there is no reason or occasion for the reader to know or to think of the circulation manager by name. The signature of the big-name editor is also not personal but machined.

The appeal to the person falls flat through insincerity. Besides insincerity the letter also violates tact through its tone of superiority—the idea that the thanks of a famous editor is a reason for renewal; the attitude in all paragraphs but the fifth that the welfare of the company is more important than the pleasure of the readers. The reader-interest index is –6 (13 "I's" to only 7 "you's")—not very effective.

Exaggeration

Extreme words and statements suggest insincerity, simply because they make claims that we know the writer cannot carry through. Sincerity is usually open to question with

```
                                    MODERN REVIEW
            NORVAL CUSHING          520 Trent Avenue
               Editor              New York, N.Y.  10022


            November 18, 1977




            Matthew Harrison
            Central State University
            University Park, PA 16802

            Dear Matthew Harrison

                On behalf of my colleagues, I want to thank you for taking
            Modern Review and to express the hope that you will continue
            to do so.

                Jeff Reece, our circulation manager, tells me that your
            subscription has just come up for renewal.  By calling this
            fact to your attention now, I hope we can obtain a prompt
            renewal and thus save the very substantial expenses involved
            in sending additional notices.

                Our close relationship with MR readers is central in all
            our thinking.  For this reason, each renewal order is a matter
            of importance to the editors.  It helps us strengthen our
            long-term editorial planning.

                About the magazine itself:  You will be pleased to know,
            I think, that the magazine is once again on high ground
            economically.  Response from readers has been most gratifying.
            We hope to justify the readers' confidence by publishing an
            increasingly valuable magazine.

                Please use the convenient renewal form and postage-free
            envelope enclosed to renew your subscription.

                Again my thanks for your support.

                                        Sincerely,

                                        Norval Cushing

                                        Norval Cushing
```

Figure 7-1

four kinds of expressions: words claiming *positive knowledge, adjectives and adverbs* of extraordinary meaning, *superlatives*, and suggestions of *surprise*.

POSITIVE KNOWLEDGE.   We can guess, but we cannot know about future events or the likes and dislikes of the reader.

> We are *positive* that you will be pleased with your new Tru-Vision television set.

> We *know* that you will agree that $35,000 is a fair price for the property.

With just a little modification these claims can be made both sincere and effective.

> We *believe* that you will be pleased . . .

> We *feel* sure that you will *agree* . . .

ADJECTIVES AND ADVERBS.   It is often necessary to use straight descriptive and functional adjectives and adverbs like *red* paint and answer *soon*. The emotionalized, subjective adjectives and adverbs of exaggeration should be used sparingly, because their lack of verifiable meaning creates distrust. Avoid words like "fabulous," "terrific," "sensational," "marvelous," "fantastic," and "revolutionary."

> This *fantastic* tool kit sells for the *low, low* price of $79.50.

The underlined words undermine trust. The reader may think the writer called the tool kit "fantastic" just to sell it. He will probably think the price is high, but he is being persuaded to believe it is low. The reader's distrust could have been avoided by saying simply:

> This tool kit sells for $79.50.

From the other information given, the reader could have arrived at his own conclusion as to the quality and price of the tool kit.

SUPERLATIVES.   Such common words as "best," "most," "latest," "least," "largest," and "highest" provoke the reader to question the sincerity of the writer. Note how the superlative words in these sentences cause doubt:

> The Do-All electric iron is *positively* the *best* money can buy.

> Our stores give the *largest* discount and the *best* service available anywhere.

> The Speed-Cutter is the *most efficient* machine anywhere in lawn-mowing territory.

How could these sentences be true? The reader knows the exaggerated claims could not practically have been measured by the writer.

Surprise.   Expressions suggesting surprise often sound insincere. Sometimes they are obviously false; sometimes they suggest accusation or superiority.

We are *surprised* that your new Ease-Dryer does not work perfectly.

There are two counts of insincerity in this statement: (1) Why should the company be surprised? Defects in new machines are a common occurrence. (2) The "surprise" gently suggests that the customer is not telling the truth.

POSITIVENESS

To get the desired response from your reader, your letter must have a positive tone. You must appeal to his best side and let him see the best side of your idea or message. Positiveness is the attitude of presenting an idea in its most positive, favorable light. It is simply, "looking at the bright side of things."

Being positive is like what we do when we take a photograph. We select the best angle, the best light, the best selection of details to include. We do not alter the nature of the subject. We just capture the most favorable view.

NEGATIVE: My bank account is almost depleted.
POSITIVE: I still have some money in the bank.

NEGATIVE: We had hardly any customers today.
POSITIVE: We made several good sales today.

Being sincerely positive is not just a matter of selecting words and details. It springs from an optimistic attitude toward life, your goods, and your services. You should have a happy view as you write your letters. Believe in your reader, yourself, and the message. You can look more on the brighter side of life and less on the darker. Which person would you rather sit and drink a cup of coffee with—the whiner and complainer or the person who talks about the good things in life?

In writing to someone, don't resent the letter as a burden or as a job that has to be done. Welcome it as an opportunity to establish or enhance a pleasant relationship between you and your reader.

Here are three basic rules for achieving the highest positive tone in your business letters:

1. Emphasize what can be done.
2. Avoid negative words.
3. Be positive instead of neutral.

Emphasize What Can Be Done

Stress what things are or what they will be, rather than what they aren't or won't be. Stress what you have done, what you can do, or what you will do, rather than what you haven't done, can't do, or won't do. Tell the reader what you *can* do for him. By making clear what you can do or will do, you also often make clear (by gentle implication) what you cannot do—without using a single negative word. Compare the following pair of negative and positive statements:

NEGATIVE: It will be impossible to send the merchandise to you until you send us your credit card number.

POSITIVE: Just as soon as we receive your credit card number we will gladly send the merchandise.

Avoid Negative Words

Sometimes you have to say "no." Frequently "bad-news" messages must be written. But even troublesome things can be expressed in an optimistic tone—especially if you avoid negative words.

We are sorry for the trouble you've been caused by the broken lawn mower.

You neglected to state which color you wanted; therefore, your order is being delayed.

The disagreeable tones of these sentences are caused mainly by the negative words: "sorry," "trouble," "broken," "neglected," and "delayed." See how the tone is improved by avoiding these negative words—and the same informative message is still given.

We want to apologize for the experience you had with your Fast Boy Lawn Mower.

You will receive your new Cane-Craft lawn chair within three days after you let us know which color to send.

Be Positive Instead of Neutral

To avoid a negative tone is most important, for it may alienate your reader. But to use a neutral tone is unsatisfactory because you may fail to stir the reader to the desired action. Give your letter extra appeal by turning neutral phrases into positive ones:

NEUTRAL: Your television set can be picked up on Friday.
POSITIVE: Your television set will be waiting for you on Friday.

NEUTRAL: If you would like us to come for a demonstration . . .
POSITIVE: We would be happy to come for a demonstration . . .

Let the power of positive suggestion work in your favor. Compare the following pairs of statements for use of positive tone:

Negative or Neutral	*Positive*
We cannot refund if the returned item is soiled and unsalable.	We gladly refund if the returned item is not soiled and unsalable.
If we can help, don't hesitate to get in touch with us.	Please call us when we can help.
I hope this is the information you want.	Should you need additional information, please telephone me at 692-6611.
The tank is half empty.	The tank is half full.
If you set the blade too close to the ground, it is likely to be damaged by small stones. Besides, the grass may die if cut too short in hot weather.	If you set the blade to cut about three inches from the ground, it should give you years of good service. And it will help your grass look green in hot weather.
Because of recent heavy demand, we will not be able to deliver your goods before June 10.	Although recent demand has been heavy, we will be able to deliver your goods by June 10.
The only work experience I have is two summers as a shipping clerk.	I had full responsibility for expediting the packaging and delivery of goods as a shipping clerk for two summers.
This unfortunate incident will not happen again.	Future transactions will be serviced with the utmost care.

We do not have any black station wagons in stock.

At present, we have only one blue, one gray, and two green station wagons in stock.

We do not sell directly to retail customers.

We will sell only through dealers.

We make no deliveries on weekends.

Deliveries are made on weekdays only.

We're sorry, but you cannot buy more than $500 worth of merchandise on credit.

You can buy up to $500 worth of merchandise on credit.

Beginning and Ending

One final aspect of positiveness in a business communication is the positive beginning and ending. As we saw in Chapter 5 on the sentence, the writer makes his or her strongest impressions at the beginning and at the end of a sentence. The same principle works in a total letter. The beginning is most important in a letter, for the tone is set for the whole letter, and the reader's favorable attention must be captured or he or she may not even read on. The ending or parting shot is next most important, for the end of the message is where the reader's reaction is crystallized toward you and toward the message.

This is not to say that the middle of a message is not important. It is. But what comes in the middle does not make as strong an impression on the reader as what comes first and last.

The skillful writer will put this principle to work. Open your letter with as positive a tone as the situation allows and close just as positively. With some messages, of course, cordiality is difficult (such as complaints or collection letters). But so far as you are able to open and close positively without violating sincerity or sounding unnatural, do so.

Here is an example of a negative opening and close:

```
Dear Mrs. Anderson:

     We received your complaint today about

the broken mantel clock.  We immediately . . .

          /  The central message. /

     We hope that this adjustment is satisfactory

to you.
```

The disgruntled customer is more likely to have her goodwill restored if the opening and closing of the letter invite a pleasant disposition:

```
Dear Mrs. Anderson:

     We appreciate your informing us so quickly

about the breakage of your mantel clock.  As soon

as we received your letter, we . . .

          / The central message. 7

     We shall rush your replacement to you as soon

as we hear from you.
```

A letter with a neutral opening and closing can be made more effective with a slight shift to the positive:

```
Dear Miss Swanson:

     We received your recent order for . . .

          / Central message. 7

     Your order will be delivered shortly.
```

Instead, a positive beginning and ending would enhance customer goodwill.

```
Dear Miss Swanson:

     We thank you for your recent order for . . .

          / Central message. 7

     Your order will be packaged immediately and

delivered to you as soon as possible.
```

Improving the tone of your communication through *tact, sincerity,* and *positiveness* will not guarantee you the exact response that you want from your reader. But certainly the skillful use of these principles will substantially increase your chances of success.

EXERCISES

1. Rewrite the following sentences to improve the tone of tact, sincerity, and positiveness.

    a. This is the third time you have permitted your account to be delinquent.
    b. Obviously you failed to read Section III of your policy, or you would know that you are not covered on accidents that occur on water but only on those that occur on the grounds of your residence.
    c. You must take advantage of savings like this if you are to be successful. Pennies saved pile up, and in time you will have dollars.
    d. I was delighted today to see your name among McClurkan's new charge customers.
    e. We are extremely pleased to be able to help you and want you to know that your satisfaction means more than anything to us.
    f. Already thousands of new customers are beating paths to the doors of Kelvin dealers.
    g. You failed to give us the color specifications of the chair you ordered.
    h. We cannot deliver your motor until Monday.
    i. We regret that we overlooked your insurance coverage on this equipment and apologize for the trouble and concern it must have caused you.
    j. We have received your claim in which you contend that we were responsible for damage to the three Schwinn bicycles. We assure you that we sincerely regret the trouble that . . .
    k. This information is being sent to you now so that we will avoid later misunderstandings about our credit terms.
    l. We know you will agree that our prices are not any higher than those of competitors.
    m. On COD orders we require a 15 percent deposit to protect ourselves against loss in case of refusal of merchandise.
    n. We will hold shipment of the television sets until we receive your confirmation.
    o. Unfortunately I will not be able to give you any definite price until you let me know the size and quantity of cartons you need.
    p. We are sorry that we cannot add a car to the policy without a specific description of the vehicle.
    q. There will be a delay of four days in filling your order because the material for your coat has to be ordered from Chicago. We are sorry about this delay, but there is nothing we can do about it.
    r. Because of shortages of material, we will not be able to ship before June 10.
    s. We regret that we cannot extend your payment date for more than two months.
    t. I hope this adjustment will be satisfactory with you.

u. We trust this mistake will not happen again, because it is our desire to serve you at all times.

v. If you are so inclined, please send us $37.20 today for your two-month delinquent account.

w. We regret to inform you that your organization cannot use the conference room tomorrow. In fact, it won't be available to you until next Monday.

x. The alterations you have requested should not present too much of a problem.

y. Because you mailed your application too late, we regret that we cannot enter your display in the trade show.

2. Rewrite the following letters to give them a *positive tone*.

a.

> Dear Mrs. Haycroft:
>
> This will acknowledge receipt of your letter of October 9 enclosing order for a tan wool suit, Style 37k, and check in the amount of $135.
>
> In reply we wish to advise that same has been shipped under separate cover and should reach you without undue delay.
>
> Permit us to take this opportunity to enclose a recent brochure which describes our new line of winter furs, and to call your attention to a special sale of fur scarves and hats to be held November 1.

b.

> Dear Mr. Jensen:
>
> This will confirm your order of May 9 for 12 dozen No. 210 Mountain Rock Collections.
>
> Price of $2.50 quoted you last March has been advanced to $2.80. We are billing you at this price for 4 dozen which are going forward today.
>
> We have only a limited supply of these rock sets on hand, as manufacturer is behind on orders. Therefore must backorder 8 dozen, as there are many orders to be filled ahead of yours.
>
> Trusting you will understand this situation, we remain,

3. The following letter was sent to Ski-Master Industries:

```
                                        982 Hill Rd
                                        Pueblo, Colorado
                                        November 14, 19__

Ski-Master Industries
201 Madison Avenue
New York, New York 10086

Gentlemen:

I've looked all around Pueblo for a place that sells
Ski-Master boots, but I could not find any.  Can you tell
me anybody in Pueblo who handles them?  If not, where can
I get some?

                            Yours sincerely,

                            Ralph Downer

                            Ralph Downer
```

This is the answer Downer got:

```
Dear Mr. Downer:

Ski-Master boots are sold in sporting good stores and
department stores mostly in larger cities and near ski
resorts.  You might try those in your city.  I hope you
will be able to find some.

                        Sincerely,

                        Henry Borton

                        Henry Borton
                        Customer Service Manager
```

It is not a very cordial and helpful reply! Rewrite the letter so that its tone will encourage (rather than discourage) Downer's going to buy or sending for boots in the nearest large city. (Company records will show, that Ski-Master boots are stocked by the The Sport Shop at 283 First Street in Colorado Springs, about 40 miles away.)

4.   Rewrite this answer to a customer's complaint, giving it a more tactful tone.

Mrs. Barnes:

We find it difficult to understand your stated cause for complaint. As far as we know, you have not yet paid your bill for $88.20. If, as you say, you remember writing the check, perhaps you forgot to mail it, or you addressed it wrong. Such things do happen.

Unless you receive a cancelled check from your bank, you have nothing to worry about. In the meantime, we're sure you will understand why, in a business as large as ours, it is impossible for us to credit your account merely on your say-so.

Don't worry though. Everything will clear up when you get your next bank statement.

Very truly yours,

Parker-Timberwood Co.

Part 2

Kinds Of Communications: The Profit And The Loss

8 Routine Communications

Routine Requests and Inquiries
Routine Replies
Form Letters and Prototype Letters

Routine communications are those everyday letters and memos through which businesses carry on much of their normal exchange of ideas and information. Such letters typically contain neither serious problems nor high pressure. They are practical and assumed. The reader is expected to be neither pleased nor displeased—but interested. And the last word is important—*interested*. The reader is interested, and we must treat that interest fairly if we expect to get a favorable response. An inexact letter may lead to confusion. A dull, boorish letter may lead to a delayed, insufficient response or none at all. What we want is a routine inquiry or reply that will lead to a prompt and specific response and a feeling of goodwill toward the writer and the company.

The writer of the following routine request letter treated "routine" as if it meant "indifferent" or "unimportant."

Crown Office Supply
128 Hill Road
New London, Connecticut 06320

Gentlemen:

I am interested in layout and design devices.
Please send me complete information.

Yours truly,

Robin Black

Robin Black

The letter has two big faults. First, its request is so vague that Crown Office Supply will find it hard to give specific information. Second, the tone is so impersonal and brief that the Crown reader might say, "I've got enough problems now. I'll take care of it later—maybe." Compare the following improved version of the letter to Crown Office Supply.

```
Crown Office Supply
128 Hill Road
New London, Connecticut  06320

Gentlemen:

Would you please send me detailed information on
preliminary layout devices, such as templates,
designing boards, and three-dimensional models?
We are planning a new layout for our Credit
Department and since our department is large, it
is not feasible to test layouts simply by moving
equipment and furniture around.

If you don't handle layout devices, can you refer
me to a company that does?  I have been unable to
find anything in dealers' catalogs or in local
stores.  If you know a dealer, you may jot the
name and address at the bottom of the enclosed
copy of this letter and return it to me.

                        Sincerely yours,

                        Robin Black

                        Robin Black
```

The precision, the style, the information, and the courteous tone will likely bring a prompt and satisfactory reply. The letter is businesslike, but appreciative. The information is specific, and sufficient background is given. The writer makes it easy for the reader to respond.

So, "routine" does not mean "indifferent" or "unimportant." Let's look at some of the strategies of organization and approach that can make your routine requests and replies effective.

ROUTINE REQUESTS AND INQUIRIES

These are the everyday letters and memos in which you ask the reader to do something. You might ask a customer to clarify an order, to supply missing answers on a credit application, to correct an irregularity in a check sent to your company. You might ask a supplier or a transportation company to sign an enclosed signature card or document. You might write a memo to a member or members of your own organization asking for information or action. You might order merchandise or ask the distributor for information about a product. You might make a credit check to approve or reject a customer's application for credit. These are some kinds of messages that are related to routine business procedures.

For a routine request or inquiry you assume the reader will do as you request when he or she understands what you want and why you want it. You do not need to use persuasion. All you need is clarity and normal cordiality. Your letter should follow a three-part organization.

ORGANIZATIONAL PLAN

1. *Direct statement of your request.*   Be pleasant, not blunt, but state your request early in the letter.
2. *Explanation.*   Tell why you are making the request and give details necessary to help the reader respond.
3. *Courteous close.*   Make action easy (such as including a reply envelope, your phone number, or office hours), and express appreciation.

Following an organizational plan can help you get control of the overall letter. But if you are going to have more than a mere skeleton, you must make use of several techniques of attitude, tone, and procedure to make your letter effective. Keep in mind the following guidelines for effectively writing inquiries, requests, or orders.

GUIDELINES

1. *Begin and end positively,* especially if rapport between you and your reader will induce a more satisfactory response.
2. *Identify yourself.* Unless it is self-evident, make clear early in the communication who you are (what position you hold or what situation you are in that has caused you to write).

3. *State your request* specifically and completely.

4. *Give your reason.* State why you are making the request, unless self-evident. The reason or reasons you give make it easier for the respondent to provide precisely what you need.

5. *Tell why you are writing to the person you address,* unless it is self-evident. People like to know why requests or inquiries are being made of them.

6. *Ask for as little information as you have to.* It is annoying to be asked for information that is readily available elsewhere or that is obviously superfluous.

7. *Watch your timing.* Time your request, inquiries, and order letters, if possible, to coincide with your respondent's least busy period.

8. *Promise to be confidential* when confidential information is requested, as in a credit check.

9. *Indicate reader benefit, if possible.* How will the reader benefit from answering the inquiry or performing the requested actions?

10. *Write with empathy,* injecting the everyday courtesies into your communications.

Typical Letters

Study the following examples of some of the many kinds of routine request letters to see how they use the typical three-part organizational plan and the standard guidelines.

Request for Free Materials

Letters written by a potential customer asking suppliers for free materials, information, or routine services are among the easiest to write. The customer will usually receive what he or she is asking for since it is to the supplier's advantage to provide it. The potential customer needs only to use clarity and a little courtesy. In writing routine request letters, give all the information the supplier will need in order to be really helpful, keep your request as brief as possible without omitting important details, and express your wishes courteously and tactfully.

In the letter at top right, the writer is correct, congenial, and factually precise. He will probably receive the information he asks for.

Let's take a look at a similar inquiry and three different ways it can be written—good, bad, and indifferent (not in that order). As assistant retail buyer of Midwest Electronics, Inc., you must have on hand the latest catalogs, price lists, and other materials of major manufacturers and distributors of electronic products. Since you have only a few of these items—most of them out of date—you need to write to several suppliers requesting up-to-date catalogs and price lists.

First look at the poorly written request at bottom right.

Fidelity Insurance Company
2931 Oak Drive
Sacramento, California 95819

Gentlemen:

Through conversations with your Northwestern Regional representative, Mr. Ralph Lowes, I have learned of the manual, <u>Your Telephone Personality</u>, which Fidelity Insurance provides for its secretaries and agents. Judging by Mr. Lowe's comments, the manual is very successful.

As Personnel Training Director, I plan to conduct a special training class for secretaries and others in the Office Services Department beginning August 1. I would certainly appreciate your sending me a copy of the Fidelity telephone manual to draw upon in conducting the training session.

Sincerely yours,

Carl Benson

Carl Benson

October 19, 1978

Williams & White Electronics, Inc.
9982 Northfield Avenue
Harrisburg, Virginia 22801

Gentlemen:

In consulting my files of catalogs of electronic equiptment and supplies and checking them off against various manufactures, it was noticed that I did not have your most current issues, which possibly were received but if so I misplaced them, and I like to keep up to date on all manufacturer's catalogs and price lists.

For this reason I would like to request that you send me your latest catalogs of equiptment and supplies (plus price lists) at your earliest convenience.

Thanking you in advance, I remain,

Yours truly,

Ted Bell

Ted Bell

How many examples of the following did you spot in the letter?

1. Incorrect grammar and punctuation
2. Misspelled words
3. Poor sentence structure
4. Circumlocutions
5. Trite expressions
6. Unnecessary words
7. Irrelevant details

In writing even the most routine letters, some people seem to want to tell their life story, wasting time for everyone and obscuring the purpose of the message. The writer did not need to give such an involved explanation of why he wants a new catalog and price list; the reader is neither helped by it nor interested in so many details. Although this letter probably will get the results the writer wants, it marks him as sloppy and bunble headed. More serious, it wastes the reader's time.

It is generally unwise to open a letter with an "In" phrase ("In consulting my files," "In answer to your letter," "In response to your question") or with words ending in "ing" ("Replying to your letter," "Acknowledging your inquiry," "According to our statement," "Referring to your question"). Such poor openings make equally weak closings. For example, don't close a letter with "thanking," "hoping," or "expecting." The sentence that begins with one of these words will not be complete unless you end with the old-fashioned and meaningless "I remain" (as shown in the example) or "I am."

Also, most people consider it presumptuous to thank someone in advance. The appropriate time to thank the reader is after he has complied with your request.

An indifferent request is no better than a clumsy one. It is just a different kind of ineffectiveness.

```
Gentlemen:

Send me your latest price lists and catalogs.

                              Yours very truly,
```

This abrupt note may be perfectly satisfactory. It certainly has the virtue of brevity. Yet, although the writer committed no serious faults, he or she might have spared a "please" or a "thank you" or some other expression of courtesy. Also, if the writer had thought carefully about the situation, he or she might have come to the conclusion that giving the purpose of the request would have been helpful. (Some companies, upon receiving requests for catalogs and other promotional material, are inclined to rush a salesman out with the material.) The writer might have asked, "How can I be sure of receiving all new catalogs and similar materials as they are issued? If I could get on the mailing list to receive such information automatically, I wouldn't have to worry about remembering to write for them."

Now let's look at an effective request for the catalog materials.

October 19, 1978

Williams & White Electronics, Inc.
9982 Northfield Avenue
Harrisburg, Virginia 22801

Gentlemen:

May I have your latest catalog and price list? I am
setting up a product information file for reference
in future buying, and I need the latest data about
electronic equipment and supplies. More specifically,
I am interested in components and replacement parts for
stereo sound systems, tape recorders, and CB radios.

Will you please put me on your mailing list for all
of your promotion and catalog material?

                              Sincerely yours,

                              Ted Bell

                              Ted Bell

The letter is effective for these reasons:

1. *The tone is appropriate.* Even though the prospective customer could say almost anything in his letter and get what he wants, he wisely observes the rules of good human relations. He could have said in the first paragraph, "I want your catalog" or

"Send me your catalog," but those are demands. "May I have your latest catalog and price list" is a courteous request, and the tone makes a world of difference. In the last paragraph the writer could have written, "Put me on your mailing list," but asking and using the word "please" changed a demand to a polite request.

2. *The letter is brief but complete.* It gives only the information the reader needs in order to help.

3. *The reason for the request is clearly stated,* even though it is not absolutely essential in this case.

4. *The letter starts with a question.* Of course, a question isn't the only way to begin such a letter, but it did get the writer into his subject immediately.

5. *The writer obviously thought about his continuing need for new materials* (last paragraph); his request can save additional letters in the future.

Request for Information or Action from a Customer

In processing a customer's order or account, you frequently need to ask a customer for additional information (such as a size or a model number), or you may want him or her to perform some small but necessary action, such as signing the check he neglected to sign or returning a claims form.

You can use form letters, either processed or individually typed, but it is often a good idea to personalize the request. Remember all letters are sales letters, and you must keep the goodwill of the customer to keep his or her business.

If you do use a letter, make sure it has clarity and character. The writer of the letter on p. 141 was probably not intentionally offensive, but the tone is cold, hostile, and self-concerned. Miss Tower will feel ill will toward the company and perhaps transfer her insurance account to another company.

The letter on p. 142 says exactly the same thing, but in a better manner. It has a positive opening and closing; it gives necessary, precise, factual information; it does not accuse Miss Tower of neglect, as the other writer did. It has a you attitude, yet it firmly indicates that the next step is entirely up to Miss Tower.

If you write a letter to a customer requesting additional information before you can fill an order, you must first of all be clear. But you must also keep the goodwill of the customer. There is a possibility that he or she might be annoyed. Remember that the customer is expecting merchandise. Instead, he is getting only a letter asking for more information. So, make your reader feel that the request is in his best interests. The following organizational plan can be followed in asking for additional information on an order. It is an amplification of the three-part plan for routine requests.

Akins & Campbell, Insurance

819 Valley Drive

Kansas City, Missouri 64111

July 28, 1978

Miss Anne Tower
3705 Hill Place
Lawrence, Kansas 66044

Dear Miss Tower:

We sent you accident claim forms on July 10 and
requested that you complete said forms and return
to this office. To date, we have received no
reply from you.

Unless we hear from you within ten days concerning
this matter, we will assume that you have no
claim to present and will close our file accordingly.

Very truly yours,

Raymond Clinton

Raymond Clinton
Claims Consultant

RC:cr

ORGANIZATIONAL PLAN FOR ADDITIONAL INFORMATION

1. Indicate appreciation for the order.
2. Identify the order, with explicit reference to details. Acknowledge check, if received.
3. Clearly state the information needed, and the reason for it.
4. Tell how the reader can easily comply with the request (such as an enclosed card).
5. Refer in closing to reader benefit, perhaps mentioning delivery date.

Akins & Campbell, Insurance

819 Valley Drive

Kansas City, Missouri 64111

July 28, 1978

Miss Anne Tower
3705 Hill Place
Lawrence, Kansas 66044

Dear Miss Tower:

In preparing to process your insurance claim, we discovered
that we haven't yet received the insurance claim forms we
sent you on July 10.

If you wish to make any claim, it will be necessary for you
to complete these forms and send them in to us within the
next 10 days.

Sincerely yours,

Roland La Porte

Roland LaPorte
Claims Consultant

RL:iam

cc: Carl Bennett
      Raymond Clinton

Enclosure

The following letter observes the five-part organizational plan.

Opening appreciation.

Order acknowledged, with details.
Remittance acknowledged.

Exact information needed.

Reader-benefit: reason.

Action clear and easy.

Reader-benefit: delivery date.

You attitude throughout.

Dear Mr. Johnson:

Thank you for your order of July 18 for
one dozen Zephyr Short Jackets, green
with white trim; catalog No. 1079A.
Your check for $240 is gratefully
acknowledged.

As we were about to fill your order, we
discovered that although we have the chest
measurements--2 at size 38, 6 at size 40,
and 4 at size 42--we have no record of the
desired sleeve sizes. Because we want to
assure your full satisfaction with new
Zephyrs, we would like you to jot down the
precise sleeve sizes on the enclosed
postcard and return it to us.

Your order will be filled as soon as we
hear from you, and you should receive
your jackets by the delivery date you
specified.

Sincerely,

Jason Cartwell
Sales Manager

Request for Special Consideration

Businesses have their practices and policies, but a business that goes strictly by the book is likely to go out of business; for it does not allow for shifting needs and practices that will come with growth and vitality. In this light, requests for special consideration, if reasonable, are actually routine. They can follow the three-part organization of direct statement of request, explanation, and courteous close.

The letter in Figure 8-1 deals with one of those common but unforeseen situations that arise in carrying on a business project. In financing its office building project, Gerald D. Hines Interests must get special certification of the availability of utilities. A letter is sent to the Director of Public Works. Ogilvie states his clear, definite request and explains the reason for the request. The second paragraph preserves cordiality and sympathy by acknowledging that the request is a little special.

Again, the same entrepreneur must request another special consideration in connection with the same Oak Park Central project (Figure 8-2). The tone of the request

 Gerald D. Hines Interests   2100 Post Oak Tower   Houston, Texas 77056   Area Code 713, 621-8000

April 13, 1978

Mr. Carl Beckett
Director of Public Works
City of Houston
P.O. Box 1562
Houston, Texas   77001

Dear Mr. Beckett:

I would appreciate your writing me a letter at the above address stating that water and sewer are available in quantities sufficient to serve the 25-story office building and 40,000 square foot retail area at the property line of Oak Park Central, 2000 South Oak Park Road. I anticipate closing the permanent financing on the Oak Park Central office building in the next several weeks. One of the items which the mortgagee has requested for his full documentation is a statement of the current availability of utilities at the property line.

It is, of course, redundant for us to reaffirm the availability of utilities since the building has been open and operated since July of 1977. Nevertheless, the lender desires this reaffirmation and information for the lender's benefit.

Very truly yours,

Staman Ogilvie

Staman Ogilvie

Figure 8-1

varies from that written to the Director of Public Works. It is more informal because Ogilvie is dealing with a friend ("Dear Frank" instead of "Mr."). The letter is also more deferential and courteous because (1) Ogilvie is dealing with a client and (2) he is asking a favor because of his own oversight. The letter follows the basic three-part organization. It opens with a pleasant reference to the enclosed Lease Amendment and then requests the favor with a reader-benefit reason. The final expression of appreciation is tied in with praise of the client ("business success").

 Gerald D. Hines Interests   2100 Post Oak Tower   Houston, Texas 77056   Area Code 713, 621-8000

April 5, 1978

Mr. Frank Wendell
Wendell Surplus Lines, Inc.
Oak Park Central
2000 Oak Park Road
Houston, Texas 77056

Dear Frank:

Here is your copy of the Lease Amendment covering the 1,785 square feet on Level 22 of Oak Park Central. In the heat of paper work, we failed to get a copy of my letter to you regarding the deferral of rental commencement until August. So that no successor or assign of mine may mistake the intent of our agreement, would you please send a xerox copy of that letter back to me for inclusion in my files.

I am very pleased that your business success has warranted additional space needs and am equally pleased to have this opportunity to reiterate my thanks to you for selecting Oak Park Central as an office home.

Very truly yours,

Staman Ogilvie

Staman Ogilvie

SO:lv

Encl.

Figure 8-2

In the following letter (Figure 8-3) requesting special consideration from a friend, the writer manages to be quite informal and friendly and still efficiently businesslike. Allen delays a little in getting to the direct request because the letter is a follow-up. Paragraph 1 ties in the previous telephone conversation—and, of course, sets the friendly tone. Note, however, that with all its cordial tone it is not garrulous. It is sharply businesslike—the necessary background, the helpful list, the precise request, the explanation, the guarantee of deposit, the name of the coordinator.

Order Letter

Most purchase orders are made on forms or by contracts that specify the terms of purchase. But occasionally you will need to write a letter to place an order. The letter should be precise, brief, and of course, courteous. The same is true of reserving hotel accommodations, meeting rooms, or parking facilities for a conference.

Order letters include three kinds of facts: (1) details about the *merchandise* you are ordering or reserving, (2) directions for *shipment*, and (3) manner of *payment*. In both order and reservation messages, the main idea in the first paragraph is that you are ordering or reserving something. Your explanatory paragraphs give whatever details the order or reservation requires—about quantity, color, style, size, price, payment, location, shipment date, place—plus any special instructions your reader might need. The last paragraph invites prompt shipment and *dated* action, if desired.

Many order letters can be as brief as this one. Though brief, it contains all the essentials of the three units of facts necessary in an order letter.

```
                                            928 Summit Street
                                            Columbus, Ohio  43210
                                            May 14, 1978




        D. Van Nostrand Company
        450 West 33 Street
        New York, New York   10001

        Gentlemen:

             Please send two copies of your new publication,
        The Complete Secretary, thumb-indexed edition, to me
        at the above address.  My check for $19.90 is attached.

             I would appreciate prompt shipment.

                              Yours truly,

                              Ann Pointer

                              Ann Pointer
```

METHODIST

HOSPITALS
OF DALLAS

June 1, 1978

Mr. Robert Sutherland
Division Manager
Southwestern Telephone Company
610 Parkside Tower
P.O. Box 552
Dallas, Texas 75222

Dear Bob:

As I mentioned during our telephone conversation last Friday,
Methodist is bringing several English nurses into the country
to work for one year. Some of these women have been asked to
make large deposits for their telephone service. The attached
list will provide the names of those individuals who have paid
the large deposit.

Since we intend to bring approximately thirty (30) more nurses
into the country during the coming year, we would be desirous
of establishing a waiver on the telephone service deposits for
these individuals. Methodist Hospital will stand good for the
ordinary amount of a deposit.

The gentleman who coordinates this program is named James Keller.
Mr. Keller will work with whomever you designate to effect the
waiver we are requesting.

Bob, thanks so much for your assistance with this problem.
This will greatly help us expedite the "settling in" of these
women and will relieve some of their anxiety about establishing
credit.

Sincerely yours,

Thomas Allen

Thomas Allen
Executive Director

TA:kr
Attachment

| Methodist Central Hospital | Post Office Box 5999 Dallas, Texas 75222 (214) 946-8181 |
| Margaret Jonsson Charlton Methodist | Post Office Box 5357 Dallas, Texas 75222 (214) 296-2511 |

Figure 8-3

With a longer, more detailed order letter, it is helpful to tabulate the items for easy reading. (See Figure 8-4.)

Gentlemen:

Please ship the following supplies to reach our main office at 9251 Grand Avenue (Flushing, New York, 11371) by Wednesday, June 3:

Quantity	Description (and Catalog number)	Unit Price	Total
2 ctn	Dry Photo Paper, Type 731	65.70	131.40
12 doz	Typewriter ribbons, polyethylene, black, Selectric, No. 3871	2.41	28.92
12	Scissors, Acme Shear, 12 in, Office use, No. 109S	3.20	38.40
			198.72

These items are to be charged to our account on the usual 2/10, net/30 terms.

Since we plan to use the scissors on a special office project beginning August 5, it is important that this order arrive on time. We count on your company's usual promptness in filling orders.

Sincerely,

Jane Pollock

Jane Pollock

Figure 8-4

Credit Check

Matters of credit can be sensitive—we are, in a sense, telling the customer we don't trust him or her. The following inquiry, however, is handled in a cordial, positive tone. The you attitude is clearly emphasized.

GULF   SUPPLY   COMPANY

428 Lennox Street

Beaumont, Texas   77905

March 3, 1978

Langston Electronics, Inc.
877 College Avenue
Kearney, Nebraska   68847

Gentlemen:

We were pleased to receive your order of February 28
for 12 Model XL20 head sets.

So that we can fill your order on account as quickly
as possible, will you please send us the names of
three firms from whom you purchase on a credit basis.

The 12 Model XL20's are being held aside to assure you
quick delivery. We enjoy the opportunity of being
able to serve you and will process the information you
provide us with immediately.

Sincerely yours,

Thomas Nelson

Thomas Nelson
Credit Manager

The same cordial, positive tone is used by Nelson when he follows up the credit reference supplied by Langston Electronics, Inc.:

Gentlemen:

Would you kindly assist us with some information we need to fill an order on account for Langston Electronics, Inc., of Kearney, Nebraska? We believe you also supply this firm.

We would like to know how long Langston Electronics, Inc., has had an account with you, how promptly they pay their invoices, and if any credit limit has been placed upon their account.

Your cooperation will be appreciated, and we will be happy to reciprocate at any time. Your reply will, of course, be kept in strict confidence.

Sincerely,

Thomas Nelson

Thomas Nelson
Credit Manager

Since, for mutual benefit, companies exchange credit information, the process is often simplified by enclosing a form with the credit applicant's name typed in. (See Figure 8-5.)

Gentlemen:

Langston Electronics, Inc., of 877 College Avenue, Kearney,
Nebraska, 68847, has given us your name as a credit reference.

We will appreciate your giving us the benefit of your
experience with this company. If you will answer the
questions listed on the form below and return this letter
in the enclosed stamped envelope, we shall be very grateful.
Your reply will, of course, be kept in strict confidence.

                         Sincerely yours,

How long has this company dealt with you? _____

The terms were _____

Amount now owing is $_____

Highest credit you will extend is $_____

Date of the last transaction _____

Remarks _____

_____

_____

                         (Signature) _____

                         (Date) _____

Figure 8-5

EXERCISES

1. The June issue of *Business Today* featured the article "Rating Employee Attitudes," by E. Bernard Miller, which you enjoyed reading. The article contained some actual test questions that psychologist Miller has devised to determine employee attitudes toward job and company as well as pertinent explanatory information and findings. Because of your position as Personnel Director, you are interested in further information. Specifically you want to obtain the complete test and interpretive materials. Write for the information in care of *Business Today*, using a fictitious address.

2. About a month ago you ordered and received from Tudor Manufacturing Company, Elizabethville, North Carolina, its new spring catalog entitled "Country Styling for City Living." The booklet was obviously expensive to produce, since it contains pages of transparent color overlays. You have made good use of the catalog and have shared it with several other interested people. However, the catalog has been misplaced and, although a thorough search has been made, the Tudor catalog cannot be found. Write the company the kind of letter that will motivate them to quickly replace your lost copy.

3. Place an order for 14 bowling shirts (cat. #384A) for your company's (National Electronics) bowling team. The basic color is white, with the lettering THE ELECTRICS to appear in bright red across the back. The design of the lettering is to follow the circular arrangement shown on page 3 of the supplier's catalog. The sizes are as follows: two small, six medium, four large, and two extra large. Since you have no account with the supplier and want to speed delivery, you enclose a check. The shirts cost $9.48 each. Because league play begins in four weeks, you need the shirts by September 1.

4. For about a year Mrs. Hepple-Martin has been a cash customer of the rather exclusive department store where you are credit manager, The Winton-Helman Co. (of 1920 Park Drive, Kansas City, Missouri). She has written to ask you to send her a Revolving-Charge credit card and has given no credit references. Your job is to write her a letter enclosing the store's standard credit inquiry form, which asks questions about her and her husband's employment, banking affiliations, and other charge accounts presently held.

   You should request that Mrs. Hepple-Martin complete the form and return it as soon as possible. It is not a difficult letter to write, but if you imply in any way that Mrs. Hepple-Martin's credit record might not be satisfactory, you may offend her and lose both a cash and a credit customer.

5. You work at Lawson Hall Leather and Shoe Company, a large mail order house. The following letter comes to your attention.

```
                              Jan. 2, 1979

        Lawson Hall Leather and Shoe Company
        1 Lawson Hall Way
        Waltham, Massachusetts 02154

        Gentlemen:

            Please send me one pair of Bermuda Woven shoes, size
        9D, no. 049A.  My check for $34.74 is enclosed.

            This is the first time I've ordered anything from you,
        and I used somebody else's catalog.  I would appreciate
        your sending me a catalog.

                              Yours truly,

                              Greg Olson
                              Greg Olson

                              428 Park Side Road
                              Akron, Ohio  44304
```

Olson's order does not indicate which color of shoes he wants—black or brown. Write a reply that requests the additional information without disappointing him over the delay. Acknowledge also his check and his being a new customer. Send him a catalog.

ROUTINE REPLIES

In writing routine replies your course of action should be clear. Somebody has initiated a communication with you, and you must respond. Someone has asked you information about goods or services, or has sent you an order for merchandise, or has asked for a credit reference, or has requested some other information or action.

Most businessmen and businesswomen realize that letters in answer to inquiries and requests present a real opportunity to turn such openings into orders and goodwill. The inquirer is often already your customer or a potential buyer. He or she may become a steady, satisfied customer *if* you send a reply that impresses him or her favorably.

If the inquirer is not already a customer, then he or she is certainly a likely potential customer. The individual has already expressed interest in your products or services. He or she has invited communication, and you have a great opportunity.

Since the other person has opened the way, your reply does not need to be persuasive. As in writing the routine request or inquiry, you should be direct, clear, and cordial. But there is another dimension. Since the person to whom you are replying has shown interest in your goods or services, your letter is a sales message. Your main message is to respond directly to the inquiry or request. But a secondary message is one of promotion and goodwill. Your letter should follow a three-part organization.

ORGANIZATIONAL PLAN

1. *Acknowledgment of request and statement of action taken.* The action may be that of sending the requested information, enclosing a booklet, forwarding the request to somebody else, filling an order, and so on.
2. *Explanation.* Give details. Answer all questions, direct or implied, about features of a product, or how to use it, or prices and terms, or shipment, or sales possibilities, and so on. Supply all necessary details of any action taken.
3. *Motivation of action or goodwill.* Avoid high pressure promotion, but don't miss the opportunity to evoke action or goodwill. Make any suggested action clear and easy. Emphasize the you attitude.

The following are some general guidelines for writing effective routine replies.

GUIDELINES

1. *Carefully read the communication to which you're replying.* It may be wise to circle all the points you want to answer. An incomplete reply is an ineffective reply.
2. *Begin and end every routine reply with a positive tone.*
3. *Acknowledge significant particulars* in the communication to which you are replying. For example, when acknowledging a purchase order, be sure to restate the details of the order (unless those details are so long that they will make your reply clumsy). Restatement is a courtesy that lets your reader know that his or her communication has been fully understood.
4. *Acknowledge remittance,* if the communication contains one.
5. *Explain why questions are unanswered,* if your reply does not answer all the questions asked of you.
6. *Give more information than requested,* if necessary to make a reply complete. if your reply contains enclosures, be sure to tell the reader where in the enclosed material his or her questions are answered.
7. *Treat potentially disappointing replies positively.* For instance, when a price has risen or there is a shortage, treat the situation as positively and as empathetically as you can.
8. *Always maintain the you attitude,* keeping the recipient's point of view uppermost in your message. If you study the initiating communication carefully, you can learn a lot about the writer's interests.
9. *Reply as promptly as you can.* If possible, reply within two days. Promptness is not only a courtesy; it keeps your recipient from losing interest or thinking you are slow.

Typical Letters

There are many kinds of routine reply letters. Some more common routine replies are illustrated in the following pages.

Reply to Request for Information

The following reply illustrates the typical three-part organization, and it observes the guidelines of effective routine replies. The writer not only sends the requested information but also promotes the product, emphasizes the you attitude, and makes it easy for the inquirer to become a customer.

March 16, 1978

Mrs. Susan Curtis
Accommodating Services, Inc.
2313 Carlton Avenue
Harrisburg, Pennsylvania 17110

Dear Mrs. Curtis:

Action taken

We are pleased to send you a copy of our brochure "The Best for Your Office," which you requested.

Explanation—details

You will be interested in the sketches of typical office layouts on pages 14-20. Surveys by our architects and engineers show that these arrangements effect savings of 50 percent by using space efficiently. And because our lightweight Star Modules are designed to individual needs, more privacy and greater efficiency result, as shown in the five typical installations on pages 36-40.

Motivation and action

Action clear and easy

After you have read the pamphlet, you may have questions pertaining specifically to the design of your offices. Our agent in your territory is Mr. James Jackson, 29 Elm Street, Scranton, Pennsylvania 18510 (phone 692-6687). As a graduate architectural engineer, Mr. Jackson can give you additional information on design, costs, and installation--all without obligation on your part.

Reader benefit

You attitude throughout

Drop him a card or give him a call. He can come with a day's notice to demonstrate how Star Modules can make your offices more efficient, more comfortable, and more economical.

Very truly yours,

Conrad Pender

Conrad Pender

CR:hb
Enc.

Negative Reply to Request for Information

It is risky to say "no" in any way to a customer. The person is almost sure to feel some ill will. Therefore, extra effort must be made to create goodwill. The following letter is ally bad, but it falls short. The first paragraph is negative and the whole letter is self-centered and didactic (as if giving the "amateur" a lecture).

W E S T   C O A S T   T I R E   &   B A T T E R Y

458 W. Wells Street

Los Angeles, California

June 23, 1978

Mr. Gerald Boland
3280 Juniper Avenue
Laverne, California 91750

Dear Mr. Boland:

In answer to your inquiry, we wish to inform
you that we do not market retreads--regardless of
the brand. We believe that their quality is wholly
substandard, and we advise that you do not use them
if you want satisfactory driving results. Often,
retreads are nothing more than old, worn-out tires
with a few layers of rubber laid over them so that
they look acceptable. The people selling such
tires would not think of using them, and certainly
you would not want to use them either.

We suggest that for satisfactory results, you
use Coastal 400's. They are available at your
local dealer for only $120.00--actually not much
more than reprocessed tires. And they are fully
guaranteed.

Very truly yours,

Carl Frank

Carl Houck
Customer Service Department

The following writer handles the problem with skill and diplomacy. The opening and closing are positive. The tone of lecturing is totally absent. The arbitrary tone is avoided, giving Mr. Boland an easy and positive option.

W E S T   C O A S T   T I R E   &   B A T T E R Y

458 W. Wells Street

Los Angeles, California

June 23, 1978

Mr. Gerald Boland
3280 Juniper Avenue
Laverne, California 91750

Dear Mr. Boland:

We were glad to receive your inquiry regarding retreaded tires. Many of our customers have expressed curiosity as to their quality.

West Coast Tire & Battery has decided, after careful investigation, not to market retreads. We want to be able to guarantee fully any product we put on the market. Because out-worn tires are involved in the retreading process, we are unable to guarantee the quality of such tires. Some of our customers have purchased retreads and been dissatisfied with their performance.

Actually, the tires we recommend--Coastal 400's-- cost little more than reprocessed tires. And, we fully guarantee them. We are eager to provide only the best tires because we know how much dependability can mean to you.

Sincerely,

Larry Frank

Larry Frank
Customer Service Department

LF:lg

Confirmation of an Order

A first-time order should always be acknowledged to encourage the customer's continuing patronage. Notice how many of the guidelines the following letter observes. The tone of the letter is positive from beginning to end. It restates the essential data. It expresses genuine appreciation. It identifies the customer with the product and the company. It appeals to "you" throughout, and it uses the brand name Sure-Shine four times to build product identification into the reader's mind.

The most attractive item, on cost, gets its own single-sentence paragraph, the third.

July 6, 1978

Hamil-Horiston Company
104 East Commerce
Baltimore, Maryland 21217

Gentlemen:

This is to thank you for your recent order and
for your check for $408.28 in prepayment. We've
already shipped your fifty cartons of Sure-Shine
dusting cloths. They should reach you within a
few days.

We feel sure you'll find the same rapid turnover
that other dealers have found with Sure-Shine.
Housewives find their multipurpose value and
disposability hard to resist, to say nothing of
the attractive package.

Needless to say, for you there is a Sure-Shine
substantial mark-up.

Enclosed is a handy reorder blank for your
convenience when your Sure-Shine stock gets low.

Sincerely,

Michael Surles
Distribution Manager

MS:ld

Enclosure

Follow-Up after Personal Negotiations

A special kind of routine reply is the follow-up after personal negotiations. It may follow a telephone conversation, a discussion in person, or some other communication.

This kind of letter pins down or confirms in writing the negotiations and frequently moves on to another phase of the business project. The letter may be built on the three-part organizational plan of the routine reply:

1. *Acknowledgment.* Confirm essential data discussed and agreements arrived at.
2. *Explanation.* Provide any additional details necessary to clarify.
3. *Future Action.* State the next direction or stage in the project.

This three-part structure is illustrated in the follow-up letter in Figure 8-6. Notice also the cordial opening and closing and the general tone of goodwill underlying very serious business negotiations.

 Gerald D. Hines Interests   2100 Post Oak Tower   Houston, Texas 77056   Area Code 713, 621-8000

October 25, 1978

Mr. P.J. Warner
President
P.J. Warner and Company
P.O. Box 97
Jackson, Mississippi 39205

Dear Paul:

Both Louis and I appreciated the hospitality of your firm yesterday in Jackson. We felt it was an exceptionally good information gathering trip. As we said yesterday, our initial look justifies an in-depth study of the Jackson office market. We believe you have a beautiful site, an excellent concept, and, with a good office building project, the ability to capture a large portion of the speculative office space market.

I anticipate being in Jackson with one of our marketing specialists in the beginning of next week. I will of course coordinate with you later in the week as to the days we actually expect to be in Jackson.

After our visit, we could give you some preliminary feedback at the end of the week. Assuming a continuing interest to proceed on both of our parts, we would be prepared to discuss the particulars of our involvement in the Twin Lakes Development during the week of November 8.

Thank you again for your gracious hospitality yesterday. I look forward to seeing you in Jackson next week.

Very truly yours,

Staman Ogilvie

SO:jp

Figure 8-6 Follow-up letter

    We can look at two other letters to see how follow-up letters may vary with different phases of the total project (Figures 8-7 and 8-8). The first letter from Topham is a confirmation of a meeting with a fairly new acquaintance. The tone is formal, the information sufficient and precise. The second letter is a confirmation of telephone negotiations with a closer acquaintance. Negotiations are well under way, common ground has been established, and the tone is informal. As in the first letter, though, the information is quite sufficient and precise.

Figure 8-7

Gerald D. Hines Interests   2100 Post Oak Tower   Houston, Texas 77056   Area Code 713, 621-8000

August 21, 1978

Mr. Terence Sullivan
President
International Realty Corporation
Suite 2222
555 Pacific Street
San Francisco, California 94104

Dear Terry:

As I mentioned to you on the telephone yesterday, we are most
interested in pursuing an office building development in Kuwait
City. We have incidentally established a new corporation
"Hines Overseas Limited" which will be responsible for these
developments in the Middle East, and I am enclosing a sheet
which outlines these functions.

The attached proposal, needless to say, would be subject to
a complex analysis on our part of cost, economics, legal,
and tax questions of such a development in Kuwait City. It
is merely an outline of a possible structuring which we have
found to be acceptable in comparable developments in other
Middle Eastern countries.

I look forward to hearing from you at such time as you have
been able to discuss this with some of your Kuwaiti clients.

With kind regards.

Very truly yours,

Michael Topham

Michael Topham

MT:jp
Enclosure

Figure 8-8

David Cowden Production Co.

4726 Jacksboro Hwy. Suite C • Wichita Falls, Texas 76302 • Phone 817 723-6875

November 25, 1977

Mr. J. S. Wintergrove
Trust Oil Department
First Mercantile National Bank
P.O. Box 123
Dallas, Texas   78946

                        RE: A. L. Smith Trust
                             13.92 acres interest
                             Proposed Oil & Gas Lease
                             Grayford County, Texas

Dear Mr. Wintergrove:

I have reviewed the proposed oil and gas lease which your trust
officer would prefer to grant on behalf of the A. L. Smith
Trust.

Our company is willing to accept a one-year lease term. We
cannot, however, grant a 90-day drilling contract with a 3/16
override to such a small mineral interest as is contained in
the Smith Trust.

I would appreciate your recommendation to the Trust Oil Committee that a one-year pooling lease at $5.00 per acre be
signed on behalf of this trust. Drilling on this acreage is
scheduled to commence on December 15. If agreeable terms
have not been reached by that date, we will be forced to
unitize the entire lease and set the Smith interest out.

Very truly yours,

Vikki L. Chaviers
Land Supervisor

VLC/bg

Figure 8-9

A follow-up letter after several stages of negotiations can forgo some amenities and be more tersely businesslike. Much common ground has already been established. The letter in Figure 8-9 represents Stage 5 in negotiations that have been going on for over three months. Here is the record of those negotiations.

STAGE 1:   David Cowden Production Co. made an initial offer to the First Mercantile National Bank to lease the A. L. Smith mineral interest for two years at $3.00 per acre. A standard oil and gas lease form was enclosed with a request that it be signed by the Trust Officer on behalf of the Smith Trust.

STAGE 2:   Mr. Wintergrove, Chairman of the Trust Oil Committee, replied that the offer would be considered during the next regular committee meeting.

STAGE 3:   Three months elapsed. The Land Supervisor again wrote Mr. Wintergrove requesting confirmation on the acceptance or rejection of the initial offer.

STAGE 4:   Mr. Wintergrove replied that he could not recommend to the committee that a lease be granted under the proposed terms. The Trust Department would, however, consider signing the enclosed one-year lease at $5.00 per acre, provided that a ninety-day drilling contract and 3/16 override were included as terms of the lease. (These terms would insure more money for the Smith account held in trust.)

STAGE 5:   The Land Supervisor wrote the letter in Figure 8-9 in response to Mr. Wintergrove's offer.

The tone is firm because at this stage firmness is what the two bargaining agencies understand. Deadlines require decisions. The letter follows the standard three-part organization of acknowledgment, explanation, and future action.

Stopgap Reply

Another kind of reply frequently necessary in business is the stopgap reply. A stopgap reply is used to prevent impatience when there will be a delay in filling a request for action or information. If, for instance, you get a request for information that will take you some time to compile, don't remain silent until you compile the information. Send a stopgap reply like the one on p. 164.

Gray saw that he could not immediately comply with the boss's request; so as soon as he determined when he could comply, he wrote a stop gap reply. His memo is precisely informative, and it bears a tone of brisk efficiency.

Credit Check

A credit manager, in addition to writing inquiries, must be able to write effective replies when others request information. The replies must exhibit a delicate balance, being

MEMORANDUM

To: Jane Grey   Date: July 3, 1978

From: Research Department (S. Gray)

Subject: Your Request for Data on the Physical Plant
          at the River Oaks System.

We have begun compiling, for cross reference, the
data on the physical plant at River Oaks which you
requested in your memo yesterday.

The data was not as accessible as we thought; four
different sources were necessary. But we've
obtained each source and the staff is busy on the
compilation. I expect to have it on your desk by
Thursday morning at 9.

---

informative enough to help the inquirer, yet not so informative as to violate the
confidence of customers by divulging too much. The following letter is a well-written
reply to Thomas Nelson's request for credit information (a request we examined on
p. 149).

Notice the writer's technique in replying. He answers all Nelson's questions and
provides some additional information he feels pertinent (that Langston Electronics is an
all-purpose supply and service firm with a brisk trade). He does not specify precisely
how much business his firm does with Langston Electronics; he uses relative terms—
"regularly," "seldom"—to answer Nelson's inquiries. Usually, when a credit manager
must divulge a customer's poor credit record, he avoids putting any remarks on paper
by using the telephone.

Mr. Thomas Nelson
Gulf Supply Company
428 Lennox Street
Beaumont, Texas 77905

Dear Mr. Nelson:

We are happy to supply the information you requested
about our customer--Langston Electronics, Inc., of
Kearney, Nebraska.

The company has purchased from us regularly for the
past nine years. They are an all-purpose electronics
supply and service house, with a remarkably fast
turnover in supplies and components. We have placed no
limit upon their credit purchases. Seldom in the
past nine years have they failed to qualify for the
discount on our regular terms of 2/10, net 30. They
never pay late.

We hope this information is helpful to you in qualifying
Langston Electronics for a credit account.

Very truly yours,

CHICAGO SUPPLY HOUSE

Howard Morris

Howard Morris
Credit Manager

Recommendations

A letter furnishing pertinent information about an applicant's qualifications and character should preferably be addressed to the specific person interested, instead of "To Whom It May Concern." A to-whom-it-may-concern letter is sometimes given to a satisfactory employee before he or she leaves the company. But because it must necessarily be general and not confidential, it carries less weight than the confidential specific recommendation.

You have a three-fold responsibility when you write a recommendation. You must be fair: (1) to the applicant, so that he or she can obtain the position for which he or she is best qualified, (2) to the inquirer (prospective employer, creditor, landlord, and so on), for he or she is depending upon your frank comments, and (3) to your own conscience and reputation for integrity.

The following organizational plan for recommendations is a variation of the three-part structure for routine replies.

ORGANIZATIONAL PLAN FOR A RECOMMENDATION

1. *The main idea.*   Identify fully the applicant and his or her job description.

    a.   State the applicant's full name and his or her relationship to you—employee, customer, friend, tenant, club member. Mention dates, length of time, and type of job, credit, tenancy, or whatever is pertinent. Use facts; don't guess.

    b.   Work in an expression of appreciation and goodwill, if sincere, combined with your statement of purpose in writing the letter.

2. *Explanation.*   Supply all pertinent details.

    a.   Answer all questions—direct or implied. (Omissions cast suspicions.)

    b.   Arrange answers in the most positive order, depending upon facts.

    c.   Back up your statements of evaluation (excellent, outstanding, or others) with specific facts about performance. For a job applicant:

        (1)   Describe specific duties that the applicant performed.

        (2)   If the inquiry states requirements of the job for which the applicant is being considered, talk about those duties that will be significant.

        (3)   When desirable, describe work habits that show personality characteristics.

    d.   Be honest and fair with negative material.

        (1)   Include negative material only if it is pertinent to the inquiry and likely to affect the applicant's success.

        (2)   De-emphasize negative material through amount of space and word choice.

3. *Positive ending.*   Include, if possible, a candid statement of your personal opinion about the applicant's probable fitness for the position (or lease, credit, recommendation)—qualified or unqualified.

Many large companies write to references supplied by job applicants—usually a form letter obviously designed to look "routine." Often the sender types in only the date, the inside address, the name of the applicant, and the title of the position applied for.

```
        Mr. Paul Collins
        240 Howle Street
        Madison, Wisconsin

        Dear Sir:

        Your name has been given as a reference in the application of
                          Kathy Teal
        for the position of
                          Accountant
        Would you please give us your assessment of this applicant--
        work habits, ability, character, potential, personality, and
        any other traits and characteristics that would help us to
        evaluate her as a potential employee in our company?  Your
        statement will, of course, be kept in strictest confidence.
        An addressed, stamped envelope is enclosed for your reply.

                          Very truly yours,

                          Carl Steger

                          Carl Steger
```

Answering such an inquiry, as the example below illustrates, is easy if you have a high opinion of the applicant and believe he or she would fit the job.

```
        Dear Mr. Steger:

        It is a pleasure for me to write in behalf of Kathy Teal,
        who has applied for the position of Accountant in your
        company.

        I have known Miss Teal for over four years, first as a
        fellow accountant and later as her supervisor.  I
        consider her an extremely competent person, completely
        dependable and extremely intelligent.  She works well
        with people--she was always cooperative and pleasant.
        Her record here was outstanding.

        When Miss Teal told me that she was leaving us (she had
        to return to Detroit to care for her invalid aunt), I
        was sad indeed.  She will be missed here.  Any organization
        that hires Miss Teal will be most fortunate.

                          Sincerely yours,

                          Paul Collins

                          Paul Collins
```

It is more difficult to write a letter concerning someone about whom you are not so enthusiastic. Here you must wrestle with your conscience and your integrity. You could take the attitude that even though you consider the person incompetent or otherwise undesirable, it is of no concern to you—let the company to which the person applied take the risk. True, it is somewhat painful to assume the responsibility for denying a person a job. Yet you would do well to remember that if you were a manager seeking information about a prospective employee, you would expect honesty from those who write a recommendation.

The following are two fair methods of handling the weak recommendation.

THE NONCOMMITTAL LETTER.   Some people, rather than say something negative about an applicant whom they can't praise, resort to a noncommittal letter.

```
Dear Mr. Golding:

It would be unfair of me to comment on the qualifications
of Clement Burch for a position with your firm.  He was
under my supervision for a very short time, and I did
not have an opportunity to evaluate his competency.

                    Sincerely yours,
```

If the writer of the letter above is hedging, then the letter is a denunciation. That is, if the writer knew anything at all favorable about the applicant, he would have said it. Therefore, what was left unsaid speaks as loudly as an outright denunciation.

If the writer is honest, however, the letter is satisfactory. The reader can consider it neutral and seek information elsewhere.

THE DIRECT EVALUATION.   The best approach is to be fair—to yourself, to the applicant, and to the inquirer. Describe both the assets and deficiencies of the applicant. Study the letter opposite to see how many good things are said and how many bad.

The writer of the letter was not heartless. No one can say that such a letter is bad or that it is good. The writer apparently believe that his integrity is at stake, and he must act according to his own conscience. He has, however, said some positive things.

1.   Clement Burch is a competent draftsman.
2.   Mr. Burch is likable and got along well with his co-workers.

Dear Mr. Golding:

In the best interests of both you and Clement
Burch, about whom you inquired, I cannot give
him an unqualified recommendation.

Mr. Burch was a draftsman under my supervision
for six months. While he is competent as a
draftsman, his attendance was sporadic. He was
frequently late to work, often called in sick,
and stayed away from work two or three days at a
time. In spite of my having several discussions
with him, the problem was never resolved, and
finally I had to release him.

Perhaps, Mr. Golding, the position Clement had
here didn't challenge him enough--or perhaps he
had personal problems he couldn't resolve. Certainly
he is a likable fellow and seemed to get along well
with his co-workers here. Unfortunately, however,
I just couldn't get him going. Perhaps he will do
better in another working environment.

                    Sincerely yours,

                    Gerald Hampstead

                    Gerald Hampstead

3. The writer suggests the possibility that he himself may have been at fault because of his inability to motivate Burch.

In this case, the inquirer may be looking for a competent draftsman and may believe that the other problems can be handled.

FORM LETTERS AND PROTOTYPE LETTERS

Many of a company's routine communications tend to be recurrent. Therefore, to save time and money, some companies use *form letters.* Such a practice does have advantages. It saves the writer and the typist the time and effort of framing a new reply and typing it. Figure 8-10 illustrates an effective form letter. The time-saving blanks can be filled in quickly. Care was also given, however, to personalize the letter, to be cordial, to give precise and sufficient information, and to make it easy for the customer to act.

The economy of form letters is often a false economy because most recipients don't like the impersonality of form letters and don't react to them very well. Consequently, any time you consider using a form letter, you must decide whether the inevitable loss of appeal is worth the dollar savings. If it is, then use the form letter. If it isn't—don't.

One alternative to the pure form letter is the *prototype letter.* A company will provide its writers with a ready-written reply that can be typed out individually each time it is used. Blanks in the prototype can be left to the writer to insert details specific to each reply. A carefully composed prototype letter can provide distinctive and original-sounding letters, but unless a prototype letter is carefully composed, it is as likely as a form letter to displease its recipient by not seeming to refer to his or her particular situation. Good examples of effective letters made from prototype letters are those on p. 199 (Burton from Turner in "Goodwill") and p. 213 (Hill from City Furnishings, #4 in "Collection series").

The four prototype letters in Figures 8-11, 8-12, 8-13, and 8-14, illustrate how a well-constructed letter can save time and money and still be easily adapted to different situations. Figure 8-11 shows a negative-response prototype to an employment inquiry. Figure 8-12 shows a positive response. In Figure 8-13 the employment manager adapts the positive response to give ordinary encouragement and continue negotiations. In Figure 8-14 he uses the same prototype to indicate very strong encouragement to Catherine Bolton in requesting her to telephone collect. He obviously would like to employ her. Both letters are economically built from the prototype, deal with different materials and purposes, and are personal and authentic.

Order No: 532279

Item No: 010

Dear Customer:

Thank you very much for your order. I am sorry to write
that we are temporarily out of stock on style 44044
in size 8½D , which you ordered. We expect to make
shipment on _____ 6/15 _____.

Unless we hear from you to the contrary, we will plan to
make shipment as soon as your shoes become available. If,
by any chance, your shoes are not shipped by
_____ 7/11 _____,
we will automatically refund your money at that time.
You may prefer not to have an automatic refund and want to
wait beyond this date; if so, please indicate this on the
enclosed postpaid card and return.

You may prefer to have us send an alternate selection.
If you wish us to do this, please indicate your alternate
selection on the enclosed card and return it to us. We
are enclosing a catalog for your convenience.

If you prefer not to wait at all, please indicate this
on the enclosed card and return it to us.

Please accept my apologies for this delay and inconvenience. I do hope you will find your shoes well worth
waiting for. Thank you for your interest in our shoes.

                         Cordially,

                         Marcia Hill
                         Marcia Hill

CS 53

LAWSON HILL
LEATHER AND SHOE COMPANY
LAWSON HILL WAY • WALTHAM, MASSACHUSETTS 02154

Figure 8-10   Sample form letter

METHODIST

HOSPITALS
OF DALLAS

Retirement Plan for Employees

Dear

Thank you for your interest in Methodist Hospitals
of Dallas.

At present we do not have any positions open in
your field; however, it is difficult to anticipate
when a vacancy may occur. Enclosed is an application
form that you may fill out and return to us at your
convenience.

We will keep your inquiry of employment on file and
contact you if anything becomes available. Again,
we appreciate your interest in our hospitals.

Sincerely,

Allen Friehoff

Allen Friehoff
Employment Manager

AF:ac
enc.

Methodist Central Hospital | Post Office Box 5999 Dallas, Texas 75222 (214) 946-8181
Margaret Jonsson Charlton Methodist | Post Office Box 5357 Dallas, Texas 75222 (214) 296-2511

Figure 8-11

METHODIST

HOSPITALS
OF DALLAS

Dear

Thank you for your interest in employment with Methodist
Hospitals of Dallas.

Currently we do have a position available for someone
with your education and experience. Enclosed please
find an application we would like for you to fill out
and return to us at your earliest convenience.

Once we receive your application it will be reviewed by
the appropriate personnel and we will then contact you
regarding a personal interview.

Again, we appreciate your interest in our hospitals.

Sincerely,

Allen Friehoff

Allen Friehoff
Employment Manager

AF:ac
enc.

Methodist Central Hospital | Post Office Box 5999 Dallas, Texas 75222 (214) 946-8181
Margaret Jonsson Charlton Methodist | Post Office Box 5357 Dallas, Texas 75222 (214) 296-2511

Figure 8-12

March 20, 1978

Mr. Carl Weller
509 Greenway Drive
Newcastle, Virginia 24592

Dear Mr. Weller:

Thank you for your interest in Methodist Hospitals of Dallas. As the
Employment Manager for the hospitals, I have been asked to reply to
your letter.

At the present time we are seeking an experienced Histology Technician
to supervise that section of our Pathology Department. Enclosed is
an application we would like for you to complete and return to us at
your convenience. It is also imperative we know your salary requirements.

Once we have received this information, it will be reviewed by our
Pathology Director and we will then contact you regarding a personal
interview.

Sincerely,

Allen Friehoff
Employment Manager

AF:ac

Figure 8-13

METHODIST

HOSPITALS
OF DALLAS

Retirement Plan for Employees

June 12, 1978

Miss Catherine Bolton
Rt 1, Box 103T
Little Rock, Arkansas 72204

Dear Miss Bolton:

Thank you for your interest in Methodist Hospitals of Dallas.

At the present time we do have a vacancy and would very much
be interested in talking with you. We have also enclosed an
application for you to complete and return to us at your
convenience.

We would like for you to call our Chief Therapist, Mr. Ralph
Brett, collect (214) 946-8181, ext. 442 so he can give you
further information regarding our Physical Medicine Department.

Again, thank you for your interest in our hospitals.

Sincerely,

Allen Friehoff

Allen Friehoff
Employment Manager

AF:ac

Figure 8-14

EXERCISES

1. You are sales manager of Haynes Enterprises, Inc. During lunch with your friend, Joe Wilson, he ordered 50,000 key rings with a chain and plate imprinted with the slogan "Kirk and White—Grand Opening," at 8½ cents apiece. You promised delivery within three weeks. Write a confirmation letter to Joe to avoid any confusion over the terms of the oral agreement, as well as to convey a friendly attitude.

2. Your company, Moran Brothers Realty of Roanoke, Virginia, today received the following letter from a prospective client:

March 3, 1978

Moran Brothers Realty
504 South River Road
Roanoke, Virginia 24015

Gentlemen:

    I am interested in purchasing a home with at least five acres of land outside Roanoke, somewhere in the $40,000 to $50,000 range. I understand that such properties are frequently available and that you are the outfit most likely to be handling them. Please let me know what you have. I will reply immediately by phone or in person.

              Very truly yours,

              Beverly Studdard

              Beverly Studdard

Obviously, you would like to sell property to Miss Studdard, and you do have several area listings of over ten acres. Because of a recent boom in land prices, however, none of these properties can be purchased for less than $60,000.

Write a letter to Miss Studdard informing her that there is property available in the Roanoke area and that although the prices are higher than her suggested range, the properties are among the best values still available in the county. The likelihood is that county real estate prices will continue to rise. Tell her, too, that you'd like very much to show her these choice properties.

Your task isn't simple. Consider the reactions you desire from Miss Studdard. Your primary objective is to maintain, or even enhance, Miss Studdard's enthusiasm for buying property near Roanoke, in spite of the fact that she underestimated how much it would cost.

3. Assume that you are the manager of the mail order department at Nan's Interiors, Inc., of Evanston, Illinois. You received Jess Johnson's order letter, which appears below, and have just filled the order and shipped it by freight express as Mr. Johnson requested. Now, because it is your policy to acknowledge all orders with a letter, write an effective letter of acknowledgment to Mr. Johnson. Keep in mind that this is the first order you have received from Mr. Johnson and remember to acknowledge the check he included with his order.

October 2, 1978

Nan's Interiors, Inc.
404 Lancaster Boulevard
Evanston, Illinois 60201

Gentlemen:

Please ship the following prepaid order via United Parcel:

6	Brass Cricket Boxes @ $10.50	63.00
8	Cross-stitch Pillows (4 rust, 4 teal) @ $8.50	68.00
6	12" Brass Candle Sticks @ $13.25	79.50
	Total	$210.50

My check for $247.70 is attached to cover both the goods ($210.50) and the freight charges ($37.20). I would very much appreciate your sending out this order in time to reach me by October 12, 197

Sincerely yours,

Jess Johnson

Jess Johnson
Manager

JJ:bs

---

4. As administrative assistant to the personnel director of the Nondale Corporation, you supervise two clerk-typists. One of these positions was until a month ago filled by

Clare Randolph. Mrs. Randolph left of her own accord (her husband was transferred to another city), but you were about to release her. Her typing skills were weak, and she never did catch on to the filing system. Also, her attitude was sullen and uncooperative—there was always a scene when she was asked to do a job over because of errors.

You receive a form letter from Clearwater Holding Company asking you to assess Mrs. Randolph's work record while in your employ. Write the letter.

5. Another clerk-typist who once worked under your supervision, Rebecca Cowart, was first-rate—a rapid typist, accurate, devoted to her job, and pleasant to be around. You were about to recommend her for a promotion to senior clerk when she left the Nondale Corporation to be married. Two months after she left, you receive an inquiry from Clymer Insurance Company about Miss Cowart (now Mrs. John McDuffy); she has applied for a position as clerk-typist. Write a reply.

6. As correspondent for Curtis Electric Products Company, manufacturers of electric curling irons, hair dryers, and other grooming aids, you need to answer an inquiry from Wells Beauty Supply, one of your new distributors in Kansas City, Missouri. They carry your complete line of products in their two stores, and they need the free newspaper mats to use in their local advertising campaign and window display materials. In addition, they would like to examine a sample of the envelope stuffers (illustrative sales leaflets) that they might enclose with their customers' monthly statements. These leaflets are not free, although of course the one sample you're sending today is free. The distributor will have to pay $8.00 a thousand for these colorful leaflets, but customers get good ideas from them. This is the first inquiry you have had from this new distributor since the welcome letter you sent him two weeks ago.

7. Improve the following reply.

```
        Dear Mr. Reynolds;

            Thank you for your postal card regarding rates for
        Winter.
            Our rates for two are; $80.00 per week & xxxxthexxxeeh
        sea side are $90.00 per week.
            These Apartments consist of Bed Sittling room, fully
        equipped kitchen, bathroom and Shower and Garage.
            We are located in the East section of Ravella about
        a mile from the main business District.  The market is a
        block away and we are about two hundred yards from White
        Sands Bathing Beach.
            We do not allow Dogs or Cats.
            On receipt of $10.00 deposit we will be pleased to
        reserve the accomodation you require.
            Thanking you for your courtesy, I am,
```

8. We suspect that the writer of the following letter was trying to deceive us. It is contradictory. The first paragraph praises, but the second paragraph hints, by its vagueness, that all was not well.

   Rewrite two different versions of the letter, giving specifics for the second paragraph. In one letter make the specifics positive and in the second letter make them negative.

Dear Mr. Walker:

It is a pleasure for me to recommend David Merton as a commercial artist. He worked under my supervision for six months, and I found him competent in his job. He was well-liked by his fellow workers.

David left our employ because the hours of work did not fit in with his personal schedule.

        Sincerely yours,

---

9. The Noble Hardware Company, 379 Broadview Road, Seattle, Washington, has written to you for credit information on Mr. Harlan Johnson, 29 Warren Street, Smithville, Washington. Mr. Johnson has been very slow in his payments; at present he owes the firm $487.29. Altogether, you regard him as a very poor credit risk. Write an appropriate answer to the inquiry of The Noble Hardware Company.

10. Write a positive letter on Mr. Johnson as a good credit risk. Instead of the above information, use the following: he paid his bills promptly for five years. His account carries a top limit of $2000.

9 Favorable Communications

Good-News Messages
Goodwill Messages

Happy messages are, of course, usually the easiest to write. There is no ugly problem to solve, no trouble to upset the reader, no difficult strategy to plan. The reader is favorably disposed toward you, and you need only to extend that state of good feeling. Yet the two kinds of happy messages—good news and goodwill—are not to be taken lightly. If you are indifferent, you may miss a great chance to undergird easy goodwill. If you blunder, you may turn a happy reader against you. So we need to look at the strategy of happy communication.

GOOD-NEWS MESSAGES

A good-news message is one in which you say "Yes" to something the reader is hoping you will say "Yes" to. Granting credit, approving an adjustment on a claim or a complaint, refunding an overpayment, providing positive information on an inquiry, granting a favor, accepting an invitation, announcing a promotion or a raise, or hiring a job applicant—these are some situations that call for good-news messages.

Good-news messages are not hard to write because you are telling your reader something that is pleasing and makes him or her feel good about you and your company. That is the special purpose, or the extra purpose, of the good-news message. You want to clearly get the news across, but you also have a wonderful chance to build goodwill. A businessperson who is insensitive to the impact of good news on the reader may miss the opportunity to build future sales.

Consider the following poorly written letter, which is actually a good-news letter but is treated as a straight, factual missive.

180

Dear Sir:

Enclosed is our check for $82.40, which is the amount over your deductible for which Ebner Body Shop, the garage you chose, agreed to repair your automobile. Enclosed also is a copy of the estimate on the basis of which they agreed to repair the car.

Yours truly,

Harrison Docker

Harrison Docker
Claims Manager

The news is clear. The reader gets $82.40 that he probably did not expect. That sounds like good news. But something is missing. Compare this method with the following letter written in response to the same situation.

Dear Mr. Clark:

I am pleased to send you our check for $82.40. It represents the repair cost of your car in excess of the deductible amount of your policy. The enclosed estimate was made, as you requested, by Ebner Body Shop in Parma Heights.

Ebner's will, we are sure, put your car back into first class condition. You'll soon be back on the road again.

Cordially yours,

Edward Griffin

Edward Griffin
Claims Manager

Both letters convey the same news, but Griffin's does it much better. After reading Docker's letter, you feel that the company begrudges the settlement. Docker is not cordial, and his tone is dull. Griffin, on the other hand, takes advantage of a good-news situation. He presents the check and sounds glad that he can really help ease the burden of repair for the client. Clark will be glad he is a client of Griffin's insurance company. He will remain so and will tell others about it. The Griffin letter illustrates a basic structural organization to follow in good-news letters.

ORGANIZATIONAL PLAN

1. *Statement of the good news.*   The beginning is easy. We don't need to hedge or offer a cushion. State the pleasant idea directly.
2. *Explanation, with details.*   Give facts, reasons, terms, or whatever explanation pertains directly to the best news or main idea.
3. *Positive, cordial close.*   The best closing is one that is related to the good news being conveyed.

The guidelines for writing the good-news letter can be few and brief. They are inherent in the basic structure of the letter.

GUIDELINES

1. *Be direct.*   The reader wants to hear the news immediately.
2. *Be brief.*   Since factual content is fairly unimportant and persuasive techniques are not needed, you can keep your message short. You don't need many words to create good feeling when good news is leading the way.
3. *Be cordial.*   Standard in all letters, of course, is to be positive and pleasant— not dull or grim. This guideline is stated here because goodwill is the special function of the good-news letter.
4. *Use reader interest.*   Remember that your purpose is to build customer relations.

Typical Letters

The following letters are typical of effective good-news communications.

Approving Credit

Here are three ways to send notice of credit granted. The first is a form letter. It sends news but does not work to generate goodwill.

Dear Mr. _____:

We are pleased to grant credit terms to you. You
may purchase up to _____ worth of merchandise
on credit. Our terms are 2/10, n/30. We
welcome you as a credit customer to our organization.

A second letter is individualized and attempts to evoke goodwill, but the impact of the good news is lost because the good news does not come first, and the tone of the letter is suspicious and trite.

*Delays answer to the
reader's big question,
"Can I pay later?"*

*"Investigated" may make
the applicant feel he
was under suspicion.*

*The stereotyped expression
weakens the sincerity of
the message.*

*Another worn-out
expression that weakens
sincerity.*

Dear Mr. Holverson:

Thank you for your order for four
dozen socket wrench sets. They are
being shipped today.

We are happy to inform you that your
credit rating was investigated and
found to be satisfactory.

Our credit terms are the usual 2/10,
n/30. Welcome to our growing list
of satisfied customers.

We trust that this will be the
beginning of a long and profitable
business relationship.

Sincerely,

Raymond Cathers

Raymond Cathers
Credit Manager

A skillful credit person gives the following kind of arrangement and positive tone to his or her good news.

Good news first: He gets
the merchandise. He gets
the credit. The writer
has some consideration
for the problems of the dealer.

Recognizes the dealer for
having earned credit rating.
Reminds him
there is a reason
for his credit grant.
Introduces the credit
terms.

Promotes resale.

Confidently looks forward
to future orders.

Dear Mr. Holverson:

Your four dozen Handy-Man Socket Sets should reach you in time for the week-end shoppers.

Pay us later.

Because of your prompt-pay practices with your other creditors, we are sending the shipment subject to the usual credit terms--2/10, n/30. By paying this invoice within ten days, you save almost enough to equal the mark up of two wrench set sales.

By using the fold out display rack included with the shipment, you can save counter space and still be assured that the customers will see these handy socket sets.

The enclosed booklet lists several other fast-moving items that you might find interesting.

Cordially,

Richard Wellington
Credit Manager

Granting an Adjustment

Adjustment letters are good opportunities to actually build business. We can assume that the claims writer thought his or her claim was valid. To reply in effect "We're granting your request, but we're not sure we ought to or want to" is a clear invitation to the customer to take his or her business elsewhere.

By making things right and explaining why they went wrong, we can gain a reputation as a business that "stands behind" its goods or services. A loyal customer may become even more loyal after a business has demonstrated its integrity. The good-news adjustment letter can actually work for us as a low-pressure sales letter. Since we are sure to be writing about our product or service, we have the opportunity to speak of it in a favorable light—to reassure the customer that he or she actually made a good choice. We can then perhaps interest the customer in some related item. You can be sure that such sales-promotional material will be read. You don't have that assurance with an advertisement or a sales circular. More importantly, by cordially granting the adjustment, you have put the reader in a very pleasant frame of mind about purchasing from your company. It doesn't make any difference whether or not you think the adjustment is justified; the adjustment must not be made grudgingly. The customer must be made to feel good about it.

For example, a woman who has ordered hundreds of dollars worth of merchandise from a mail-order house during the past few years writes that the three wash-and wear white cotton dress shirts she bought two months ago are turning a "dirty gray." She returns them for new ones. You discover that this is her first complaint and decide to replace the shirts, even though it is obvious that she did not follow the laundering instructions on the label. If you insensitively thought that her goodwill would be retained as long as she got what she asked for, you might send her a letter like the following one. It turns good news into bad news by its negative, accusing tone.

No good news, yet.

No need to remind her of the disappointment.

Best not to accuse the reader by making her the subject of the sentence.

Accusatory and unpleasant.

Should not remind her about "dirty gray."

Grudging. Suggests we should not grant the request, but are making an exception.

Dear Mrs. Merton:

We received the three wash-and-wear shirts that you returned to us for replacement.

We can imagine how disappointed you must have been with them, but we can explain the problem. You have been sending your shirts to a laundry which evidently washes them by machine. (We noticed the marks in the collar.) The washing instructions clearly visible on the label say "Hand Wash." Did you call this to their attention at the laundry?

Some bleaches used in washing machines will keep other cotton fabrics white, but they turn wash-and-wear cottons a "dirty gray."

Because of your past record with us, however, we are sending you three new wash-and-wear shirts free. Just follow the directions on the label, and the shirts will give excellent service.

Sincerely,

Herman Martin

Herman Martin
Customer Service Manager

The main faults of Martin's letter are that it accuses the customer and grants the adjustment grudgingly, only after other details have been presented. The following letter corrects these weaknesses.

Good news first.
   Promotional material.

Resale: Assures her she
   has made a wise choice.

Explains, but hides the
   negative. Does not accuse.
   She will probably realize
   her mistake. Presents
   a plan to prevent future
   trouble. Calls attention
   to the label without
   accusing.

Confidence that she will
   order more merchandise.

Dear Mrs. Merton:

Three new long-wear stay-white Perma shirts are on their way to you. There is no charge.

Compared with the standard shirt, Perma wash-and-wears stay whiter, last longer, and remain wrinkle free.

But for maximum service they must be washed by hand without strong detergents and bleaches. When you take them to the laundry, ask them to follow the instructions on the collar label.

You should receive our annual Spring Sale catalogue within a few days.

Cordially,

Ralph Colton

Ralph Colton
Customer Service Manager

Granting a Favor

One of the chief reasons why a business person or professional grants a special favor, such as giving a talk, is to promote goodwill for his or her company. In accepting an invitation, he or she should accept enthusiastically and should follow the three-part structure of the standard good-news communication: (1) good news first, (2) explanation or details, and (3) positive, friendly close.

An unplanned, dull acceptance letter like the following suggests that the talk will be just as disorganized, thoughtless, and dull.

No good news first.
Leaves acceptance hanging.

Talks about himself in
trite language.

More about himself.

Accepts at last.
The ninth "I" in the
letter. Probably a
speaker who is
self-centered, stuffy,
and windy.

Dear Mr. Jenson:

1 appreciated your letter of January 15 in which you invited me to speak to your students on Career Day. To answer, I wish to state that I have been in the home and auto supply business for 25 years, having spent a good deal of time on the sales floor as well as doing market analysis.

I have a special talk I could give on "The Customer Is Not Always Right, but He Is the Customer." I could supplement it with a ten-minute film.

I consider it a pleasure to accept your invitation. I shall look forward to seeing you at ten o'clock on Wednesday.

Cordially,

John Winderman

John Winderman

The writer of the preceding letter could just as easily have used enough snap, cordiality, and substance to indicate that careers in his business have such qualities. Here is a revised acceptance letter.

Good news immediately.
The reader is pleased—
now he won't have to find
another speaker.

Uses the you attitude.

Necessary details.

Makes course of action
for the important
event clear.

Dear Mr. Jensen:

Yes! I accept your invitation to talk with your students about a career in merchandising.

Your students are probably mainly interested in managerial careers, but I can also talk about market analysis, if any should indicate interest. To aid the discussion, I would like to show a ten-minute film. I shall bring the projector and screen. Perhaps you could arrange for an appropriate room.

So I will plan to see you in Dayton Hall at ten o'clock next Wednesday morning.

Sincerely,

George Meadows

George Meadows

Announcing a Raise

Occasionally a blanket good-news message goes out to a group of people. Though general, it still should be personalized. Though brief, it follows the three-part format.

Good news at once.

Definite, necessary details.

You attitude.
Sincere praise.

```
To:  All members of the Design Department

From:  H.L. Stillwell

Subject:  Salary increases


I am happy to inform all members of the
Design Department that you will receive
a 6% increase in salary beginning
November 1.  Raises will be first
reflected in your November 15 pay checks.

Since we launched our new design program
last March, it is primarily your excellent
work that has made it such a success.  You
certainly deserve the increase.

                    H.L. Stillwell
                    Manager
```

EXERCISES

1. The writer of the good-news letter opposite could simply have written, "We are sorry your lamp arrived damaged. We are sending you a free replacement." Analyze what makes the actual letter an effective good-news message.
2. Frie's Office Supply Company, 202 Elm Street, Cleveland, Ohio, recently sold a desk-sized calculator to Mr. Winfred Marks, a public accountant, at 4506 Pierce Drive, Medina, Ohio. After using the machine for about ten days, Mr. Marks observed that the calculator no longer produced a digital readout. He was certain

Dear Mrs. Harmon:

A new Crestline lamp should reach you in a few days to replace the one you received in damaged condition. We sent it today by prepaid express.

As the freight company gave us a receipt acknowledging that they received the original lamp perfectly crated, the porcelain base must have been cracked in transit. We are sorry this happened, for we know how much you want this beautiful gift for your cousin's wedding anniversary. Although our responsibility ended when the freight company accepted the package, we are glad to make this replacement for you.

Will you please give the damaged lamp to the delivery man when he delivers the second lamp? We will enter a claim with the freight company, so that you will not be inconvenienced further.

Thank you for writing promptly. Our main concern is that you receive the lamp in time for the anniversary and in perfect condition.

                               Sincerely,

                               Frank Lee
                               Custom Service Manager

he was operating the machine according to instructions. Write a letter from Mr. Marks's perspective, asking that a representative call and either replace or adjust the machine.

   Then send a good-news letter to Mr. Marks, saying that certainly Frie's will send a representative to replace or adjust the faulty calculator. The representative will call at 10:00 A.M. on the following Wednesday. Write the letter to Mr. Marks for Frie's Office Supply Company.

3. In your position as personnel manager for American Glass, Inc., in Philadelphia, Pennsylvania, you write a lot of letters, some of them good-news letters. Here is one such case: You have received an application from James Jay, a senior at Cornell University, Ithaca, N. Y. His well-written letter and resumé divulge the following information about him.

He is twenty-three years old, single, and has served in the military for two years.

He is graduating as a humanities major and a business-administration minor, in the top 5 percent of his class.

He seeks a position as a management trainee with American Glass.

You are impressed with his application and wish to have him fly to Philadelphia for an interview at the company's expense. Write a letter to Jay acknowledging his application and expressing your interest in seeing him during the first half of April. In the letter, ask him to call you collect to inform you exactly when he will be able to come for the interview.

4. From a department store or some other large retail outlet that provides customers with charge-account cards, obtain a copy of the letter sent to customers informing them that their request for credit privileges is being granted. In a memorandum to your instructor analyze the letter's effectiveness as a good-news business message.

5. Assume that you are credit manager for Caswell Electronics. On May 16 your firm received an order for four Model TX10 Caswell Amplifiers from Supreme Sound, Inc., of Atlanta, Georgia. The amplifiers are priced at $148.50 apiece; Supreme Sound has requested credit terms of 60 days. You acknowledged the order by letter and requested that Supreme Sound supply you with three credit references. You pursued the references they supplied and learned that their credit rating was good. Now you can grant credit terms. Write to Supreme Sound telling them their order is being filled as requested. Make it a really effective good-news letter. This is the first order that Caswell Electronics has received from Supreme Sound, but you certainly don't want it to be the last.

6. Read the situation in Exercise 3 above. Assume that Jay came in for the interview and was met with approval by all who spoke to him. You now want to write a letter to Jay making him a formal offer of the position he seeks.

As agreed in the interview, the starting salary will be $860 per month. Also as discussed at the interview, Jay will serve the first four weeks of his job at the American Glass regional manufacturing plant in Union City, Georgia, after which time he will move back to the Philadelphia home office. The job will begin on Monday, June 15. Jay will take his preemployment physical in Philadelphia on Friday, June 12, and fly down to Union City on June 13.

You want to sound confident, but not presumptuous, that Jay will accept the offer. You do not want Jay to feel the path to success at American Glass is going to be easy, but you do want to sound enthusiastic about having him join the company.

7. Mrs. Diane Spiller, #6 Decker Road, Humphrey, Nebraska, shopped locally for a pair of brass door handles and plates. The best she could do was to obtain the address of an Omaha firm: Snider Hardware Company, Omaha, Nebraska. She drew a sketch of the type of hardware she wanted, giving dimensions, and wrote a letter asking whether such handles and plates could be obtained from them.

Snider's had a variety of door hardware, some similar to the type Mrs. Spiller wanted. For Snider's, write a letter to Mrs. Spiller. Explain that any of the four handles and plates pictured in an enclosed brochure would be suitable for her needs. Each one is priced at $47; freight to Humphrey would be $6.70. The brass door hardware comes in either high polish or antique finishes.

8. You are this year's chairman of AIMS (American Industrial Management Society). This year's AIMS Award for the Executive of the Year will go to James B. McKinney, vice-president of AMCO Motors, Inc. (Dearing, Michigan), for his outstanding efforts in mediating a wage dispute last spring between the automotive industry and t e Association of Electrical Suppliers of America. As AIMS chairman you must write a letter to McKinney, informing him of the award and inviting him to come to New York on October 25 at AIMS's expense for the annual awards banquet.

9. You are the shipping manager for the Albatross Seas Lines, a steamship company based in New Orleans, Louisiana. One of the smaller loads carried on the last trip of your ship the S.S. *Langston* from Le Havre to Mobile was a shipment of five trunks of personal effects belonging to Mr. David Durham of Logan, Alabama. Two of Mr. Durham's five trunks were damaged en route—damage that your agent was able to confirm when Durham picked up the luggage in Mobile. Durham has written a claim to the Albatross Seas Lines for $150, the replacement value of the damaged goods.

   Now you want to write a letter to Durham accepting the claim, apologizing for the damage and the inconvenience, assuring him that such occurrences are rare on Albatross Seas ships, and informing him that your insurance company will settle his claim as filed. Tell Durham that he'll be receiving his check, probably within ten days.

10. Mr. Frank Ledford, who has purchased a clothing store in Cairo, Illinois, is anxious to establish credit with major wholesale suppliers. One letter was addressed to the Jackson Wholesale Supply in St. Louis. Jackson Wholesale was completely satisfied with Mr. Ledford's application for credit. His current ratio was very favorable, and his references spoke highly of him. Write a letter informing Mr. Ledford of his credit privileges. Include some sales-promotional material.

GOODWILL MESSAGES

Goodwill messages have one thing that makes them different from other business messages. They are not necessary. The other messages that we have studied are necessary in the routine transaction of business. Requests, replies, announcements—whether good news, bad news, or neutral—must be sent. In contrast, goodwill messages are not absolutely essential for the operation of business. Their main purpose is to convey a friendly, usually unexpected message to build goodwill. The aim is, of course, that the goodwill, in turn, will build business.

No matter how large or how small an organization is, one of its main tasks is to promote and maintain goodwill. So sensitive, thoughtful executives often write messages just to foster cordial relations with customers, distributors, employees, and others.

They will find an occasion or make use of a special occasion to hang a goodwill message on. Some typical occasions are these:

1. Congratulations—for a promotion, a success
2. Seasonal greetings
3. Appreciation—for help, a gift
4. Sympathy—for illness or difficulty
5. Deserved praise—for a job well done
6. Welcome—to a new customer, a new worker

Goodwill messages follow the general format of the good-news message listed below.

ORGANIZATIONAL PLAN

1. *Statement of the goodwill occasion.* Point of praise, important item, or whatever
2. *Comment and details*, if any
3. *Cordial ending*, if needed

Goodwill messages, unlike most other messages, should not be heavily promotional. Most people dislike messages that pose as goodwill messages but are actually sales letters. Also, though goodwill letters, like all letters, must have a positive tone, beware of overdoing it. Because the letter is free and friendly with no strings attached, you might be tempted to be gushy or wordy. The guidelines for the general good-news letter should be followed, with these additions for the specific goodwill letter:

GUIDELINES

1. *Avoid sales promotion,* unless merchandise or service was the specific occasion, and then the sales pitch must not be obtrusive.
2. *Be sincere, direct, and brief*—not gushy.
3. *Add a personal touch,* if in order—a handwritten notation, the letter sent to the home address, use of special paper, and so on.

Typical Letters

A sincere, enthusiastic message of goodwill can have an unforgettable impact on the receiver. Some examples of goodwill messages follows.

Congratulations for Achievement

The following letter, though mentioning no sales, actually brought the writer's company (floor coverings) thousands of dollars of business through subcontracts.

Begins with the happy
  occasion.
You attitude.
Personalized, but not
  gushy.

Comment

Direct, sincere
  praise.

Cordial close.

> Dear Mr. Bender:
>
> Your promotion to vice president of Midwest Development Company was great news. I was happy to read about it in the Dispatch. They even printed a fairly good picture of you.
>
> You certainly deserved the recognition your company has given you. Your enterprise and hard work at developing new ways to promote the services of Midwest have won the admiration of many--including your competitors.
>
> Congratulations! And best wishes for your success.
>
> Sincerely,
>
> *George Marlon*
> George Marlon

Check the Reader-Interest Index for the you attitude. It is +7. There are eight "you's" to only one "I".

Thanks to Customer for a Special Favor

Here is a note that is tailored to the favor. It is a personal thank you. Though not a sales talk, services are mentioned, since they were part of the occasion.

The good-news occasion.

Mrs. Ash and "you" get
  top billing throughout.

Praise through factual
  details.

Appeal to esteem—but
  presented as objective
  reporting without
  gushiness.

Positive, friendly
  close, with reader benefit.

> Dear Mrs. Cole:
>
> When Mrs. Ash visited us Monday upon your recommendation, I was very much pleased. It was good that she came in and good to know that you like our store well enough to recommend it to your friends.
>
> You might be interested in knowing that so far seven members of the Craft Club have become our regular customers. All of them mentioned that you had recommended us and that they respected your judgment.
>
> Thank you, Mrs. Cole, for your confidence in The Adept Shop and its services. We will always do our best to give you the services you expect.
>
> Sincerely,
>
> *Inga Brown*
> Inga Brown
> Manager

Praise for a Job Well Done

Messages of goodwill within an organization are important. A wise business person knows that words of deserved praise can spur employees on to better efforts and help keep the whole work force functioning smoothly.

Good news

Dear Joe:

You must have felt a genuine sense of satisfaction when you were able to walk forward and receive the 100 Percenter Award this year.

It must have been especially rewarding since you came so close last year.

Details

Your achievement of 108% of quota, with a tough new territory, is certainly an achievement that you can be proud of.

Positive, friendly close

I am looking forward to an even more successful year from you this year. It is good to be working with you.

Sincerely,

Carlton Beyers

Carlton Beyers
Regional Manager

The three letters in Figures 9-1, 9-2, and 9-3 were written to an employee of Continental Motels at different stages of her career. Two are from the Director at the home office; one is from the Director of Personnel at a new unit that Miss Schumann helped open. Three different levels of tone are shown in the three communications— formal letter, informal letter, and memo. But all have one feature in common: they explicitly and cordially express well-deserved praise for a job well done. Such messages are one reason why the company is able to keep such excellent people as employees.

```
Philadelphia Continental / Hill Ave. off Schuylkill Expwy
                Phila., Pa.,  19131
```

CONTINENTAL
Motor Hotels

February 8, 1977

Miss Sheila Schumann
Continental Motor Hotels
7060 Lake Drive
Washington, D.C. 20016

Dear Sheila:

I appreciate the fine work you did here at the Philadelphia Continental
during the Expanded Facilities Opening.

Not only were you directly involved in assisting the Personnel
Department to screen over 1000 persons who applied for positions
during a very short period of time, but you also made a significant
contribution to the Restaurant Manager of the King's Wharf Complex.
Your long productive hours of hard work did contribute immeasurably
to our successful opening.

                        Sincerely,

                        Robert W. Cotton
                        Director of Personnel
                        Philadelphia Continental

RWC:sc

Figure 9-1

C *Enjoy life, Enjoy*

Executive Offices / 3060 Lake Drive Washington, D.C. 20016

CONTINENTAL
Motor Hotels

May 17, 1978

Dear Sheila,

Miami is open and we couldn't have done
it without you.

Just a note to tell you how much we
appreciate the hard work and long hours
you put in. You did a great job and we
want you to know we are sincerely grateful.
You may take pride in the fact that you
have once again proved that Continental
has the expertise to do an outstanding job.

Thank you for a job well done.

Sincerely,

Allan West

Allan West
Director
Regional Services

Figure 9-2

C

Enjoy life, Enjoy

CONTINENTAL
Motor Hotels

June 8, 1978

Dear Sheila,

We want to give you an extra special word of thanks for
your great help in managing our employees at Hogate's.
We are ever grateful for the time and effort you have
given us during the opening.

Sheila . . . it's always a pleasure to work with you,
and reassuring to know that we can call on you whenever
we need you.

Thanks to people like you on our task force, we managed
a smooth and successful opening.

Please accept our sincere appreciation.

Sincerely,

Allan West
Director
Regional Services

Figure 9-3

General Appreciation for Patronage

Many businesses write to established customers every year or two to express appreciation for patronage or for prompt settlement of accounts. Though the following letter is not an individually written letter but a personalized prototype, it can do a lot to generate goodwill toward the company.

Dear Mr. Langston:

Thank you for the many opportunities you have given us to serve you over the years and for the fine manner in which you have settled your accounts year after year.

Customers such as you, who purchase without commotion and pay without notice, may seem to go unobserved and unappreciated. But we want you to know that we do notice you and appreciate you.

We are pleased to have you as a McClurkan & Company customer. We are proud to serve you.

Sincerely yours,

Isabel Ralston

Isabel Ralston
Vice President

Welcome to a Newcomer

This letter of welcome from a furniture store to a newcomer in town is an effective use of the goodwill letter to build toward later business. Most people settling in a new home do need some new pieces of furniture to complete their new decor. Home Furniture Company calls attention to itself through a welcome letter. The promotion appeal is entirely subordinate to the goodwill message and is hinted only. The free city map, which the Burton family will find useful, and the unobtrusive "we've been supplying furniture" combine to make the newcomers think pleasantly of Home Furniture Company when they have furniture needs.

Dear Mrs. Burton:

Welcome to Bridgeport. We hope that by now you've found most of the things the movers left and are able to walk through the house without too much bumping.

Bridgeport isn't large, but there is a lot to it. We've enclosed a map of the city for your use whenever you're ready to start looking around town. Notice the list of restaurants, shops, professional services, and cultural centers. Most of these are within ten minutes' drive of your home.

For any information about the city, please feel free to call on us. We've been supplying furniture and carpeting to the people of Bridgeport for over 50 years, and we know the city fairly well.

Our best wishes go with you and your family during these trying first days of organizing your home. But it'll be worth it. Bridgeport's a good town to live in.

Sincerely yours,

William Turner

William Turner
Manager

These good-news and goodwill messages are important in their effects. Though there is no tangible result, such as a sale or the payment of a bill, the sales value of goodwill and good-news messages may emerge months, even years, later when a recipient is ready to buy and remembers your company with pleasure.

The well-written good-news and goodwill message is the bread cast upon the waters that shall return after many days.

EXERCISES

1. Analyze what's wrong with the following letter intended to generate goodwill. In preparing your analysis, think about Chapter 7 on tone. Rewrite the letter making it effective as a goodwill letter.

> Dear Mr. Harmel:
>
> This is to acknowledge your spotless record in paying your bills over the past three years. All of our customers should be so prompt.
>
> Thank you.
>
> *Carl Rowell*
>
> Carl G. Rowell

2. Analyze this letter to an executive secretary as an effective goodwill letter.

> Dear Miss Turner:
>
> Just a brief note of thanks for your help last week in getting me in to see Mr. Robinson. It was important that I speak to him, and climbing through twelfth-floor windows is not my strong point. Once in conference, I believe he and I had a productive meeting.
>
> If I can ever return the favor, I'd be more than happy to. Thanks again.
>
> Sincerely,
>
> *Kelly Brighton*
>
> Kelly Brighton

3. Yesterday you were elected to the Board of Aldermen, getting fifty-one percent of the total vote cast in your district. Your success would not have been possible without the thirty-six campaign workers who gave tirelessly of their time, ringing doorbells, making telephone calls, and handling correspondence in your behalf.

    Write an effective letter of thanks that can be individually addressed to each of your campaign workers. In addition to being genuinely grateful to them, remember—you'll be up for reelection in a short two years and needing campaign help once again.

4. Wilbur's Novelty Store, at 14 Foster Street in Alexandria, Virginia, is one of the retail stores hat your company—Tidal Basin Wholesalers, in Washington, D.C.—regularly supplies. Unfortunately Wilbur's had a fire last week. The store was not totally burned out, but Wilbur Still's office at the back of the store was severely charred.

    Write a goodwill letter to Mr. Still conveying your sympathy over the fire, your confidence that he can overcome the temporary hardship, and your willingness to replace any Tidal Basin samples, brochures, or price lists that may have been destroyed. You would also be quite willing to duplicate for Still any records of transactions he has had with you.

5. Assume that you own and manage a clothing store in your town. Compose a prototype letter welcoming newcomers to your town.

6. Procure a seasonal greetings letter from a local department store, and evaluate its effectiveness. Look especially for the following items:

    a. Is it personalized enough?
    b. Is it trite or gushy?
    c. Does it have an obtrusive sales pitch?

7. Arthur Carpenter, a research assistant in your division, responded very promptly to your request and compiled data on last year's sales in the St. Louis market, submitting then to you in a memorandum that you received this morning. You, as Regional Manager, need to incorporate these figures into the semiannual report for submission to D.D. Lincoln, your company's executive vice-president. Thanks to Carpenter's quick work, you will be able to complete the report before the day is out. First, though, you ought to write a brief memo of thanks to Carpenter. Write this memo.

10 Unfavorable Communications

Demands
Conciliation
Bad News

So far we have been dealing with letters that are fairly easy to write—routine requests, routine replies, and various favorable communications. They are fairly easy because they usually deal with ordinary business matters that both reader and writer are pleasantly interested in. Only clarity and normal positive tone are required.

Now we turn to those communications that must make *demands,* or *conciliate,* or present other *bad news.* Such letters are more difficult because they arise out of some form of disturbance, and the reader must be given a cushion to ease his or her discomfort.

Familiar kinds of letters needing a cushion are claims, collection letters, complaints, reprimands, replies to complaints, refusal of credit, acknowledgment of orders you can't fill, or bad news about prices or services.

These kinds of letters involve somebody who is angry, annoyed, or jolted—or is likely to be angered, annoyed, or jolted. You must handle the disturbance. You must convey your message without losing the goodwill or good feeling of the reader.

DEMANDS

You write letters of demand when you believe somebody owes you something. You must plan your letter with care because the reader may disagree with and resist your demands. Complications follow. You insist, he resists further, and a successful outcome is threatened. So you have a double aim—you must have your demand met, and you must do it without losing goodwill. Strategy is necessary in writing the various kinds of demand messages.

Some standard demand letters are *claims* for faulty goods or services, *reprimands* or constructive criticism, and *collection letters*. You may use the following structural organization for a claims letter or a reprimand. The collection letter requires a more elaborate process that will be described later in the chapter.

ORGANIZATIONAL PLAN

1. *State the major demand*—without anger and as positively as possible.
2. *Explain your case.* Give pertinent details of the situation, and tell why you wrote and why the reader should respond as you requested.
3. *Request the action to be taken*—clearly, specifically, and completely. (If you have explained your case well, of course your demand will be reasonable.)
4. *Close positively*—indicating confidence that the demand will be met.

Typical Letters

Both claims and reprimands may follow the same four-part organization. Guidelines for each, however, are somewhat different and are listed separately within each section.

Claims

You write a claims letter when you are dissatisfied with a product, a service, or a policy. Typical situations concerning merchandise may involve defective materials or workmanship, malfunctioning parts, soiled or shopworn items, or misrepresentation of products. Claims about services might include delivery mix-ups, broken promises, discourtesy, carelessness, and clerical errors. When you state your complaint, you usually make a claim or request some kind of adjustment, correction, or improvement. You will usually request one or more of the following:

1. A new shipment with the correct item ordered
2. Cancellation of an order or part of an order
3. Free replacement of the defective part(s), the whole item, or the whole shipment
4. Free repairs
5. Refund for all or part of the purchase price
6. Credit to your account (or a credit slip)
7. Reduction in the price (because of a product or service defect)
8. Free inspection, leading to redecorating or complete overhaul
9. Explanation or change in policy or procedure

To get the best possible adjustment, observe these guidelines:

GUIDELINES

1. *Write promptly.*   Be fair to the seller.
2. *State all pertinent facts.*   Give dates, amounts, model numbers, sizes, colors, or any other specific information that will make a follow-up easy for the reader. Avoid exaggeration, irrelevant material, guesses, and opinions as to causes and culprits.
3. *Avoid anger and blaming.*   Remember that the reader is not the person who made the mistake. He or she is the one you are expecting to make a satisfactory adjustment. Antagonism will diminish your chances.
4. *Use the best strategies of tone and the you attitude.*   If you write a discourteous, antagonistic letter, the company may in turn be angered and give you the barest adjustment possible or decide they would rather do without your business. For the you attitude, you might state something you like about the company's products or services.
5. *Motivate action by appealing to the reader's best nature.*   Appeal to the reader's sense of fair play, honesty, or pride. Don't threaten him with loss of business.
6. *Make the demand itself*—clearly, specifically, and completely. State what specific adjustment is considered fair, only if you really know. If you don't know, let the adjuster suggest a satisfactory settlement. Surveys show that when the customer has a reasonable claim and has left its settlement completely up to the company, the adjuster will usually grant more than the customer would ask.

Consider the poor chances of success from this letter written by a thoughtless or mistaken person who has violated several guidelines for claims letters.

Dear Sirs:

Where in the world did you get that bumble-handed clown running your shipping department? We place a simple order, delivery gets here almost too late, and when it finally does get here, most of the pieces are broken. And on top of that, in the same day's mail, we get your bill. What a deal!

We can get along without such rotten service. It's too late for our sale for us to place an order with a decent company, so get the lead out and send us a replacement order right away.

Yours truly,

-Carlton Bristol

Imagine yourself the receiver of the letter from Bristol. Your company is probably successful, you usually take the greatest care in preparing orders for shipment, and you wouldn't be seriously hurt by losing such a customer. How would you respond? Now compare another letter written in the same situation.

The major claim.

Details.
Reasons.

Action
  requested.

Positive close.

Expresses
  confidence.

Gentlemen:

On February 8, we placed an order for 48 dozen Swedish tumblers. Yesterday the order arrived, much to our dismay, with only 210 pieces in salable condition. All the others were chipped or broken. We are asking for an adjustment on these tumblers.

The situation was especially disappointing because we had already advertised that the tumblers were to be on sale today. I personally examined a dozen tumblers, four of which we are sending you by express for your examination.

We ask that you send us immediate replacement for the 366 broken tumblers, and allow us to adjust our payment to cover only the salable items.

As soon as you get this shipment to us, we will reschedule our sale.

Sincerely,

Sybil Scott
Retail Buyer

The letter is courteous, objective, specific in details, and clear in its demands. It expresses confidence in the company's meeting the demands. Everything is designed to fit the writer's purpose—fast replacement of the damaged shipment without destroying the business relationship.

Reprimands

A reprimand to an employee, or constructive criticism, is another kind of demand often necessary in business. This is the demand for improvement in performance. Executives and supervisors are responsible for correcting deficiencies in the work of their staff.

This task requires the ability to criticize effectively without injuring morale or decreasing initiative. A delicate job—for most people don't want to be told they are deficient.

Ultimately, of course, most managers have the power to fire their subordinates for incompetence. But the businessperson who continually fires people, without improving output, is a failure.

Consider, for example, the following memorandum written by a department store manager to a staff of 20 salesclerks. He wanted to reprimand them, to demand that they spend less time in the coffee shop and the rest room and be more concerned about customers and sales.

July 18, 1978

TO: All Sales People

FROM: Vincent Scrimmer

SUBJECT: Lack of Sales

My heartfelt thanks, girls. I'm proud to announce that, as a result of your brilliant and energetic efforts this month on the sales floor, we fell only 15% below our last month's record low.

I'm sure much of this huge success can be attributed to your extended coffee breaks and your numerous trips to the rest rooms for cigarettes and gossip.

I hope it is not too much to ask to give some of that dedication and energy to the customers on the floor.

VS

Because of its sarcasm, its accusatory manner, and its failure to call forth the best in the staff, the memo only made things worse. It aroused tempers, lowered morale, and created resistance to working any harder for "that creep Scrimmer."

The following memo is an example of a constructive criticism effectively written. The memo follows the four-point organization of the demand message:

1. State the deficiency, positively.
2. Explain your case.
3. Request the action to be taken.
4. Close positively.

October 20, 1978

To Jeff Moreland _____

From C.J. Stevens _____

Subject The sales calls we made together. _____

Jeff, after going along with you last Wednesday on some of
your demonstrations, I understand why you're one of our best
salesmen. You show such enthusiasm and love for your work.
It is obvious why you are second highest on our staff in total
sales. Realizing this, you are probably more disturbed than
I am over your low standing in sales over demos.

I think the answer is in the way you handle the demonstration.
At times, you seemed a little flustered, as if you weren't
quite clear on the process. Once, for example, you referred
to the "reactor" as the "resistor." It is likely, of course,
that the client wouldn't be clear either and would not respond
favorably. You need to get a better handle on the demonstration.
I think that is one key to getting your results up over quota
where they belong.

How about practicing a little more? Use some of us for guinea
pigs, if you want to. Bill or Tom would be glad for the chance.
I'm willing to bet that with a couple of good run-throughs, your
sales will increase by at least 25%.

Stevens's memo illustrates the guidelines that should be followed in writing an effective reprimand.

GUIDELINES FOR REPRIMANDS

1. *Write promptly.* Be fair to the employee. Be fair to the company. If a deficiency exists, don't let it linger to impair business.
2. *State all pertinent facts.* Give dates, figures, incidents, or any specific information that will indicate that improvement of some sort is needed. Avoid exaggeration, irrelevant material, guesses, or unsupported opinions.
3. *Avoid anger and blaming.* Remember that what you want is improvement—not conflict, termination, demoralization, or punishment. If you want to fire the employee, do so—and any letter of reprimand is out of order. If you want to get better performance from an employee, then reprimand with the purpose of spurring him or her on to strengthen some weakness.
4. *Use the best strategies of tone and the you attitude.* If you write a discourteous, caustic letter, the employee may be angered or demoralized, and you may not get the improvement you desire. To employ the you attitude, genuinely honor the person. Look for some good qualities. You might state something you like about the way he or she is doing things.
5. *Make the reprimand clearly, specifically, and completely.* State explicitly what the employee has done or is doing wrong.
6. *Help the employee.* Suggest some tangible ways the employee can work to improve.
7. *Motivate action by appealing to the reader's best nature.* Appeal to the employee's sense of fair play, ambition, or pride.
8. *Indicate confidence in your reader.* You certainly do have confidence in the employee, or you would fire him or her. Why not state your confidence?

Collection Letters

Collection letters are a special kind of business demand. The nature of the collection problem often requires the creditor to send more than one communication.

Every organization goes about the task of collecting overdue bills in its own fashion. For example, firms that do considerable selling on credit, such as large department stores, furniture stores, appliance stores, and jewelry stores, may develop several different collection series that they use over and over, constantly testing different combinations. Most businesses, however, develop a series along the following lines, perhaps with more than one letter or memo in each stage:

COLLECTION SERIES

1. Statement—sent at end of billing period
2. Second statement—twenty to thirty days later

3. Reminder—one or two, about fifteen days apart, often form letters, obviously duplicated to appear routine and impersonal
4. Inquiry—becoming more urgent, expressing concern
5. Appeal
6. Strong appeal or urgency
7. Ultimatum

Three basic types of appeals are used to persuade people to pay:

FAIR PLAY.   This appeal is to one's sense of duty, honesty, and justice. It is as if you say, "We treated you right by providing you goods or services; now you do right by us."

PRIDE.   This includes reputation, prestige, accomplishment, and ownership. It is as if you say "A credit reputation is a valuable asset; don't risk losing it."

FEAR.   This includes loss and threats—loss of financial status, security, and possessions, and threats of legal entanglements. The appeal to fear is the strongest of all, and is used only when all other appeals fail. It is as if you say "We are considering placing your account in the hands of an attorney. Don't force us into such an action."

A series of communications, one demand after another making use of the various appeals, creates a sense of insistence that usually brings about payment. In a collection series each letter or memo is a fully articulated request that payment be made. The assumption underlying each collection element is that the recipient will respond with payment, and that no further demand will be necessary. From experience, however, the writer knows that often the next element will have to be sent out, and perhaps the next, and so on. Each successive element is somewhat stronger in its demand that payment be made, until finally, if payment is not made, the account is turned over to an attorney or a collection agency, and the company's collection effort is terminated.

Every collection element, whether it is a "one shot" letter or whether it comes early or late in a series, has a double aim (as most demands do). It tries to collect, *and* it tries to retain goodwill. Why should the businesses worry about the goodwill of delinquent customers? For the same reason they will send delinquent customers a whole series of collection letters. Even though the customers are delinquent at present, they are prospects for future business once the present bill is paid. Unless you would rather *not* sell any more to a customer who presently is slow to pay, any collection message you send should have a goodwill objective. The further along in a collection series, the more difficult it becomes to retain goodwill because the demand must be more strongly stated. The skillful writer, however, can retain goodwill right up to the end of a collection series.

The following letter is an example of a poor collection letter. It is hasty, vague, uncooperative, and peevish. It gives the debtor a chance neither to pay the bill nor to retain goodwill.

Dear Mr. Johnson:

Your bill with us is now more than a month
past due. How do you expect us to pay our
bills if you don't pay us what you owe us?
You could at least have the common courtesy
to give an explanation of why you have been
so negligent.

If I don't receive your check within the next
few days, I'll have to turn your account over
to the Peerless Collection Agency, and you
know what that means.

Your truly,

George Simmons

George Simmons
Credit Manager

Mr. Johnson had not even been sent a reminder. Perhaps all he needed was a reminder, or a little help, as suggested in the following letter.

Specific amount

Helpful tone

Fair-play appeal

Specific demand

Cooperative option

Dear Mr. Johnson:

Your account with us has a one-month past-due
balance of $298. Can we help you clear your
account? Because we did not receive a response
from our statement, we believe there must be
a good reason why you have not paid.

Please send us either a check within the next
week, or if some problem has arisen, give us
an explanation. I am confident we can work
something out.

Sincerely,

Betty Thatcher

Betty Thatcher
Credit Manager

An entire series of collection letters which are effective at each stage is shown in Figure 10-1 (a-h).

Step 1: Statement

Assumption: Recipient needs only the statement.

Tone: impersonal

CITY FURNISHINGS, INC.
219 E. Columbus Avenue, Dayton, Ohio 45409
Tel. 354-7690

June 6, 1978

Account: Dr. William Hill
4000 Jacksboro Rd.
C248   Dayton, Ohio 45409

	Charges	Credits	Balance
5-1-78	$628.00		$628.00

Figure 10-1a   Collection series

Step 2: Second Statement

Assumption: Customer needs only a reminder.

Tone: impersonal

Appeal: special stamp

Figure 10-1b

```
                    CITY FURNISHINGS, INC.
          219 E. Columbus Avenue, Dayton, Ohio  45409
                       Tel. 354-7690

                                          July 3, 1978

        Account:   Dr. William Hill
                   4000 Jacksboro Rd.
        C248       Dayton, Ohio  45409
```

	Charges	Credits	Balance
5-1-78	$628.00		$628.00

Please Remit
Account Is Overdue

Step 3: Reminder, brief form note

Appeal: cordiality and cooperation

Assumption: Customer overlooked the bill and needs a more direct reminder.

Tone: friendly, impersonal

Figure 10-1c

```
                                 July 25, 1978


        Dear Dr. Hill:

        This is just a friendly reminder that
        payment on your invoice #C 248 for
        $628 is still due.

        If you have already sent your check,
        please disregard this notice.  It has
        been a pleasure to serve you.

                          Yours truly,


                          City Furnishings, Inc.
```

*Step 4: Reminder with
slight personal touch*

*Appeal: cordiality with a
little sense of prodding*

*Tone: slightly
personal—company is
getting involved*

Tangible urge to action

Figure 10-1d

August 15, 1978

Dear Dr. Hill:

We'd like to remind you once again that
payment on your invoice #C 248 for $628
is still due.

We would very much appreciate receiving
your check as soon as possible. The
enclosed envelope is for your convenience
in remitting.

                        Very truly yours,

                        City Furnishings, Inc.

---

*Step 5: Inquiry, a fully
personal letter*

*Appeal: fair play,
alternate action offered*

*Assumption: Customer is
having financial
problems.*

*Tone: friendly and
helpful but emphatic*

Figure 10-1e

August 29, 1978

Dr. William Hill
4000 Jacksboro Rd.
Dayton, Ohio 45409

Dear Dr. Hill:

I hope this letter finds your new practice
prospering and all the problems of opening
an office about solved. Several years ago,
when our business got underway, we were sure
our creditors outnumbered our customers by
at least three to one. We understand your
situation.

If you have found the initial expenses a
little too heavy, perhaps you would find
your account for $628 more easily settled
in periodic payments. If so, you need only
drop us a note, or call, and we'll be glad
to make a mutually convenient arrangement.

                    Cordially yours,

                    Kenneth Benson
                    Kenneth Benson
                    Credit Manager

Step 6: Appeal

Special Appeal: fair play

Assumption: Customer has not just forgotten, and more stringent measures are necessary.

Tone: less friendly, more direct

Urgency implied for first time

Figure 10-1f

September 12, 1978

Dr. William Hill
4000 Jacksboro Rd.
Dayton, Ohio 45409

Dear Dr. Hill:

We just don't know what to think--we can't understand why we haven't heard from you in response to our recent letter. As you know, your bill of May 1 is still outstanding. We have been as fair as we can be, I think, in offering a way of easing the burden of payment for you. But so far, you've ignored us.

We must ask you to send a check this week, or get in touch with us promptly.

Sincerely,

Kenneth Benson

Kenneth Benson
Credit Manager

Step 7: Strong Appeal

Special Appeal: pride

Assumption: Pressure is needed but something can still be worked out.

Tone: urgent, stringent but still cordial in hopes of making the collection and retaining goodwill

Figure 10-1g

September 22, 1978

Dr. William Hill
4000 Jacksboro Rd.
Dayton, Ohio 45409

Dear Dr. Hill:

When we provided the furnishings for your office and waiting room on a credit basis, it was because of your good credit standing and your sound reputation. Such a reputation is something to be proud of, and we are sure you are proud of it.

As a doctor beginning a new practice in our city, surely you do not wish to do anything to jeopardize your good reputation. Yet your unpaid bill for $628 dates back to last May.

We have enjoyed serving you. All that's necessary is a payment or an explanation by return mail.

Sincerely,

Kenneth Benson

Kenneth Benson
Credit Manager

Step 8: Ultimatum

Appeal: fair play
Assumption: Hill may still pay; if not, action will be taken.

Appeal: pride, fear

Tone: definite and firm.

Respectful, still reflects hope of making the collection. Many ultimatums are more ominous.

```
                                    October 2, 1978


        Dr. William Hill
        4000 Jacksboro Rd.
        Dayton, Ohio  45409

        Dear Dr. Hill:

        So far, four reminders and three letters
        have not been able to bring forth a
        response from you concerning your unpaid
        bill.  Payment of your invoice of May 1,
        for $628, is now long overdue.  Though
        we appreciate your business, we can no
        longer afford to carry this unpaid account
        on our books.  Believe me, we do not
        like to think of taking action against
        you.  We are here to serve customers,
        not summonses; and it does us no good
        to see your credit rating destroyed.
        This is, of course, the inevitable outcome.

        So we ask that you save both you and us
        the trouble.  I shall not turn your
        account over to an attorney for another
        seven days, feeling sure that you will
        remit payment within that time.

                              Respectfully,

                              Kenneth Benson

                              Kenneth Benson
                              Credit Manager
```

Figure 10-1h

The collection series involving Dr. Hill had eight items. The tone was friendly and respectful throughout and stopped short of threatening. Series may have either fewer or more items; some have a more ominous tone. Individual cases are different. It is a matter of what will get the job done.

The series of collection messages from a loan company in Figures 10-2 through 10-7 lean a little towards the sledgehammer effect. The loan company probably believes that their customers are tougher-skinned than Dr. Hill. The series is short, with only six messages. They are prototype letters—used as models with the addition of the appropriate inside address and salutation, dates, and amounts of money. As prototype letters, they are not as impersonal as the strict form letter. Notice that they have complimentary close and signature.

The series moves with increasing stringency through the various stages—statement, reminder, appeal, and ultimatum. Only the standard inquiry stage is bypassed. Notice that, although the letters do become stringent, they remain courteous throughout the series and leave the way open to negotiations even through the ultimatum stage.

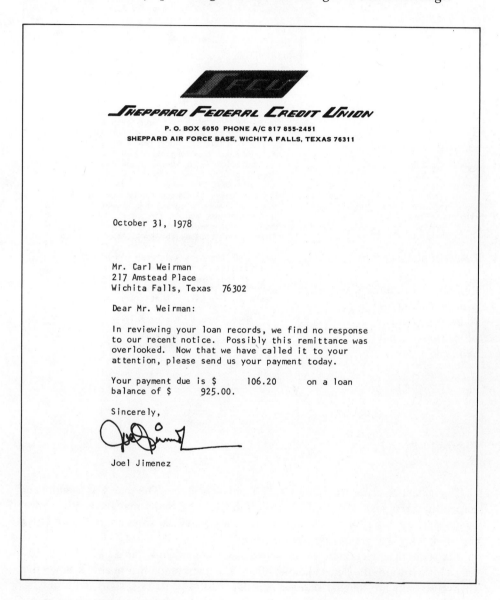

Figure 10-2a Step 1: *Statement.* **Hint at oversight. Request action.**

SHEPPARD FEDERAL CREDIT UNION

P. O. BOX 6050 PHONE A/C 817 855-2451
SHEPPARD AIR FORCE BASE, WICHITA FALLS, TEXAS 76311

November 10, 1978

Mr. Carl Weirman
217 Amstead Place
Wichita Falls, Texas 76302

Dear Mr. Weirman:

Your account presently reflects a balance of $ 926.35
of which $ 106.20   is past due. The last remittance
received was on   September 5, 1978.

Please remit the amount past due by   November 20, 1978,
and make all future payments as per contract.

For arrangements, please write or call this office at
817-855-2451.

Sincerely,

Joel Jimenez

Figure 10-2b Step 2: *Statement. Tone:* cordial. Urge to action.

SHEPPARD FEDERAL CREDIT UNION

P. O. BOX 6050 PHONE A/C 817 855-2451
SHEPPARD AIR FORCE BASE, WICHITA FALLS, TEXAS 76311

November 20, 1978

Mr. Carl Weirman
217 Amstead Place
Wichita Falls, Texas 76302

Dear Mr. Weirman:

Your account reflects 2 months past due of $ 927.35
not including accrued interest since the last transaction
of $ 9.22.

If we are to cooperate with you by accepting monthly
installments, your payments must be made to us promptly
as promised in your contract.

Just place your remittance in the enclosed envelope and
mail to us today.

Sincerely,

Joel Jimenez

Figure 10-2c Step 3: *Reminder-Appeal*: fair play. *Tone*: cordial. Urge to action.

SHEPPARD FEDERAL CREDIT UNION

P. O. BOX 6050 PHONE A/C 817 855-2451
SHEPPARD AIR FORCE BASE, WICHITA FALLS, TEXAS 76311

November 30, 1978

Mr. Carl Weirman
217 Amstead Place
Wichita Falls, Texas   76302

Dear Mr. Weirman:

Your account balance of $ 928.00   is past due $ 212.40.
No payment has been applied since   September 5, 1978.

It is imperative that you pay the amount past due or
call this office for arrangements. If you fail to do
either, sterner collection measures will be initiated.

I am enclosing a pay-off form good through   December 6, 1978,
by which date I will expect a call from you, the amount
past due, or remittance in full.

Sincerely,

Joel Jimenez

Figure 10-2d Step 4: *Strong Appeal. Appeal:* **fear.** *Tone:* **urgent. Arrangements offered.**

SHEPPARD FEDERAL CREDIT UNION

P. O. BOX 6050 PHONE A/C 817 855-2451
SHEPPARD AIR FORCE BASE, WICHITA FALLS, TEXAS 76311

December 6, 1978

Mr. Carl Weirman
217 Amstead Place
Wichita Falls, Texas   76302

Dear Mr. Weirman:

The last payment received on your account was on September 5, 1978.

We have been very lenient in allowing you to repay your loan in
such a manner, realizing that you are possibly experiencing financial
difficulties. However, we feel that you are now taking advantage of
our leniency by not paying on your account or contacting us.

If it is your choice to ignore your obligation here, then we will have
no other alternative than to turn the balance of $ 928.90
including interest over to a collection agency, which will result in
further expense to you.

If I do not receive the balance in full by December 15, 1978, or a
call from you to make arrangements for repayment, then I will assume
you do not intend to pay and will act accordingly.

Call collect at 817-855-2451 or address all correspondence to my
attention.

Sincerely,

Joel Jimenez

Our accounts protected by
Nationwide Surety Systems.
Unless paid in ten days
delinquency charge added
and forwarded for collection.

Figure 10-2e Step 5: *Strong Appeal. Appeal:* **fear, fair play.** *Tone:* **stringent.
Further fear added by notice of collection agency.**

SHEPPARD FEDERAL CREDIT UNION

P. O. BOX 6050 PHONE A/C 817 855-2451
SHEPPARD AIR FORCE BASE, WICHITA FALLS, TEXAS 76311

December 17, 1978

Mr. Carl Weirman
217 Amstead Place
Wichita Falls, Texas 76302

Dear Mr. Weirman:

Please allow this to serve as final notice of pending legal action.
Your continual disregard toward this just obligation to the Sheppard
Federal Credit Union has made such stern measures necessary.

If the entire balance of $ 931.12   including interest is not received
in this office by   December 20, 1978,   or a call advising me of
satisfactory repayment arrangements is not received by that date, then
the aforementioned action will be initiated. This will only result
in further expense to you as per contract.

Please feel free to call me collect to make arrangements, and
address all correspondence to my attention.

Your prompt attention to this important matter will be advantageous
to you.

Sincerely,

Joel Jimenez

Our accounts protected by
Nationwide Surety Systems.
Unless paid in ten days
delinquency charge added
and forwarded for collection.

Figure 10-2f Step 6: *Ultimatum. Tone:* **stringent and definite, but still leaves hope for settlement.**

The timing of collection letters is important. How much time should elapse between each message in the series? The following general guidelines should be useful.

COLLECTION SERIES TIMING

1. *Allow time for an answer.*   Frequent messages give a sense of insistence, but the time lapse must be enough to allow the earlier appeal to be complied with. The Dr. Hill series messages moved from a month apart to seven days apart.
2. *Check the credit rating.*   If at the time of purchase the debtor's credit rating was excellent, you would be wise to allow liberal timing. If, on the other hand, the customer was only a fair or moderate risk, timing would probably be shorter.
3. *Consider the nature of your business.*   A prestige department store will pursue delinquent accounts more slowly and gently than a high-interest, short-term loan agency will.
4. *Check your competition.*   Don't outdo them. If, for example, your three major competitors all wait twelve months before taking action, you would be unwise to insist upon turning your delinquent accounts over in ninety days.

EXERCISES

1. Gerald Munson, representing the Atlantic Indemnity Co., was a recent guest of Holiday House. During his two-day stay he incurred a bill of $275.70; at the time of checkout he paid his bill by check. However, the bank on which the check was drawn returned the check to you stamped "Insufficient Funds." Write Mr. Munson asking for payment. He has been your guest several times before.
2. Your Christmas catalog was printed by the Boulder Printing Company, 109 Rockcliff, Boulder, Colorado. Because of a printers' strike, publication was delayed three weeks, and therefore you had no chance to see proofs because it was essential that the catalog be in the hands of your customers by October 1. When the 15,000 copies of the catalog arrived on September 26, you found errors in the prices listed for eleven of your major items. Write to the Boulder Printing Company asking for an adjustment.
3. How could the claimant's letter at top right be improved? Rewrite it.
4. Last Friday you took an interesting tour with a group of 12 other business people through the Tyler Foundries. All of you had attended a conference, and the tour was scheduled as part of the conference. As you walked under an overhead crane, a large gob of oil dropped on your right shoulder, staining your new suit beyond the possibilities of cleaning. One of the employees suggested that you ask the Foundry to buy you a new suit. Write a courteous letter requesting the desired amount of money.

Dear Sir:

My order did not arrive on time, and as a
result I did not have the hampers for my
spring sale. It seems you ought to be more
careful to fill your orders on time. If
this happens again, I'll have to stop doing
business with you.

Sincerely yours,

Betty Marchman

Betty Marchman

5. Which of the following collection letters is more effective? Give reasons.

a.

Dear Mr. Winters:

It has long been the custom for collection people
to pretend that bills aren't paid because they have
been "overlooked" or that the customer needs to be
"reminded."

In this instance, however, I'm going to come right
our and say that I think the reason you ignored our
last letter and the previous statements is that you
didn't have the money at that time. Am I wrong in
this assumption?

If the situation were reversed and we owed you money,
I know that you would certainly expect at least a
reply from us. I am, therefore, appealing to your
sense of fair play in asking you to send us a check
for $58.40 to settle your account. Were the situation
reversed, you would expect the same consideration
from us.

We are awaiting your remittance in the envelope
enclosed for your convenience.

Very truly yours,

b.

```
Dear Sir:

Surely you knew when you ordered automotive parts from
us that you must some day pay for them.

That day is here.  We have given you every consideration
in this matter, and in return, we have not even had a
reply from you.  You seem willing to ignore the fact
that your credit reputation is at stake.  By doing so,
you jeopardize your whole future.

Won't you, therefore, relieve us of the unpleasantness
of taking necessary action by sending us your check for
$58.40 without delay?

                        Yours very truly,
```

6. William Jefferson, Manager of General Electronics, Pittsburgh, PA 15213, insisted on installing an efficient intercom system when the present new building was being constructed. The building contractor was the Byrd Construction Company, Youngstown, OH 44503. Included in the "specs" was a statement that the system was to be transistorized, requiring no warm-up time. Now that the store is operating in the new building, Mr. Jefferson observes that the intercom system requires "warm-up" time. Write a letter for Mr. Jefferson requesting that the system be changed to comply with the specifications.

7. Assume that you are advertising credit manager for *Modern Times* magazine. Six weeks ago your publication sold a quarter page of advertising space to the following company, at a cost of $348.

    Contemporary Galleries, Inc.
    2820 Brook Avenue
    Urbana, Illinois 61801

    The owner and general manager of the firm is Mrs. Helen Timmons. It is a small and relatively new business (two years old). The Central Credit Association of Urbana rates Contemporary Galleries as a "fair to good risk" because, although their assets are merely adequate for their present level of business, their growth potential is excellent.

You received copy from Contemporary Galleries and ran it, as contracted, in your edition of four weeks ago. According to that contract, payment was to be made immediately upon error-free publication of the ad. Although your proofreaders assure you that the ad was run without error, no payment has been received.

Two weeks ago you sent Contemporary Galleries a duplicate invoice stamped "payment due," but payment still did not arrive.

a. Today you want to send a reminder note to Contemporary Galleries. Write a cordial and brief note explicitly calling their attention to the overdue charge.

b. Assume that by two weeks from today you still have not received payment. Write a second reminder note with a somewhat different and more persuasive approach.

c. Assume that by four weeks from today you still have not received payment. Now write what may have to be the first of several personal letters—perhaps addressed directly to Mrs. Timmons—appealing for payment.

d. Assume that by six weeks from today still no payment has arrived. You must write a second personal letter in your attempt to collect this account.

Your instructor may want to give you additional instructions regarding how many more letters will be sent before action is taken against Contemporary Galleries. If not, make this decision on your own and indicate it at the bottom of communication d.

8. When the North Park Xeron Service Station, 1011 Northwest Highway, Dallas, Texas, sends an order to you as manager of the Automotive Wholesale, Inc., of Dallas, you check the North Park account. It contains a past-due balance of $566.45, and the credit limit placed on the account is $600.00. The owner of the station, Mr. Phil Keeter, has placed the new order for $175.00 in merchandise, tires, tubes, and batteries. Write Keeter seeking some action on his part that will enable you to keep the account open by collecting before you ship the new merchandise.

9. As owner of the Gamble Office Supply Company, a distributor of stationery and other office supplies, write appeal letters to the following customers.

a. Mr. David Suth, Office Manager of the Cry-Vac Manufacturing Company, has a reputation for prompt payment, is well thought of in the community, and is a leader in professional activities. His account is now 60 days past due; the balance is $105.00.

b. Miss June Prentice, owner-manager of the Speed-Y Secretarial Services in your city, is an aggressive businessperson who started the business on her own and has built it into one of the most reliable secretarial services in the city. Her account balance of $58.20 is now 40 days past due.

10. Miss Prentice, owner of the Speed-Y Secretarial Services, fails to respond to your appeal letter. Her account is now sixty days past due. Your check reveals that she is still in business and has recently placed an order with another supplier of stationery supplies. Write her an urgency letter.

11. Your urgency letter (Problem 10) has not been answered. Write Miss Prentice an ultimatum letter.

12. As manager of Huff's Furniture Store, 730 Mesa Avenue, Phoenix, Arizona, you have extended credit to Mr. Louis Kingston, Flagstaff, Arizona. Mr. Kingston purchased a seven-piece dining ensemble—a table and six chairs—for $978.36. According to the terms of the contract, he was to pay $81.53 for twelve months. After paying regularly for eight months, Kingston missed the ninth payment; the tenth is almost due. He has received two reminders and a letter of inquiry. One week has passed since the inquiry letter was mailed. Kingston is known to be a prosperous motel operator with a good credit reputation. Because only two days remain before the tenth payment is due, you want to get an appeal letter in the mail in an attempt to get both the ninth and tenth payments at the same time and, thus, forestall a serious delinquency. Write the letter to be sent by special delivery.

13. Louis Kingston (Problem 12) chose to ignore your appeal letter. His account now stands two monthly payments behind schedule. Fifteen days have passed since the appeal letter was mailed. Accounts more than 45 days delinquent must be reported to the Arizona Retail Credit Association. The Association does not collect amounts for its members, but it does circulate the names of delinquent customers to its membership. Your normal recourse against delinquencies is your right of repossession as stated in the conditional sale contract, which Kingston signed. Send Kingston an urgency letter.

14. Because Kingston does not respond to your urgency letter (Problem 13), you have no choice but to send him an ultimatum. His ninth payment is now 60 days past due, the tenth is 30 days late, and the eleventh payment is due. Write the ultimatum that will be sent by registered mail.

15. You are the collection manager of the Tri-State Finance Company, Kansas City, Missouri. Stephen Burns, a butcher with a local meat packaging company, borrowed $100 just prior to Christmas with the agreement that he would pay back $10 a week until the debt was cleared. It is now the middle of January, and Burns has not made any payment. In such cases you attempt to make collection on the basis of a single letter. You can and will use the courts as a collection means and have found the packaging company cooperative in garnishment proceedings, in which you can get a court order to withhold the money due from the debtor's paychecks. The garnishment procedure will give the debtor a bad name with his employer. Write Mr. Burns an effective collection letter detailing the advantages of prompt payment.

CONCILIATION

A conciliatory letter is one written in response to a demand. Such letters are among the hardest to write because, obviously, if somebody has complained, that person's confidence in you is impaired. Even if it is only the mildest of demands asking for a guaranteed adjustment, somebody sees you as having committed an error or done a wrong. Maybe it's poor service, damaged merchandise, or an overcharge; but somebody is at least disturbed, perhaps angry. You will need all the help you can get from effective use of tone to relieve the distress and to remedy its cause.

The following organizational plan is useful for structuring a conciliatory letter.

ORGANIZATIONAL PLAN

1. *Apology.*   Make whatever apology is necessary—perhaps all that is needed is an expression of regret over the inconvenience caused.
2. *Explanation.*   In most cases, give a complete explanation of what happened to cause the troublesome situation. People feel they are entitled to know why.
3. *Remedy.*   Offer an adjustment, if appropriate, or reassurance, or otherwise state what will be done for the person to be conciliated.
4. *Positive close.*   Build goodwill.

The following guidelines give some additional strategies to follow in the four-part conciliatory letter.

GUIDELINES

1. *Check the chapter on "Tone."*   You will need all the help you can get from tact, sincerity, and positiveness.
2. *Avoid an accusing or suspicious tone.*   Even though the customer may be at fault, your purpose is to conciliate, not to blame.
3. *Don't be gushy.*   Do apologize, but an exaggerated apology may suggest insincerity.
4. *Conciliate graciously.*   If you offer an adjustment, don't do it grudgingly. You have decided to please the customer, haven't you?
5. *Indicate how the reader is to respond,* if a response is necessary. Make it easy for the reader to respond.
6. *Check the chapter on the you attitude.*   Indicate some reader benefit or continued relationship with your firm.
7. *Emphasize customer identification.*   The disturbance has alienated the customer or reader somewhat from your organization. Try to pull the customer back. Send a new catalog, refer to a new product or service, assume (but not presume) that your relationship will continue to be "business as usual."

Typical Letters

Let's look at some letters that illustrate different combinations of conciliatory efforts—*apology, explanation,* and *adjustment.* Although an apology is almost always in order, not all complaints are susceptible to adjustment or even explanation. If somebody demands that you pay a bill and for the time being you cannot, about all you can do is offer an explanation. If you receive a reprimand or a petty complaint of discourtesy, explanation will not satisfy, and adjustment is not in order. A sincere apology and reassurance must suffice to conciliate.

Apology—Explanation—Adjustment

With a letter like the following one from a longtime customer, the problem is clear. You have to calm his anger and keep his patronage. That means giving an apology, an explanation, and an adjustment, using a positive tone throughout.

May 15, 1978

The Boat House
809 Bond Street
Oklahoma City, Oklahoma

My dear Sir:

    To call it like it is, you sure fouled up delivery of my Mercury outboard motor. If I told you once, I told you five times you should deliver it to my week-end place at Lake Altus, not at my regular address. So there I sat, with my fishing buddies who were going boating with the thing, while you tried to deliver it to the regular address. If the neighbors hadn't seen your delivery man with the motor, we still wouldn't know what happened. I've got a good mind to cancel my charge account and take my business someplace else where they've got ears!!!

Disgustedly yours,

Donald Keeter

Donald K. Keeter

The answer to this customer service complaint follows the pattern of apology-explanation-adjustment. Positive tone and customer identification are maintained throughout. The final paragraph makes it easy for the customer to respond as you wish him to.

May 17, 1978

Mr. Donald Keeter
405 North 19 Street
Frederick, Oklahoma 73838

Dear Mr. Keeter:

Apology: "Mix-up" avoids unpleasant word

Please accept our most sincere apologies for the delivery mix-up on your Mercury outboard motor. Upon receiving your letter this morning, I checked the delivery slip and found that, in completing it, our shipping department had copied the address straight from your account folder. When your neighbor told our delivery man that you were on vacation, he brought the outboard motor back to the store assuming he would redeliver it as soon as you got back. We in the sales department assumed delivery had been made to your summer residence. Both departments are indeed embarrassed.

Explanation

Reassurance

Continued relationship

Having purchased from us for many years, you know that we do our best to avoid these slip-ups in communications. Somehow, this one got away from us.

Adjustment

Reader benefit: business as usual

What we'd like to do is deliver your Mercury to you at either address you wish. And, because we didn't get it to you in time for your fishing trip we'd like to pay for your not having had it by delivering it at a twenty-five percent discount. By doing this, we can say we're sorry and still provide you with the finest in recreation equipment for your many fishing trips to come.

Response made easy

Mr. Glenn, our shipping manager, has said that he will call you for your "OK" on a delivery time that will meet your earliest convenience.

Sincerely yours,

Thom Atkinson

Thom Atkinson
Sales Manager

TA:bs

Apology—Explanation

No adjustment is possible or necessary with the following case; so conciliation must be brought about by apology and explanation. There is nothing tangible to offer the customer, such as a discount on a piece of merchandise. Conciliation is managed by goodwill and explanation. Note the special appeal to the customer by saying "You are correct."

October 27, 1978

Mr. Alexander Leapold
4490 Belgrade Circle
Green Bay, Wisconsin 54305

Dear Mr. Leapold:

    We sincerely apologize. Upon receiving your letter, we rechecked your invoice of October 17. You are correct. Your check for $549.25 does cover the charges fully. Shipping costs incurred by another customer had been mistakenly added to your account.

    You have our assurance that, however cross-eyed from overtime our bookkeepers may become, our policy is still to make your bills as low as we possibly can.

Cordially yours,

Elaine Janke

Elaine Janke
Vice-President

EJ:me

Apology

In some conciliatory situations there is no tangible remedy, and even an explanation is meaningless or unnecessary. In the following letter conciliation is brought about with just an apology. But the right tone is used, and a little chatter is added to humor the customer and keep her identified with the company.

```
                                        December 12, 1978



        Mrs. Betty Schneider
        2492 Longview Road
        Richmond, Virginia  23220

        Dear Mrs. Schneider:

            I am very sorry!  I know personally how
        it feels when someone misspells my name--they
        usually leave out one of the r's.

            Please excuse the typist's mistake.  The
        intention of our letter--to say we appreciate
        serving you--still stands.  We do appreciate it.

                            Sincerely yours,

                            Karren Brown

                            Karren Brown
                            Manager

        KB:jr
```

If Ms. Brown had written only the following brief note, she would have increased the offense with her curtness.

```
                                        December 21, 1978



        Mrs. Betty Schneider
        2492 Longview Road
        Richmond, Virginia  23220

        Dear Mrs. Schneider:

            We're sorry we misspelled your name.

                            Yours truly,

                            Karren Brown

                            Karren Brown
                            Manager

        KB:jr
```

EXERCISES

1. Improve the conciliatory effect of the following letter. No adjustment is in order, but apology and explanation are. Use positive tone to evoke goodwill.

                                        March 17, 1978

        General Office Supply
        827 Fountain Street
        Cincinnati, Ohio 45221

        Attention: T. S. Butterfield

        Dear Sir:

            We were quite surprised to read your
        letter of last week in which you claimed
        that you wrote "Rush--United Parcel" on
        your order form. There was no such notation
        on the order form we worked with. So we
        sent your order by rail freight, the way
        we usually send all orders.

            But our company policy here at National
        says the customer is always right. So
        we are certainly sorry for all the trouble
        you might have been caused.

                            Sincerely yours,

                            Rudolph Jenkins
                            Rudolph Jenkins

---

2. Rewrite the following letter to improve the conciliatory effect. Write on the assumption that one of your new employees had made an error and included 500 old baskets in the order. Remove the accusing tone, sincerely apologize, explain fully, and cheerfully offer an adjustment.

Mr. Harvey Walker
Purchasing Agent
Peerless Imports
2290 Elmwood Road
St. Louis, Missouri 63105

Dear Sir:

We were quite shocked to learn from your letter of
May 19 that the 1000 Handi-Baskets ordered on May 1
were unsatisfactory.

You claim that many of the baskets were discolored
and streaked. If this is true, we are at a loss to
understand how such damage could have occurred
because all of our merchandise is carefully inspected
before it is shipped. You also state that several
hundred of the baskets give evidence of having been
in our stock room for a long period of time because
they are dusty and faded. We cannot understand this
because the baskets sent to you were manufactured
only one month ago.

Since you have been a good customer of ours, however,
we are willing to take back the baskets which you
claim are discolored and to replace them. We hope
this will be satisfactory.

                                        Sincerely yours,

                                        Gilbert Bond

                                        Gilbert Bond

3. As an assistant in the public relations department of Edison Light and Power Co.,
    you receive the following letter. Write an answer to Mr. Spiller's letter based on
    your investigation showing his meter is accurate. Make use of such other informa-
    tion as the fact that while the price of other commodities has increased greatly, the
    cost of electricity has gone down; that the bill was for the month of December when
    the Spillers probably had a lighted Christmas tree and additional lighting; that Mrs.
    Spiller informed your investigator that the family had received a new TV set, an
    electric oven, and an iron for Christmas.

Gentlemen:

Every time I get an electric bill from you
it is higher than the one for the month
before. My December bill was $67.70 which
is the highest I have ever had, and I am
getting sick and tired of paying such
exorbitant bills. You big utility companies
take advantage of small customers like me,
and it's no wonder you make the huge profits
that I see reported in the papers. I want
someone to come out and examine my meter
because I know I'm being overcharged.

Sincerely yours,

Howard Spiller

Howard Spiller

4. Joseph Thrasher, 268 Nelson Lane, Buffalo, New York 14221, has written to you indignantly protesting that twice within the last year he has received bills for merchandise for which he had paid cash. Write Mr. Thrasher explaining that the errors were made by a bookkeeper who has since been dismissed for negligence.

5. The Pioneer Furnishings Company, 1312 Miami Ave., Ann Arbor, Michigan 48104, has written that one of three walnut dining room tables shipped by you on August 15 arrived with its top badly scratched. Apparently your shipping department was negligent in inspecting this merchandise before shipment. Rather than pay charges for shipping a new table and for returning the scratched one—which is the adjustment the customer asks for—offer a discount of 20 percent on the table and suggest that this saving be used to repair the damage.

6. As adjuster for Atlas Carpeting, you received a complaint from Mrs. James Dawkins that the carpeting she received does not match the sample she was shown at the time of purchase. Since her drapes and furniture were ordered to blend with the sample of carpeting, her whole decorative scheme is ruined. Your salesperson had apparently neglected to tell the customer that no two dyes of carpeting are exactly the same and that samples and the delivered carpet do not match exactly. Since the carpeting is already cut to the dimensions of the customer's rooms, you face a considerable loss if the customer does not accept it. Write, offering her a discount of 20 percent and endeavoring to get her to accept this adjustment.

BAD NEWS

Bad-news messages are among the hardest to write, but they have to be written. You might be refusing credit or adjustment claims, answering inquiries when the information is unfavorable, acknowledging orders you can't fill now or at all, turning down job applicants or work offers, announcing bad news about prices or services, or enforcing company policy.

When you must write a bad-news message, you must do it in such a way as to cushion the disturbance. You have to give the bad news, but you want to keep the goodwill of the recipient so that he or she will remain a customer, or at least a friend of the organization.

Such a task requires all your skill in effective use of tact, sincerity, positiveness, the you attitude, and effective phrasing. Yet a skillful letter writer can actually win or keep a friend for the company even when saying "No" or "Too bad for you" in one way or another.

Compare the following two letters that refuse credit—the last effectively concerned with the customer and the first thoughtless.

Dear Mr. Jensen:

I am sorry we cannot grant the 60-day credit terms you asked for in connection with the fall meeting of the Lofty Scalers. We had an unfortunate experience with your group when you were here at Valley Resort two years ago. You did not pay us for over four months, and we had to get very unpleasant about it before we collected. I am sure you will understand why we think you are not a good credit risk.

Very truly yours,

Carl Bowen

Carl Bowen

With such a negative response Mr. Bowen has destroyed the possibility that the Lofty Scalers may patronize Valley Resort on a cash basis. The following writer, though direct, is tactful and sales minded. The tone of the letter is cordial, appreciative, and thoughtful. No mention is made of the previous unpleasant experience with the Lofty Scalers. The last paragraph cushions the refusal and encourages patronage by offering other customer benefits.

Dear Mr. Jensen:

Thank you and your fellow members of Lofty Scalers
for thinking of Valley Resort for your fall meeting.
It will be a pleasure to have you, although we do
ask you to make full settlement at the time of
checkout. This is our standard arrangement with
similar organizations.

If you find these conditions satisfactory, Mr.
Jensen, you may be sure that we at Valley Resort
will see to it that your group is extended every
courtesy and service. In fact, you will be glad
to know that a new trail has been opened on the
South Slope which you will want to explore.

Please return quickly the enclosed card confirming
your reservations so that you may be assured of
getting the exact accommodations you want.

                              Sincerely yours,

                              Jill Timms

                              Jill Timms

The Timms letter illustrates the typical structural organization for a bad-news letter.

ORGANIZATIONAL PLAN

1. *Opening cushion*—cordiality, appreciation, agreement on something
2. *Reason for rejection or bad news*—with adequate explanation
3. *The refusal itself*—de-emphasized, but clear
4. *Positive alternative*—or other reader benefit

Let's look at some guidelines for treating the reader as sympathetically as possible and the bad news as positively as possible.

GUIDELINES

1. *Begin with a cushion, not the bad news.* Don't say "No" in the first sentence. Find something to agree on—thanks, or appreciation, or a neutral thought about which there will be no disagreement. If both reader and writer have begun by agreeing on a less important issue, the likelihood of strong disagreement about the important issue is decreased.

2. *Give a full explanation.* To be reasonable and convincing, use sufficient detail. Facts and figures are helpful.

3. *Give the explanation before the refusal.* A logical explanation given first may make the bad news seem more reasonable and may prevent a negative reaction. Preventing is easier than curing.

4. *Don't dodge with pass-the-buck phrases.* Avoid such evasions as "Our policy prevents." Instead, give specific reasons.

5. *Try to point out reader benefit.* If you stop to think the problem through, you can usually see ways in which the reader profits from your answer. Perhaps by refusing such requests as the reader has made, you can either sell at lower prices, make quicker deliveries, or deliver better merchandise. The disappointment will be minimized if you can show the reader that in the long run he or she is the winner, not the loser, as a result of your action.

6. *De-emphasize the actual bad-news statement.* Here are some techniques for de-emphasizing negative statements.

    a. *Use impersonal language.*

    b. *Bury the bad news in the middle of a long, complex sentence.* Cushion words like "although" are helpful.

      Although we are unable to grant you . . ., we can offer you . . .

    c. *Make the bad news one of a cluster of ideas.* In this sentence "pay" is de-emphasized by being placed among several other ideas:

      May I please have information about the responsibilities of the job, the pay, the opportunities for advancement, and the availability of good housing?

    d. *Use minimum space.* Use only a few words and never a paragraph by itself for the bad-news statement.

    e. *Use polite requests.* A polite request is less emphatic than a question or a statement.

7. *Make the message clear.* Though you de-emphasize the message, make it definite. Leave no uncertainty. Don't apologize—you acted with good reason. It is inconsistent to say "We are sorry we had to refuse." Don't prolong the correspondence. A sentence like "If you have any further questions, don't hesitate to write us" indicates that the case is still open.

8. *Try to offer a positive alternative.* Offer a constructive suggestion, a counterproposal, or another course of action. Remember, your goal is to keep the

reader sold on your merchandise and your services and identified with the company. For instance, if you refuse requested credit, you can offer the layaway plan; instead of a requested personal interview, you can enclose a booklet to help answer questions; instead of the full order, you can offer half now and half in two months.

9. *Close positively.* Suggest acceptance of a counterproposal, invite other purchases, or offer other services. If the reader should take some action, make clear exactly what the action is, when it is to be done, and how it can be done easily. Emphasize reader benefit. Give the impression that you confidently expect to retain the customer's business and that this is to his or her advantage.

10. *Use words with a positive tone.* Review "Connotation" in Chapter 4 on *Words* for selecting words of approval rather than disapproval. Review "Positiveness" in Chapter 7 on *Tone* for techniques for using a positive rather than a negative tone.

Typical Letters

Let's see how some well-written bad-news letters follow the guidelines and the four-part organization given above.

Refusal of Credit

The following was written to a small sporting goods store—Outdoors, Inc.—which asked for credit on ski equipment. Upon request the store submitted credit references, but the replies from those references disclosed that Outdoors, Inc. had a poor record in discharging its debts. They paid their bills slowly during the busy season and sometimes not at all during the off-season. Consequently, the writer of this letter had to refuse Outdoors' request for credit. Yet he wanted to induce them to purchase on a cash basis. The letter opposite is what he wrote.

It is a well-done bad-news letter, especially when you consider how poorly it could have been written. Some refusals would have sounded like this:

```
    Gentlemen:

    We are sorry to inform you that we cannot extend
    credit as per your request.  However, we will fill
    your order C.O.D. if you wish.  Telephone us or
    wire us collect if this arrangement suits you.

                    Yours truly,



                    Donald Bain
```

*Opening cushion:
Appreciation,
thoughtfulness*

*Reason for rejection—
with reasons and
explanation*

*The refusal:
sde-emphasis through
use of "although"*

*Positive
alternative*

*Sales value—
customer benefit*

Alternative

Action made easy

September 15, 1978

Outdoors, Inc.
1988 Penwood Blvd.
Denver, Colorado 80204

Gentlemen:

Thank you for so promptly providing the
requested credit data. We have considered
it carefully and contacted each of the firms
you listed.

Knowing the nature of the sporting goods
market you face, we are ordinarily glad to
extend credit to merchants engaged in it.
Of concern, though, is the effect which
seasonal fluctuations in the market seem to
have upon your ability to meet short-term
credit requirements. We would gladly
lengthen the payment period for you, but
obligations to our manufacturers force a
thirty-day credit limit upon us.

So although we cannot--at present--offer
you credit terms, we feel we can serve you
equally well by shipping your order C.O.D.
As you've said, you can move the winter
sports goods most quickly during the upcoming
season. They should definitely be on your
shelves. With the extra advantage of a
two percent discount for cash, you can realize
an even more substantial profit. If ready cash
is low, your order can easily be cut in half,
with the rest held aside for subsequent rapid
delivery. We merely await your approval.

Just wire or phone us collect, and the goods
will be in your shop and selling by the middle
of next week.

Sincerely yours,

Burton Langstrom

Burton Langstrom
Customer-Service Manager

It is likely that Langstrom's letter will succeed. The people at Outdoors, Inc., certainly know their credit rating is poor. They must have goods, and Langstrom's tactful, reader-interest approach will probably produce a C.O.D. order.

Refusal of Request for Adjustment

As customer-service manager of Fun Enterprises, you receive a complaint from one of your customers, Miss Jennifer Wilkins. She has written to complain about the inferior quality of the Halloween costumes that she sold. Miss Wilkins says that customer complaints about the costumes have resulted in "loss of face and probably loss of business in the future." She maintains that you should give her credit for $96.80, a 50 percent reduction, to compensate for her embarrassment.

After investigation you decide that Miss Wilkins is not justified in her complaint. The costumes are cheaply made, but they were priced especially low, too, which helped to account for their being the best-selling costumes you have handled. Many retailers purchased the same costumes and reported selling them with great success and satisfaction.

You give this information to your new assistant and ask him to say "No" to Miss Wilkins. He brings you the following letter for your approval. What do you think of it?

Dear Mrs. Wilkins:

I am quite sorry to have your complaint about the inferior Halloween costumes you claim you were sent. Your complaint has been investigated thoroughly, and we find no justification for your contentions.

May I expect your check for $96.80?

        Yours very sincerely,

You point out to your new assistant the negative aspects of the letter. A positive writer would have avoided the accusatory terms of "your complaint" and "your contentions" and would not have referred to the product as "inferior." You write the following letter as an improvement.

Dear Miss Wilkins:

We appreciate your letter concerning the Halloween
costumes you recently ordered. Your success in selling
all of them speaks well for your business. Many of our
customers reported similar success, with complete
satisfaction from the parents and youngsters who bought
them.

As you know, we purchased these costumes (identical
in quality to those you purchased last year but lower
in cost) at a very special price, and we were able to
pass the discount on to our good customers such as you.
If you explain to your customers that a $4.98 top price
for a complete costume is quite a bargain--even for a
one-time garment--they will likely understand and
appreciate your position.

Your account is being credited for $96.80, leaving a
balance of $96.80. Please send us your check today in
the enclosed addressed envelope.

I am enclosing the new catalog of Easter novelties. You
may enjoy looking through it in preparation for the
upcoming season.

                         Sincerely,

                         Customer-Service Manager

The letter above conveys bad news with reader interest and a positive tone. There is no mention of complaint or of inferior merchandise, and there are no accusations. the letter simply explains the situation to Miss Wilkins in a reasonable, friendly, direct, positive manner, assuming that she will agree. The final paragraph carries resale interest and an assurance to Miss Wilkins that the company values her business.

Refusal of a Request for a Favor

Assume you run the largest restaurant supply company in the region. Ralph Smith, who operates one of the large restaurants that you have supplied for several years, is expanding his business into a catering service. Since he expects to pay his salespeople by commission, as you do your contact staff, Mr. Smith has written to ask you for information about the basis on which you pay your staff. You must refuse his request and still keep his goodwill. How do you do it? Compare the approach of the following two letters.

Dear Sir:

I have received your letter of June 10 asking about the basis on which we pay our salespeople. I regret that I cannot let you have this information because confidential reports have a way of getting out. I might say that our system of remuneration has been very successful and our salespeople are completely satisfied with it. It is my hope that you will not consider this refusal an unfriendly act on our part and that our pleasant business relationship may continue in the future.

Very truly yours,

Dear Mr. Smith:

Thank you for the interest you expressed in your letter of June 10 concerning the way in which we pay our salespeople. We are flattered that so successful a businessman should ask our advice.

We are sorry that we cannot release this information. Because each of our salespeople works under an individual contract, we would be violating the confidence of our employees if the terms of these contracts were given out. Because our sales staff themselves have requested this confidence and we have agreed to it, you can understand why we cannot comply with your request.

You are probably familiar with B.T. Olcans's book Treating Salesmen as Human Beings. We have found it helpful in its practical suggestions for dealing with specific employee problems. It might prove useful to you at this time.

If we may assist you in any other way, please call on us. We offer our best wishes in your new venture. I believe the territory has been needing such a catering service as you are setting up.

Sincerely yours,

The first letter makes bad news worse with its wrong emphasis. The phrase "not consider this refusal an unfriendly act" creates unfriendliness. The letter is almost insulting in its thoughtless suggestion that the reader cannot be trusted with confidential information. It is taunting in its hint that "our system of remuneration has been very successful," but you can't have it.

The second letter, by contrast, is sincere, constructive, and tactful. Goodwill and customer relations will remain intact.

Sometimes you must refuse a request for a favor in situations that do not strictly relate to business. In the following two cases (Figures 10-3 through 10-6), the executive director of a big-city hospital must refuse two sticky requests—one from the mayor of the city, who is exerting political-business pressure, the other from a business colleague who is trying to cash in on an old school tie. Although such requests and refusals should be routine business, if the bad-news letters are poorly handled, relations could become strained and the writer or his institution could suffer some loss. A mayor and the city council can do things to affect the operation of a hospital. With the school friend, both friendship and business interchange could be weakened.

The executive director handled the refusals effectively. In both instances he followed the basic plan.

The mayor (see Figure 10-3) uses considerable pressure by flashing the influence of the community—"enclosed editorials," "business community," "free enterprise system," letterhead from the City Council. He makes a refusal difficult by indicating that other businesses have already helped, by using presumptuous, obvious flattery ("only you"), and by assuming that a certain number of slots will be pledged. Nevertheless, Allen does say "No" (see Figure 10-4), but he says it cordially and effectively.

Allen's letter uses the four-part organization of the bad-news message. Paragraph 1 opens with a positive cushion. The pleasant word "encouraging" is used. The second sentence uses expressions—"concern," "shared," "doing everything"—that keep the hospital tightly linked with the community. The refusal itself comes in paragraph 2; it is de-emphasized, but clear, and given with adequate explanation. The last sentence gives an alternative that is a weak one, but still keeps possibilities open. The mayor must accept the refusal graciously.

The request from the old school friend (see Figure 10-5) exhibits some problems. Johnson himself is also an executive director of a hospital and might expect some special professional courtesy. A good businessman can accept a reasonable businesslike refusal, but some signs in the letter—citing his "W.V. Class of '57" and putting his degree after his name—indicate that Johnson has a sensitive ego that needs to be propped up. The excessiveness in phrases such as "your fine city" and the "very sincerely yours" suggests a tendency toward superficial emotionalism that must be pampered a little. Allen's solution is to refuse the request for a favor with the basic bad-news organization. He writes a friendly, but clear "No" that can give no ground for offense (see Figure 10-6).

Allen opens with a positive cushion ("Thanks," "availability"). He de-emphasizes the "no" and gives an adequate explanation. He closes positively, keeping the friendship intact by sending regards of a mutual friend. It is small letter, but it does the job well.

```
                    C I T Y   O F   D A L L A S

CHET WILSON                T E X A S
Mayor                      _____

                          City Council


    June 26, 1978



    Dr. Thomas Allen
    Methodist Hospital
    301 West Colorado
    Dallas, Texas  75208

    Dear Dr. Allen:

    The enclosed editorials outline the critical need
    for meaningful work for economically disadvantaged
    youth in the Dallas region.  The business community
    has already placed a number of disadvantaged youth,
    but we still have approximately 5,000 young people
    who need employment.  Only you, as a business leader,
    can teach these youngsters that work is the way to
    progress and that the free enterprise system works
    for all people in the community.

    Jobs for these youths are very important to our
    community, and I will personally appreciate your
    checking with your personnel division to see how
    many jobs you can make available for these needy
    youngsters.

    Please call Ted Garcia, Executive Director of the
    Summer Youth Program, at 748-4056 and let him know
    how many slots you can pledge.

    Thank you for your cooperation in this vitally
    important program.

    Sincerely,

    Chet Wilson
```

Figure 10-3

METHODIST

HOSPITALS
OF DALLAS

July 3, 1978

The Honorable Chet Wilson
Mayor of Dallas
Lane and Temple Streets
Dallas, Texas 75201

Dear Mayor Wilson:

We received your letter encouraging us to provide summer jobs
for some of our disadvantaged young people. Your concern for
these youngsters is shared by us, and we want you to know we
are doing everything we possibly can to comply.

At this time in the summer, our jobs are always filled. We
will probably not have anything available for the remainder of
the summer. However, should vacancies occur, we will be in
touch with Ted Garcia.

Sincerely yours,

Thomas Allen

Thomas Allen
Executive Director

TA:kr

Methodist Central Hospital | Post Office Box 5999 Dallas, Texas 75222 (214) 946-8181
Margaret Jonsson Charlton Methodist | Post Office Box 5357 Dallas, Texas 75222 (214) 296-2511

Figure 10-4

Founded 1908

GS   THE GOOD SHEPHERD HOSPITAL

William W. Johnson   Phone: 8 8 2 - 5 2 2 0
Executive Director   280 Front Street
                                            Normal, Illinois
                                            61761

April 25, 1978

Dr. Thomas Allen
Executive Director
Methodist Hospital of Dallas
P.O. Box 5999
Dallas, Texas 75222

Dear Mr. Allen:

I am writing in regard to Mr. John E. Todd, from Normal
Illinois, who is a senior medical student at SMU in your
fine city, and is planning on going into psychiatry. John's
father indicated he was seeking summer employment in Dallas
and at the same time wishes to continue his schooling. I
know the family well and would appreciate greatly if you
could do something to provide John with some summer employment.

If I can ever be of assistance to you, please let me know.

Thank you.

                          Very sincerely yours,

                          William Johnson, M.H.A.

                          William Johnson, M.H.A.,
                          Executive Director
                          W.V. Class of '57

WJ:bv

Figure 10-5

METHODIST
HOSPITALS
OF DALLAS

May 2, 1978

Mr. William W. Johnson
Executive Director
The Good Shepherd Hospital
280 Front Street
Normal, Illinois 61761

Dear Bill:

Thanks for informing us of John Todd's availability.
As much as we would like to assist him, we will not be
hiring any summer help this year as our financial situation
is simply too tight.

Tim Hafner sends his regards. Sorry we are unable to help.

Cordially yours,

Thomas Allen

Thomas Allen, FACHA
Executive Director

TA:pm

Methodist Central Hospital | Post Office Box 5999 Dallas, Texas 75222 (214) 946-8181
Margaret Jonsson Charlton Methodist | Post Office Box 5357 Dallas, Texas 75222 (214) 296-2511

Figure 10-6

Turning Down a Job Applicant

Even if you are only turning down a student's request to get a summer job back, you must do it tactfully, as the following letter does. The student can be a goodwill ambassador, a potential customer, and a future employee.

Dear Mr. Enloe:

We are pleased that you wish to work again this summer for the Chalmers Company.

The nature of contracts and subcontracts we presently hold has lowered our projected manpower needs at least through October. As a result, all our regular summer spots must be filled by full-time permanent employees--leaving us without a position to offer you this summer.

This reply is certainly no reflection upon your abilities and qualifications. We were quite pleased with your performance last summer, and we hope to have openings again next summer for college students like you.

I feel quite sure that a person of your energies and abilities will find appropriate employment. Thanks again for your interest in Chalmers.

Sincerely,

Henry Helman

Henry Helman
Personnel Manager

From the sample letters given—bad and good—we can see that bad-news letters all have a double purpose. They must express the news clearly and they must cushion the impact to keep the goodwill of the reader and perhaps the account.

Bad-news letters, whether adjustment refusals, credit refusals, favor refusals, or order refusals, all follow the same basic four-part plan. The four-part plan is: (1) begin with a cushion, (2) offer an explanation and reasons for the bad news, (3) express the refusal unemphatically but clearly, and (4) suggest a positive alternative. And, of course, all bad-news letters carry a positive tone and reader interest throughout.

EXERCISES

1. Analyze the weaknesses of the following refusal credit letter. Then rewrite it.

Mr. Charles Billings
The Nen's Shop
281 Peach Tree Street
Atlanta, Georgia 30314

Dear Sir:

Thank you for your promptness in sending us the necessary credit information, but we are sorry to inform you that your references spoke rather unfavorably of you. You will understand, therefore, why we cannot grant you credit terms for the merchandise you ordered on September 18. As a businessman, you yourself know how difficult it is to collect money these days, especially from those with a poor credit rating.

We think you should order about half the amount of your original order and pay cash for this merchandise. We will be glad to extend you our two percent discount for cash.

We know you will want to stock Crown Prince suits for the coming season because of their finer quality and lower price of $69.90. We hope to receive your order in a few days.

Sincerely yours,

Jason Trumbull

Jason Trumbull
Credit Manager

2. Which of these letters is more effective? Point out the weaknesses and strengths of both letters.

a.

> Dear Mr. Larkin:
>
> We are glad to tell you, in answer to your letter of March 8, that, after careful examination of the Dynatone Stereo, we find nothing seriously wrong with it. A few inexpensive repairs are needed. The player appears to have been dropped or otherwise damaged, for the compensating lever is broken.
>
> As you will recall, our guarantee covers only defects in material and workmanship, but if you will send us $8.75 for repairs and postage, we will be glad to repair the player and return it within a few days.
>
> May we put your Dynatone Stereo in first-class working condition at once?
>
> Very truly yours,

b.

> Dear Mr. Larkin:
>
> Thank you for your letter of March 8. We have carefully examined the Dynatone Stereo, which you returned to us, and we find that the merchandise is not defective as stated in your letter. The player has been dropped or damaged by careless handling and the compensating lever is broken. This is, of course, not covered by our guarantee, which expressly states that it covers only "defects in materials and workmanship."
>
> If you want this player repaired, please send us a check or money order for $8.75 to cover the cost of repairs and postage. These repairs will take at least ten days.
>
> We regret that our guarantee does not cover this work, and we thank you for past favors.
>
> Very truly yours,

3. You are customer service manager of a shop that repairs cameras and electronic equipment. One of your out-of-town customers sent you for repair a Photolux camera, Model 891, bearing the serial number 46578. He claims the camera is defective and asks for free repairs, because he has had it only six months on a one-year guarantee. Examination shows that the camera is not defective, but it has been dropped and badly misused. These repairs are needed: replacement of broken lens, $42; repair of range finder, $3.50; repair and readjustment of electronic eye, $2.25. These repairs will put the camera in first-class shape. It originally cost $189. Write to the custmer, Mr. Thomas, letting him know why he will have to pay for these repairs.

4. Mr. Michael Spiller, 3821 Oak Street, Athens, Ohio 45701, has written to your loan company in Columbus, Ohio, asking if he might borrow $450. Five years ago he had been granted a similar loan, but his payments were always behind schedule. The final payment was extracted from him four months after the due date. Write to him refusing his request.

5. Mr. Jacob Renner, 281 College Avenue, College Station, Texas 77843, is a building contractor. He builds houses on the owner's lot; occasionally, he buys a lot, builds a house on it, and sells at whatever profit he can make. He wants to buy a large lot 20 blocks from the Texas A&M University campus and build a multiple-unit apartment house. The local branch of Gulf States Savings and Loan Association has refused to finance the project. He has appealed the decision to the main office in Austin, Texas.

   Although the main office has confidence in Mr. Renner, it questions the wisdom of building another apartment house in the area. Enrollment in the university has held steady for the past five years. Other apartment houses in the area appear to have several unrented apartments. The new multiple-unit building may be difficult for Mr. Renner to sell (it will cost $10,000 per unit), and he would probably have a hard time renting to college students. For the home office, write a letter refusing his loan.

6. Inform your employees in Wing C that all electricity will be turned off between 10 and 11 A.M. next Tuesday morning, May 17. The electricity shutoff is necessary while workmen hook up a major power cable between Wing C and the power plant. New fluorescent lighting will be installed within the next month. The employees will have to plan their work in such a way that they can get along without using any electric machines that hour; in fact, they won't have any electric lighting either. However, as these are sunny days, lack of electricity for lighting should not be too much of a problem. Everyone will be responsible for getting out the necessary work that day, because business must go on. The electricity shutoff will not be an excuse for working overtime in the afternoon, because no extra pay will be allowed.

7. Mrs. Temple Ellis, 3020 Riverside Drive, Kent, Ohio 44240, has ordered "three more teaspoons in Crown Sterling" from Walters Jewelry Store, Cleveland, Ohio 44106. She encloses her check for $45, which she hopes is enough to cover postage

too. Walters, however, does not carry Crown Sterling; you have the exclusive franchise for Regal Silver, which you think is one of America's finest. The Euclid Jewelry Store, 1971 Euclid Avenue, has the exclusive franchise for the Crown Sterling brand. As the manager of Walters, you'll return her check and build whatever goodwill you think appropriate for your store. You carry a complete line of exquisite silver hollowware (teapots, candy dishes, trays, serving dishes), chime clocks, watches, necklaces, rings, and other jewelry that Mrs. Ellis might be interested in.

8. Assume you receive the following letter from Mr. Clinton Powell, chairman of the United Community Fund campaign.

Dear _____:

As you know, our city conducts a United Community Fund drive annually. Many people volunteer their help to coordinate the campaign. Will you be willing to serve as a captain this year?

Captains are responsible for a particular area of the city. Yours would be a ten-block area bounded by 8th Avenue on the east, 12th Avenue on the west, Adams Street on the north, and Jefferson Street on the south. You would be responsible for selecting chairmen in each block, who in turn will canvass each house in their particular block.

Needless to say, your effort will be for a most worthy cause. Will you drop me a line . . . soon, saying you'll accept?

Unfortunately, you must decline the request. The campaign is to be kicked off in September, and you will be out of the state on vacation at that time.

9. Robert Hinson is director of bands at the local Southwestern University. The Junior Chamber of Commerce in the city is sponsoring the Festival Bowl, one of the university football play-offs. Mr. Hinson has written the Bowl chairman a letter volunteering the university drum and bugle corps for a pregame or intermission performance. All arrangements for the entire program have, however, already been made. A troupe of clowns will perform before the game; a high school band is to perform at intermission. As Bowl chairman, write to Mr. Hinson, declining his offer.

10. Assume you are manager of the High Seas Corporation, manufacturer of sailboats, speedboats, and yachts in New Orleans, Louisiana. Your new assistant has just written the following reply (dated March 30) to an inquirer from Galveston, Texas. What improvements can you suggest? The chief reason why you cannot at present give the information asked for in the "four points" (price, capacity, construction, and power unit) is that your new High Wave 70 yacht is to be unveiled in all showrooms throughout the nation on the same day—May 1. A widespread advertising campaign is building up to that date.

Dear Mr. Millerton:

This will acknowledge receipt of yours of March 27. At the time of this writing we are not in a position to give you any information on the four points which you mentioned in your letter since no information is available to us for release at this time.

We are sure, however, that your local dealer will be only too happy to keep you informed as to when the High Wave 70 will be made available to the public.

We would like to thank you for your interest in our new yacht.

Sincerely,

Carl Timmons

Carl Timmons

---

11. Mr. James Rester, owner of Rester Clothing Store, 280 Scott Street, Louisville, Kentucky 40208, bought six dozen men's work shirts directly from the manufacturer. After four weeks only six of the shirts had been sold. He cleared them out as a sales item at a loss of 50 cents per shirt. He thought the manufacturer should share his loss because the field representative persuaded him that this shirt would "go over big." Rester wrote a letter, asking the manufacturer to credit him for 50 percent of the loss.

The manufacturer learned through the field representative that Rester had marked these shirts up 33⅓ percent. The retailer and the manufacturer had agreed earlier that the markup would never exceed 25 percent. As adjustment manager for the manufacturer, write Mr. Rester a bad-news letter.

12. Mrs. Sheila Morton, 728 Parkdale Road, Pomona, California 91766, is to host the next meeting of her book club. The subject for discussion is "Mental Horizons." She has ordered ten copies of *Extrasensory Perception*, a paperback book, at $1.85 a copy from Expansion Publishers, for which you work. The supply is exhausted, but you are expecting more copies from the printer within four weeks. Mrs. Morton must have the books before the next club meeting, which is only three weeks away.

Write to Mrs. Morton, explaining that the order cannot be shipped for a least a month. Expansion Publishers does have available for immediate shipment a small book, *Concentration at Its Best*, by a well-known psychologist of a western university that costs $1.25 a copy. You have a good alternative to offer Mrs. Morton. See if she would like to buy *Concentration at Its Best* for her discussion of "Mental Horizons."

11 The Sales Letter

The Persuasive Process
Typical Letters

Promoting sales is a constant concern for every business. Promotion can be done through sales personnel, radio, television, newspapers and magazines, circulars, catalogs, booklets, brochures, billboards, and, of course, letters. Letters can be very effective as a promotion method because they are immediate, specific, and individualized in a way that other methods are not.

In a sense, every business letter is a sales letter. You are selling either yourself, your ideas, or your company, and so eventually your product. You always need to put your reader in a positive frame of mind toward the company.

Here we will deal with the type of letter or memo that has sales as its *primary* purpose. Such letters are the most difficult to write because you must use your powers of persuasion. You must produce interest, desire, and action where perhaps there were little or none before.

Several different kinds of persuasive letters are used by businesses. Here are the standard ones:

1. *The Special Item Letter* offers a particular item for sale at a special price, usually to an individually named person or a selected list of prospective buyers.
2. *The Reply to a Particular Inquiry* responds to a letter about an item and aims to bring about a sale. It is a variation of the *Routine Reply* when the occasion indicates that additional persuasion and promotion are appropriate.
3. *The Institutional Letter* does not offer a particular item for sale, but a specific person promotes the products of the company as a whole, including its special services. This letter is intended to create goodwill by building up the idea that the company makes fine products and renders good service. The institutional letter is less individualized and less personal than the special item letter.

255

4. *The Good-News Announcement* is a variation of the *Good-News Message* that introduces a new facility, service, or product to attract new customers and keep old ones. Although direct sales promotion is often not appropriate in the standard good-news and goodwill message, it is appropriate in this case. The occasion for the announcement is the goods and services that are for sale. Such letters are often sent to a selected list of old customers who have already indicated a general interest in the new product.

THE PERSUASIVE PROCESS

The persuasive process in a letter usually follows a four-stage order of techniques.

1. Capture the reader's attention.
2. Focus the reader's attention on a basic motive for buying.
3. Develop the persuasive appeals through sound methods:
   a. Descriptive detail
   b. Logical reasoning
   c. Emotional effects
   d. Respected opinion
   e. Reader benefit
4. Induce a certain course of action.

Let's look at these four stages in detail to see how the persuasive process works.

Capture Attention

People's first impulse toward a sales letter is either indifference or skepticism. Receiving pieces of "junk mail" by the thousands, people normally either ignore them or glance at them briefly before throwing them away. Therefore, the first thing your sales letter must do is capture the attention of the reader. The very beginning of the letter must make the reader think "Hey! There's something going on here. This one might really have something for me."

Appeal to the reader's curiosity. Make him or her want to read on. To stir up interest, you may use various novelties: catch phrases, proverbs, humorous statements, cartoons, questions, curious headlines, unusual thoughts, unexpected commands, and similar devices.

Here are some examples of attention-getting openings:

Danger! Beware of falling prices! If you are not careful, a great bargain may miss you . . .

Back to school in three more weeks. But . . .

Are you eager to lower your heating bill this winter?

Pep up your car engine! Get more miles to the gallon! Let us . . .

Are you as popular as you would like to be?

A penny saved is more than a penny earned at . . .

Come and get it!

Sweepstakes! You can win up to . . .

Appeals to curiosity may grab the reader's attention. When you get the reader's attention, you must keep it and induce him or her to read on.

Focus on a Basic Motive

To induce the reader to read on, you must motivate self-interest quickly. Once you have stimulated curiosity, indicate just what you have to offer that is special to the reader. What works with one reader may not work with another, so you must be skillful enough to tailor the appeal to the particular reader. It should be relevant to his or her situation. A startling but irrelevant opening will disgust a reader as soon as he or she sees it as just a device for grabbing attention. For relevance, the opening of a letter to mechanics might refer to the efficiency and dependability of tools. A sales letter to housekeepers might discuss the speed and ease of housecleaning.

Dynamore Cleaner will simplify your housecleaning and allow you more time for your . . .

A letter to a parent might successfully open with a head like this:

Your baby is the reason our standards are high.

The following list will give you ideas for appeals to use in various situations for all kinds of people.

BASIC HUMAN DESIRES AND MOTIVES: CHECKLIST

Making money	Comfort
Success	Leisure
Personal ambition	Social approval
Protecting family and loved ones	Education
Personal health and safety	Children's success
Efficiency	Making friends
Pride of possession	Having a nice home
Attracting the opposite sex	Curiosity
Saving time	Romantic enchantment

BASIC DESIRES CHECKLIST (continued)

Saving money	Escape
Popularity	Avoiding criticism
Desire to be stylish	Protecting reputation
Emulating others	Exercising one's talent
Belonging to a club or society	Being well dressed
Pride in accomplishment	Travel
Satisfying appetites	Being respected in the community
(hunger, thirst)	Desire for knowledge and insight
Generosity	Prestige
Individuality	Beauty

Here are some examples of how these basic appeals may be used in business messages.

Appeal to making money:

> Dear Mr. Jensen:
> After carefully analyzing your primary market and your advertising program of the past year, we believe that Acme Advertising can offer you a plan that will bring you muc more return for the same expenditure you are now making . . .

Appeal to efficiency (Notice the tact in this memo in saying "we" instead of an accusing "you."):

> Mr. Turnbow, I think we have a bottleneck in the operation of the shipping department, a weak point that can be easily corrected if we do a little shifting . . .

Appeal to ease, escape, romantic enchantment:

> The single International Charge Card can take you anywhere you want to go . . .

In planning your sales letter, focus on a central appeal and develop it. Supplement your central appeal by one or more secondary appeals. A letter attempting to sell home air conditioners would probably appeal to the *comfort* motive first. Secondary appeals might be *saving money, love of family,* and *having a nice home.*

A letter promoting fine crystal ware might appeal to the reader's *pride* or *prestige*. *Beauty* and *style* could be secondary appeals. A service station promoting automotive checkups could appeal to *safety* as central and *saving money* as secondary.

Consider your product. Consider your prospective customer. Then determine what central aipeal you should develop. Your central appeal must be appropriate and clearly defined. Without a strong central appeal you will not persuade.

Then use secondary appeals to supplement your promotion. Any secondary appeal by itself would not be sufficient, but as a supplement it strengthens the central appeal by saying in effect, "Here is just one more reason why you should . . ."

Develop Persuasive Appeals

After focusing your reader's attention on a primary motive, you then develop a central appeal and any secondary appeals. All of the following techniques are useful in persuading your reader.

DESCRIPTIVE DETAIL.   You must make clear exactly what your product is—prices, sizes, colors, capacities, and specifications. Description must be tangible and truthful. Vague generalities will leave the reader with only a vague wish to buy. Misleading and sensational promises will alert the reader to insincerity, and may prompt him or her to throw your letter away.

LOGICAL REASONING.   Backing up your appeal by sound thinking usually takes one or two approaches. The *inductive* approach draws from specific instances, statistics, or verifiable facts. An employee at Standard Products who wants to persuade his supervisor to purchase an addressing machine might base the appeal on inductive reasoning. He would cite case after case of similar companies with large periodic mailings who have reduced their costs by using such a machine.

You might use *deductive* reasoning, by which you draw a conclusion from the connection between two or more valid premises. The consultant who advises the Peerless Corporation to open a new unit in Kansas City might argue that the marketing analysis shows that the income generated will easily exceed the cost of expansion and that the expansion funds are available.

EMOTIONAL EFFECTS.   It helps to enlist the feelings in support of your appeal. Emotionally toned words, pleasant associations, and reference to basic human drives can favorably dispose the reader toward your product even though there may be no rational connection.

The following examples in no way tangibly describe the product or offer verifiable facts or logical demonstration.

Carefree fun lovers enjoy the glorious excitement of Arrowhead Beach.

For up-to-the-minute news reporting, all-round coverage, and the outspoken opinions that add zest to your own thinking—why not try *The New Reporter?*

Such appeals simply create an emotional aura in hopes of captivating the reader. They can be very helpful if used to support or color your use of tangible description, verifiable facts, and logical reasoning. An appeal based solely on emotionalism, however, quickly drives off most readers, and all sophisticated ones.

RESPECTED OPINION.   An expert, speaking on the subject of his or her greatest information, persuades us. His or her knowledge, experience, and opinion are solid. You undergird your appeal if you cite the opinions of experts on your product or services.

If the writer is regarded by the reader as an expert, that writer's opinion will carry weight. If you are not an expert, you can call on those who are. A letter from a shop mechanic evaluating the condition of your car is more valid than the opinion of the auto salesperson. If a cigarette advertisement suggests that Spring Green cigarettes with menthol will give you zest and health, you are less persuaded than by the opinion of the Surgeon General who has determined that "cigarette smoking is dangerous to your health."

Whether you are the specialist or you draw on others who are specialists, you can make use of respected opinion to promote your appeal. The following excerpts make use of respected opinion:

> I believe we should shift George Sampson from the lathe department. Sarah Cravens, the labor-relations analyst, studied the situation carefully and thinks we're in for increasing friction with the employees as long as George is their foreman.

> Lili Monteux, world-famous beauty expert says: "For enticing a man, there is nothing quite so inevitable as After Dark by De Conte."

> I know I'm just your doctor and a cardiac specialist for 20 years, but I'm telling you that if you don't slow down, you'll be dead in two years.

READER BENEFIT.   Reader benefit is the ultimate appeal. The letter begins by getting the reader's attention and then fastens onto something that is important to the reader—money, prestige, family, and so on. The whole letter must be for the reader. The you attitude is especially important in the sales letter and should be particularly emphasized. Check again all the principles and techniques of the you attitude of Chapter 6. What "I" the writer can do or think is kept to a minimum. Emphasis is on the reader and how he or she can benefit. The reader must be convinced that he or she needs the product. Forcefully, yet tactfully and concisely, the reader must be shown the relationship between the product and himself or his business, and the ways in which the product will profit or benefit him.

Induce a Course of Action

The effective sales letter leads to the purchase of a product. The final paragraph should motivate to action. The prospective buyer must be encouraged to act immediately, and his course of action should be made clear and easy. A simple order form, a business reply card, or a postage-free return envelope are some of the devices to encourage prompt action by mail. Here are some examples of effective closing paragraphs for sales letters:

> For a generous free sample, just send the enclosed postage-free card to us.

> For additional information, send us the enclosed card with your name and address.

> Let us demonstrate our Lawn Master on your own lawn—with absolutely no strings attached. Call 692-6611 for an appointment.

Our representative will be glad to drop in to see you within the next few days if you will just mail the enclosed postcard back to us with your name and address.

Your name and address on the enclosed form will bring you *Our Living World* for a two month's trial period. Or if you want to subscribe for a year, send check or money order for $8.95. If after you've received four issues, you don't like the magazine and wish to cancel your subscription, let us know and we'll refund your money.

There are many techniques for inciting your reader to act. You can offer introductory prices, trial purchase terms, gifts, guarantees, or free pamphlets. You can provide redeemable coupons. You can urge prompt action for a variety of reasons, such as taking advantage of a limited sales offer or ordering in time for summer vacation or for Christmas delivery. Any of these techniques and others can be used as long as they do not conflict with the letter's purpose or its desired level of dignity. Alone, these inducements to action would not be persuasive, but when added to a letter in which a genuine appeal has been developed, they help stimulate the actual response. Let's look at several sample sales letters to see how the persuasive process is built.

TYPICAL LETTERS

Special Items Letter

The letter on p. 262 from a distributor to selected auto parts retailers is built on the four stages of: capturing attention, focusing on a central appeal, developing the persuasion, and inducing action.

Notice that Alexander captures attention with a catchy line and the pleasant associations of spring. He moves on through the other three stages of the persuasive process. The central appeal is efficiency of service. Secondary appeals are money making and customer approval.

Reply to a Particular Inquiry

The letter on p. 263 also observes the four stages in the persuasive process. Find evidence of the central appeal of efficiency and secondary appeals of saving money and saving time.

Sales letters in response to inquiries must be unobtrusive. The inquirer has asked for information, not a sales talk. A high-pressure, blatantly sales-oriented letter will offend, instead of persuade, the reader.

The writer doesn't have to work hard at capturing attention, because the reader has already indicated interest. In Wiseman's letter about the Xeron Stenotyper, the central appeals and secondary appeals to use—efficiency and saving time and money—are obvious, built into the type of machine. The letter merely emphasizes these appeals, gives abundant descriptive detail, and makes it easy for the prospect to act.

Attention getters:
  word play,
  spring and life,
  customers
Focus on motive:
  efficient service

Developing the persuasion:
  descriptive detail
  emotional word
  profit motive
  reader benefit
  sound logic
  emotional appeal
  profit

Action:
  special inducement,
  ease of action

Mr. James Spellman
Spellman Service Center
1809 Chittenden Avenue
Columbus, Ohio 43210

Dear Mr. Spellman:

Cars and customers put on new life in the spring.
Now with spring nearly here, you will be thinking
of your customers' special automobile needs for
spring and summer. And you will be checking your
stock of radiator hoses, fan belts, summer coolants,
plugs, points, and condensers.

As Road King distributor for the Columbus area, I
would like to offer you the special services of our
new consignment program for automobile supplies. We
will stock your shelves with Road King parts, at no
cost to you. You will have on hand a full supply of
quick-turnover parts for automobiles of all makes and
models. You will not pay for the parts until you
sell them. If, after four months, you are not entirely
satisfied with the program, I will pick up the parts
and issue full credit. With a program of this kind
you have all to gain and nothing to lose.

You are already familiar with the high quality of
Road King products and their competitive prices.
The enclosed brochure describes many of the popular
items you can have on your shelves. You will notice
that with most items you will realize a 33% profit.

A supply of free travel kits is also provided with
this spring's consignment. Called "Game Plan," it
has two parts--travel information for the adults and
games and diversions for the children. Your customers
will be delighted.

We believe our new consignment plan will help you not
only maintain but increase the efficient service you
want to give your customers. I would like to call
on you at your station on March 8. If you have any
questions, I will be happy to answer them.

                        Sincerely yours,

                        John Alexander

                        John Alexander
                        Columbus Area Distributor
                        Road King

X E R O N   C O R P O R A T I O N

950 Third Avenue   New York, New York 10022

July 17, 1978

Mr. Howard Hudson
Purchasing Agent
Universal Developments, Inc.
428 Hammock Road
Jersey City, New Jersey 07305

Dear Mr. Hudson:

Here is the information you requested on the new Xeron
Stenotyper. It is a pleasure to send it to you.

This automatic typing unit presents a low-cost system
for fast, reliable production of office documents, forms,
and personalized correspondence which contain portions of
repetitive information. Purchase orders, invoices,
production orders, legal documents, and unlimited paragraph
selection for correspondence are but a few of the many time-
and money-saving applications.

At your convenience, we will be glad to demonstrate the
Xeron Stenotyper to your organization. Just call us at
201-269-8400, and give us a day's notice. We believe
that further investigation on your part will convince you
that this is truly the most versatile automatic typing
system on the market.

Purchase plans, rental plans, and low-cost lease plans are
all available as described on p. 12 of the enclosed brochure.

We appreciate your interest in the versatile Stenotyper. If
we can be of service to you in any way, please let us know.

Sincerely yours,

Daniel Wiseman

Daniel Wiseman
Sales Manager
Automated Equipment

DPW:gh
Enclosure

Institutional Letter

This kind of letter is basically a goodwill letter with a little sales pitch. Instead of trying to sell a particular item, it aims to sell the reader on the whole company. Analyze the letter opposite to see the four stages of the persuasive process and the development of the various appeals.

EXERCISES

1. Assume that you are a sales manager for a large retail clothing store. A private sale for regular customers is to be held prior to its public announcement in the newspapers. Prepare a suitable sales promotion letter.

2. As the owner of Hillsides, a summer resort, you wish to maintain friendly contact with your former guests. Prepare a letter expressing the hope that you may be their host again next summer. Mention the innovations and improvements that have been made for the greater comfort and pleasure of the guests, and suggest the need for early reservations.

3. You are opening a new kind of automobile service station in your community. It is not just a gas pumper, but it provides a special arrangement for picking up cars regularly and keeping them tuned up *before* the expensive breakdown. Prepare a sales promotion letter. In addition to the description of your special service, include the following in your letter: mention of the nationally known brands of items offered in the service station for all types of automobiles, modern equipment, specially trained personnel, reasonable prices, opening date, hours of service, souvenirs during opening week, and the desire to render the best service to the car owners of the community.

4. You are director of a children's summer camp located 50 miles from the city where you live. Prepare a letter to be sent to parents suggesting that they enroll their children as campers for the approaching summer. Include the following and any other information that would be of particular interest to parents of young children: athletic and recreational facilities, educational and social programs, sleeping accommodations, food standards and facilities, counselors, nursing staff, rates, and enrollment procedure.

5. Write an effective sales letter to be sent to home owners urging them to subscribe to *Modern Home*, a monthly magazine devoted to home decoration, maintenance, and improvement.

6. You are manager of Unique Clothiers, Inc., a large retail haberdashery located at 237 Park Street, Pittsburgh, Penn. Your store's specialty is clothing for overweight women. You carry pants, sweaters, blouses, dresses, coats, underwear, nightwear, and ecening wear cut especially for women who ordinarily have great trouble buying clothes that fit well and look good. In addition, you offer expert tailoring

THE LAWSON COMPANY

1400 Tilden Street
Dayton, Ohio 45409

"Everything for the Home and Family"

January 26, 1979

Mr. Gerald Johnson
2078 Tenth Street
Dayton, Ohio 45409

Dear Mr. Johnson:

Welcome to Dayton! We hope that by now you and your
family have got the furniture and things arranged
enough so that you can start looking around to see
what our community has to offer. You will like it.

The Lawson Co. offers itself for your home needs
and shopping pleasure. Ours is one of the largest
department stores in Ohio, especially equipped to
serve the home owner. It may be furniture, clothing,
household furnishings, and supplies. It may be
gardening supplies, paint, or tools. It may be
jewelry or stationery. . . we have it if you need
it. During the years, Lawsons has earned the
reputation of selling the best brands at very
reasonable prices.

You may find it convenient to open a charge account
with us. Let us talk it over when you are in our
store. We are open until 9 p.m. on Tuesdays and
Fridays; on other nights, except Sundays, we are
open until 6 p.m. Plenty of free parking is
available in our parking lot.

Won't you and your family visit us soon? We'll be
happy to meet you and show you around. Please bring
this letter with you and receive a gift from us,
a token of our hospitality and good wishes.

Cordially yours,

Glen Sullivan

Glen Sullivan
Manager

service on any garment sold. You are the only store in your area that offers this specialty.

In order to promote your new fall line, you have obtained a mailing list of 3,000 women living within a forty-mile radius of Pittsburgh who qualify as good prospects for your specialty. Some of them have probably patronized your store in the past, but the great majority have not. Write an effective sales promotion letter to these 3,000 prospects; the desired response will be a trip to your store to see your merchandise. Your letter may embody any sales techniques you think appropriate. Consider, also, the necessity for euphemism somewhere along the line.

7. Write a promotion letter which will appear in *The Open Road*, a travel magazine, as an "open letter to all who've never seen northern California in the fall." The letter will invite readers to the Fall Open House at the Ravella Brothers Mountain View Winery (Santa Sola, California).

The open house, which is free to all, provides daily tours of the winery during which guests can view the crushing vats, the fermentation chambers, and the bottling line. The open house also includes wagon rides through the vineyards during harvesting, hours of wine sampling in the Ravella Mountain View Taste Center, and the general, friendly spirit at Mountain View Winery. your central appeal in this open letter will probably be an emotional one. Select it carefully, and develop it fully.

8. The Bronze Maiden is an exclusive boutique in Palm Springs, California. As the head buyer you have recently completed a trip to the Orient where you purchased an unusual collection of ladies' evening wear and sportswear. Among the items you have purchased are silk stoles and cocktail gowns, seed pearl evening wraps, velvet hostess gowns, embroidered slippers, beaded handbags, enameled bracelets and rings, and jade Buddhas.

For a special promotion you wish to invite all the Bronze Maiden's regular charge-account customers to an Oriental Tea and Fashion Show at which your new collection will be displayed before being put on sale to the general public. Write a persuasive invitation to your regular customers, getting them to attend the Oriental Tea and Fashion Show.

12 Specialized Writing Projects

Job Application
Business Report

Job application letters and reports are special writing projects not quite as common as other kinds of communications in the usual business routine. You may acquire your job without having to write letters, and you may never have to prepare a report. But such communications can be so important to your career that some attention is given here to the fundamentals of job application letters and business reports.

JOB APPLICATION

The most important letters you write may well be those concerned with applying for a job. A few of the many types are illustrated here. Of special importance are the *letter of application*, the *resumé*, and such follow-up letters as the *thank you for the interview* and the letters of *job acceptance* or *job refusal*.

Application Letter

The amount of effort you must put forth to land the job you want will depend largely upon the competition for that job. Depending upon the business climate or the economic cycle, jobs in your field may or may not be plentiful. But really good jobs are always scarce. Blue-chip jobs are won by those candidates who have strong qualifications and who effectively communicate those qualifications. Ability alone is not enough. You must make a prospective employer aware of that ability. Since there are usually several applicants for a position, the letter may be the decisive factor, particularly in whether or not an interview is granted. The letter of application is successful if it results in an interview.

The letter of application has three sections: purpose of the letter, background information, and request for an interview. The background information may be included entirely within the letter itself or it may be given on a separate page, referred to as a "data sheet," "personal information," "resumé," or some similar title. Regardless of how the background information is presented, however, the purpose of the letter is stated in the first paragraph, and an interview is requested in the closing paragraph.

PURPOSE OF THE LETTER.   In the first paragraph state that the letter is an application for a job (it is usually better to apply for a specific position than for an "opening"). Tell how you found out about the job, and explain your reason for wanting it.

BACKGROUND INFORMATION.   Whether you include it in your letter or in a resumé, the background information is made up of several blocks of data.

1. *Personal information*
   Name
   Address and phone number
   Birth date
   Height and weight
   Marital status
   Health
   Willingness to relocate (if applicable)
2. *Education block*
   Specific degree
   Name of school
   Date of graduation
   Overall grade average (if B or higher or if class standing is in the top third or better)
   Specific courses related to the job
   Extracurricular activities
   Academic awards, scholarships, honors
3. *Experience block*
   Any kind of work experience is an asset.
   List jobs in reverse chronological order—most recent first.
      Job title
      Name and address of company
      Dates of employment
      Number of hours per week
      Special responsibilities
4. *Personal interests*
   Activities, interests, and experiences to indicate well-roundedness as an individual. It is best not to include religious or political organizations. Also, do not list activities that might indicate temperamental oddities, such as skydiving, motorcycle racing, and fire eating.
5. *Military block* (if any)
6. *References*

You have two options. Either indicate that references will gladly be provided upon request, or give a list of the names of three or four persons who will speak for you. Include titles and addresses. Be sure to check first with the person you use as a reference.

You may include your background information in the letter or present it in a resumé. The third section of the letter will request an interview.

```
                                        6804 W. Leander Boulevard
                                        Los Angeles, California  90047
                                        October 18, 1978



California Shirt Works
458 Alameda
Los Angeles, California  90029

Attention:  Mr. Jim Cooper

Gentlemen:

I was very pleased to see your advertisement for an experienced
secretary in today's Los Angeles Times.  My qualifications for
such employment are listed below.

     Graduated from Nimitz High School, San Diego, California; received
     secretarial training at Bellamy Business College in San Diego.

     Age 28, married, no children, career-minded.

     Stenographic speed, 160 words per minute; typing speed, 90 words
     per minute.

     Secretary, six years, Palm Textiles, where I am employed at
     present.  Though Palm Textiles is presently headquartered at 1640
     Gable Avenue, Los Angeles, California, 90015, shortly the firm will
     be moving to Georgia.  For this reason I am seeking other employment.
     At present I am secretary to Mr. Lynn Edwards, plant supervisor
     (Telephone:  855-6006).

     Stenographer, two years, Lamar Advertising Co., 736 Welcher Boulevard,
     Los Angeles, California, 90121.  I worked for Mr. Fred R. Gillard,
     credit manager (Telephone:  747-5001).

Please feel free to check with my present employer, Mr. Edwards, who
is eager for me to obtain suitable employment with a reputable firm
before Palm Textiles moves to Georgia.  I believe that he will tell
you that I have the knowledge, experience, ability, personality, and
appearance necessary for the kind of secretary that is an asset to any
organization.

May I be given the opportunity of an interview?

                              Sincerely,

                              Cynthia Trimble

                              Cynthia Trimble
```

REQUEST FOR AN INTERVIEW.   Any firm interested in employing an applicant will want to interview him. In the closing paragraph of the letter of application, therefore, request an interview at the prospective employer's convenience. However, if there are restrictions regarding availability, such as classes or work, say so. If distance makes an interview impractical (for instance, living in Denver and applying for a job in Pittsburgh), suggest some alternative, such as an interview with a local representative. As a final word, be sure to include in this closing paragraph how and when you may be reached.

Solicited Applications

Many times applicants are solicited by employers through the daily classified ads, professional journals, employment agencies, and college placement bureaus. Whether your application is solicited or unsolicited, the basic principles of the letter of application are the same. The main difference is in the beginning paragraph. In the solicited application letter the first sentence should refer specifically to the employer's solicitation. You will ordinarily refer to the source of the solicitation, indicate the specific job for which you are applying, and suggest your major qualifications.

Resumé

If you present your background in a resumé, here are some standard guidelines for format. You may use a unique style of format if you tailor it to the character of the company and the position for which you are applying. For instance, a flamboyant style would be more appropriate for a job in the advertising department than in the accounting department. A sample resumé is given in Figure 12-1.

FORMAT FOR RESUMÉ: GUIDELINES

1. For neatness, maintain a "picture-frame" effect, with one inch or more of white space at top and bottom, left and right.
2. Make sure that your headings and subheadings will be clear to the reader at a glance.
3. The language and form of a resumé must be physically flawless.
4. Usually confine it to a single page in length. Anything longer may be considered wordy and wasteful of the reader's time.
5. When you prepare to mail out more than one application package, do not use carbon copies of a resumé. A carbon copy carries the implication that the neater original has gone elsewhere. If you are sending out many applications, you may wish to use professionally printed resumés.

David Alexander

2727 Miller Court   Age: 22
Oklahoma City, Oklahoma 73069   Height: 6'0"
692-9476   Weight: 186 lbs.
                                           Marital status: Single
                                           Willingness to relocate: Yes

Education

    BBA in Marketing, University of Oklahoma, June 1977
    Top 5% of class, with special courses:

    Business Law   Motivational Psychology
    International Marketing Research International Business Principles
    Overseas Operations Management Economics of Underdeveloped
    International Marketing   Countries
    Multinational Sales Forecasting Communications
      Models   Principles of Operations
    Statistics   Management

    Won Junior Chamber of Commerce Scholarship 1976, 1977
    Member of Marketing Club
    Member of International Relations Club
    Elected Secretary of Student Council
    On Dean's Honor Roll since 1975

Experience

    Assistant to Retail Buyer, Claremont Department Store,
      Oklahoma City, March 1976 to present. Part-time
      duties (3 hrs. a day) included inventory control
      and the processing of purchase orders.
    Worked with Chamber of Commerce, Oklahoma City--customer
      interest survey

Personal Interests

    World affairs, environmental control, tennis, junior
      chamber of commerce, and Little League baseball coach.

References

    Gladly provided upon request.

Figure 12-1

Covering Letter

The resumé presents a detailed, factual, and largely impersonal view of the applicant. It tells the applicant's qualifications for the job. The purpose of the accompanying covering letter is to humanize the applicant and interest the reader. It gives the reader a view of the applicant's motives, goals, personality, and ability to express himself or herself.

The first section of your letter states your purpose, as does the letter with no resumé. For the background section of the letter, you merely highlight your background by mentioning major qualifications and then invite the reader to consider the details in the resumé. Here is a sample letter written to accompany the resumé of David Alexander. The letter is brief, complete, and articulate, and it reveals a warm and sensible personality.

```
                                        2727 Miller Court
                                        Oklahoma City, Oklahoma  73069
                                        March 1, 1978




         Mr. Carl Chapman
         Director of Personnel
         Continental Enterprises, Inc.
         St. Louis, Missouri  63130

         Dear Mr. Chapman:

         With graduation only months away, I would like to apply
         for a position in marketing research with Continental
         Enterprises.  My University of Oklahoma degree will be
         in marketing.  I will finish in the top 5% of my class.

         For the past three years I have been employed part-time
         as an assistant to Gerald Barrows, retail buyer at
         Claremont Department Store in Oklahoma City.  I have also
         worked with the Chamber of Commerce.  The enclosed resumé
         will give you fuller details of these experiences and the
         rest of my background.

         With my college training almost completed, I have anticipated
         this year as a time of beginning.  The career beginning that
         interests me most is one with Continental Enterprises.  May I
         hear from you regarding my qualifications, and come to see you
         at your convenience?

                                 Sincerely yours,

                                 David Alexander

                                 David Alexander
```

Follow-up Letters

If you are especially interested in a position for which you have applied, you can follow it up with another letter. This letter may be sent after you have submitted your application or after the interview. You may even want to write a follow-up letter when you have been told that there is no vacancy at present but that your application will be kept on file and will be considered should a vacancy occur.

If you do not receive an acknowledgment of your application within a week or two, you may write a letter of inquiry. Your note should include the following: the date of your application and the position applied for, a description of your interest in the position and your ability to perform the required duties, and a request to keep your application under consideration.

Here is an application follow-up that could well be worth the time required to write it. It reinforces the candidate's application by keeping her file active, reporting additional experiences that qualify her for the job, and creating an impression of diligence—of knowing what she wants and going after it.

Dear Mr. West:

Since I wrote to you about a junior accounting position in February, I have completed three additional courses in accounting and have been doing some part-time individual income tax work for Mr. John Page of Page Products.

Please keep my application in the active file and let me know when you need another junior accountant.

Sincerely,

The letter you send after the interview should express your pleasure in meeting the interviewer and your appreciation of the courtesies extended. Include any additional facts you may have omitted in the interview.

Dear Mr. Bennett:

Thank you for granting me an interview yesterday.

After talking with you about Fleming Industries, I am all the more interested in the position of junior accountant. I appreciate the careful consideration you are giving my application.

Sincerely,

A job acceptance letter is fairly easy to write, since it is a good-news message. As in any good-news message, begin with the good news, the acceptance, then follow with necessary details, and end cordially with a pleasant anticipation of the time when you are to report to work.

Dear Mr. Johnson:

I am happy to accept the position of credit investigator with Atlas Finance Company.

Here are the security-clearance forms and health record. I'll bring a photostatic copy of my birth certificate when I report for work on Monday morning, June 1.

Thank you for introducing me to some of the staff when I talked with you last week. I will enjoy working with them.

                         Sincerely,

The job-refusal letter is a matter of standard courtesy and diplomacy. An employer likes to know as quickly as possible whether a job has been accepted. Companies also like to know the reasons why an offer has been declined. Be courteous and diplomatic; you may want a job with the company later.

Dear Mr. Timmons:

The interview with you was one of the most interesting I have had in my search for tax-accounting work. I was much impressed by the efficiency and high morale of your accounting department.

As you indicated, opportunities are especially promising for those who are mainly interested in costs. But since my primary interest is in tax accounting, I have taken a job with Fleming Industries, where my responsibilities will be entirely in tax accounting.

Thank you for the time you spent with me.

                         Sincerely,

The reference in the letter above to the other interviews is a good way to begin breaking the bad news—to lead up to the statement that the candidate has accepted a job with another company. In the second sentence the applicant reminds the reader of knowledge gained in the interview—a compliment to the interviewer. After these remarks, the applicant can easily give reasons for the refusal; state the refusal in polite, positive language; and part with an expression of gratitude.

Another follow-up situation occurs when you receive acknowledgment of your application without an immediate offer of employment or invitation to an interview. Such a notice indicates that your application is being kept on file and may be considered when a vacancy occurs. Your follow-up letter after receiving such an acknowledgment should express appreciation, should affirm your interest in becoming associated with the firm, and should close with the hope that your application will be given favorable consideration should a vacancy occur.

EXERCISES

1. Prepare a personal resumé suitable for inclusion in any job application package you might write upon graduating. If you are not yet in your last year, assume that you are so that you can offer yourself to a prospective employer as a degree holder.

2. Determine the kind of job you would like to be seeking as you approach graduation, and write an effective covering letter to accompany your resume. Address this letter to the appropriate person in the company you are writing to. Remember, your letter must make you appealing enough to receive an interview.

3. Select from a newspaper or an appropriate industry periodical the advertisement for the job that sounds most appealing to you. Write a letter applying for the job.

4. Last Wednesday you learned that a representative from Continental Products, Inc. (a firm you'd like to work for) was making an unscheduled visit to your campus placement center. You quickly arranged for an interview; met Mr. Bullard, the CP representative; and expressed your interest in working for the firm (the specific kind of job is up to you). At the end of what seemed to be a mutually satisfying interview, Bullard gave you a long application form and asked you to complete it and mail it to him "with an extensive covering letter expressing your plans and your short-range and long-range goals." He indicated that he'd be in touch with you within several weeks of receiving your letter and completed form.

   Now your problem is to write that covering letter. Remember, this is not to be an ordinary covering letter. Bullard wants a good deal of specific information. It's obvious he also wants to see how well you express yourself in writing at length.

5. Write a letter to Mr. Bullard of problem 4 above thanking him for the interview.

6. You have gotten the job with Continental Products to begin September 1. Write a letter of acceptance.

THE BUSINESS REPORT

Skill in writing clear, well-organized, thorough reports may well be a major factor in determining how far a businessperson will go in a chosen profession. Having good ideas and suggestions is not enough; the person in business must be able to put these ideas and suggestions in writing so that he or she can communicate them to others in higher positions who can put the ideas and suggestions into action. And that gives us a definition of a report. It is a written communication conveying business information about research or a situation from one area of business to another to assist in making decisions.

In all but the smallest of businesses, no one person can do all the work. Other minds must be enlisted to help carry responsibility. The efforts of each person sharing that responsibility must be coordinated so that the business can operate smoothly and meet its objectives. The business report is one of the main means by which those efforts are coordinated.

Most business reports go up the chain of command in an organization. Members of a department write reports for their supervisor so that he or she can coordinate their efforts and, in turn, report the department's activities to the executive who coordinates the efforts of the various departments—and so on up the chain of command. Other reports go across the organization from one staff member to another, or from one department to another. Others go down the chain, informing the staff of decisions made or further steps to be taken. Still other reports go outside the organization, like the report from an advertising agency to a client informing him of progress on a new advertising campaign. Reports can come from the outside in, such as reports from management consultants who are retained to study a company problem.

Regardless of direction, however, business reports are vital to the coordination of objectives and activities. Effective reports are necessary to all but the most minor decisions in business. Poor reports will cause confusion. Write effective reports, and you may be called upon for higher responsibilities.

Reports serve three basic functions. All reports convey fact (by definition, they must). Some reports also interpret the facts that they convey. And some reports that interpret also make recommendations in light of those interpretations. Within these three basic functions there are many specific kinds of reports. There are periodic, departmental, project, progress, laboratory, field, area, library, and inspection reports, as well as combinations of some types (such as laboratory-library), to name a few. Reports can include subjects such as profit-and-loss statements, market analyses, stock averages, production figures, hours of work, progress on certain projects, employee turnover, evaluation of an ongoing process, agenda and minutes of meetings, or summaries and abstracts. These and many other kinds of information are exchanged continually in carrying on business.

Suppose, for example, that a bicycle manufacturing company wants to diversify its production because the current market has become severely competitive, and the faddish nature of bicycles makes the future uncertain. Should the company go into lawn mowers, outboard motors, motorbikes, or various sports novelties? What must the company know before it launches an expensive, new production project? It must know, first of all, everything about itself and its financial and productive capacity for expansion. It must have knowledge about the market—what products are needed, what competition exists, what distribution channels are available. When we consider the requirements of such an undertaking, the task seems impossible. Yet such activity takes place every day in modern business. Every responsible position in business requires a person who can recognize the need for action, analyze the need, and contribute to the final solution. Finally, people must learn how to record their actions in words—words that will be intelligible to those who read the reports. This is the job of the report writer. Its importance cannot be overemphasized.

Steps in Writing a Report

Every report, except the briefest and most routine message, requires a series of steps:

1. Recognize and define the problem.
2. Gather the information.
3. Organize the findings.
4. Draw conclusions and make recommendations.
5. Write a first draft.
6. Use illustrative aids.
7. Revise the report.
8. Put the report into proper format.

We will consider each of these steps in detail.

Define the Problem

Definition of the problem is usually begun for you by the one who requested the report. Except for reports you initiate yourself, every report begins with an authorization. Either you are asked bs the person in charge to write a report on a certain subject, or the responsibilities of your job require that you report on certain things. If a superior has requested the report, he or she, no doubt, has specified the purpose. If your superior did not make clear what was expected, ask for a clarification of the request. If you initiate the report, you have a reason for developing it. Whatever the situation, you should write down, clearly and accurately, the purpose of the report. Four kinds of tests can help you define the problem.

FIVE W's AND AN H. Ask "who, what, when, where, why, and how?" This kind of pinpointing will help you to break a large problem into smaller ones and to see them all clearly. Studying the parts leads to studying the whole.

Usually not all of these six questions will apply to a specific problem, but asking them helps to clarify the problem. For example, suppose your boss asks you to write a report to "find out what our people think about our new system of short lunch period and early checkout." Ask the five w's and an h.

Who?   The memo says "our people," but whom does "our people" include? Whom does it rule out? Does it include executives or only nonexecutive staff? Does it include part-time employees and seasonal help or only permanent full-time employees? Does the boss want the opinions of the people in the suburban branch, or only those in the home office? All these questions need to be answered if the report is to be researched effectively.

What?   The boss wants opinions: "what our people think about the new system." Does this statement include opinions only of the new system or opinions comparing the old system with the new? Does it also include suggestions for changes in the lunch-break system?

When?   This question isn't central to the definition of this particular problem, except that your report should state how long after the policy revision the opinions were measured.

Where?   The answer is self-evident.

Why?   This question raises the issue of whether your report need concern itself with the reasons for the opinions you elicit. If the memo isn't clear on this point, you had better consult the boss. Also, ask why the boss wants the report. The answer may affect any recommendations you make.

How?   This question is obviously not relevant to the present problem, though asking it of yourself might suggest a later study on how best to comply with employees' wishes and company requirements about short lunch period and early checkout if the new policy proves unsatisfactory.

Asking the five w's and an h helps you to define the problem and then to gather information for your report.

MEANINGFUL TITLE.   A report title should clearly indicate what is covered. To determine how well you recognize the problem, write a title for the report. Remember that you can't say enough in a word or two to cover the scope of the report. This brief title, for example, gives no definition or sense of direction, but indicates only a broad area of interest:

The New Lunch Break and Checkout System

You need more definition. A better title would read:

Attitudes of Nonexecutive Employees toward the New System of Short Lunch Break and Early Checkout

If you have clearly defined the problem, you will be able to write a clear indication of the direction of your report.

YOUR READERSHIP.   Identify the reader who is to be your primary audience. How deeply should you go into your subject to satisfy that audience? How technical or nontechnical should you be? What attitudes toward your subject does the audience have? What does your reader expect? These considerations are important because the purpose of the report is to help the reader make decisions.

WORKING OUTLINE.   You should be able to break your well-defined subject into natural subdivisions. You may not know all the parts of the problem until you've actually done some research, but you should be able to write down several related areas that you will need to investigate in gathering material for the report. Write them down. If they don't give you directions for beginning your systematic research, go back and clarify the request and the problem.

Gathering Information

Once you have defined the purpose of the report, the audience, and the scope, you are ready to begin gathering data. Much of the information you will need will probably already be available—in books, pamphlets, magazines, and other pieces of writing.

Uncovering this recorded material is called *secondary research* (or *library research*, since most of this investigation is done in the library). For many reports, however, secondary research will not be enough. For current or local situations never before examined, you may have to do your own *primary research* (or firsthand research). Primary research includes observation, experimentation, and interviewing. Let's look in detail at these two methods of research.

SECONDARY RESEARCH—READ.   The first step is to read up on your subject. Most businesses keep a shelf of handy reference books containing information likely to be needed on the job. If the information you need isn't close at hand, you have to turn to the library. Most libraries are standardized, with holdings of three principle kinds: reference works, books in a general collection, and periodicals. These holdings may be packaged in various forms—books, documents, bound periodicals, single periodicals (if current), and microfilm.

In the search for published information, consult reference works first. This brief list suggests just a few of the enormous variety of reference books available.

1. *Business and trade directories* provide information about people, organizations, and activities in various trades and industries. Among the best of such directories are *Thomas' Register of American Manufacturers; Kelley's Directory of Merchants, Manufacturers and Shippers of the World;* and the *N.W. Ayer & Sons Directory of Newspapers and Periodicals* (which also provides gazetteer information on every city and town in the United States in which a newspaper is published).
2. *Biographical registers* offer information about noteworthy people. There are the *Dictionary of American Biography* (which covers persons deceased who con-

tributed significantly to American life); *Who's Who in America* (which covers the living); *Who's Who* (which covers important people in other countries); *Current Biography* (a series of monthly reports, bound into yearly volumes, on newly prominent people); various regional registers like *Who's Who in the Midwest, Who's Who in the West, Who's Who in New York;* and registers of important people in various fields, like *Poor's Register of Directors and Executives, Who's Who in Commerce and Industry,* the *Official Congressional Directory,*and the *American Architects Directory.*

3. *Encyclopedias* provide general background information on a subject. Standard general encyclopedias are the *Americana,* the *Britannica,* and the *Columbia.* There are specialized encyclopedias like the *Encyclopedia of the Social Sciences* (which provides good coverage in economics, law, government, politics, penology, and social work, among other areas) and the *Encyclopedia Canadiana* (which covers aspects of Canadian life, economy, history, and culture).

4. *Yearbooks* give information on recent trends and events. Some yearbooks are annual supplements to encyclopedias, like the *Americana Annual* and the *Britannica Book of the Year.* Others are annual records of events in specific fields, like the *Sales Management Survey of Buying Power* (an annual supplement to *Sales Management Magazine) and The United States in World Affairs* (which surveys U.S. international involvements during the preceding year). Many other yearbooks are published by professional, trade, and industrial groups, and by foreign nations.

5. *Handbooks* offer detailed facts and statistics on specialized subjects. These include the *Accountant's Handbook,* the *Business Executive's Handbook,* the *Corporate Treasurer's and Controller's Handbook,* the *Sales Promotion Handbook,* the *Personnel Handbook,* the *Foreman's Handbook,* and the *Handbook of Industrial Relations.*

6. *Almanacs* contain facts and statistics. There are general almanacs like the *World Almanac and Book of Facts* and *Whitaker's Almanac* (a British publication strong on Commonwealth organizations and institutions) and specialized almanacs like the *Economic Almanac.*

7. *Statistical source books and census reports* provide information on population, manufacturing, housing, transportation, argriculture, and other areas of American economy and society. The most widely used among these are the annual *Statistical Abstract of the United States,* the annual *County and City Data Book,* and the decennial reports of the United States Census.

8. *Dictionaries* give definitions and help in clarifying terms. There are unabridged dictionaries like *Webster's Third* and the *Oxford English Dictionary* (in thirteen volumes), desk dictionaries like *Webster's New Collegiate* and *Webster's New World,* and specialized business dictionaries like the *Encyclopedic Dictionary of Business* and the *Dictionary of Business and Industry* (a work that defines some 45,000 commercial and technical terms).

9. *Gazetteers* offer data on places around the world. Among the most useful gazetteers are the *Columbia Gazetteer of the World, Webster's Geographical Dictio-*

nary, and the *Directory of Post Offices* (which, for the United States, provides information on the service areas of all the nation's post offices).

10. *Atlases* contain maps and accompanying information. For American economic coverage, the best is the *Rand McNally Commercial Atlas* (whose maps and data are updated every year).

There are even reference books to reference books, such as Murphey's *How and Where to Look It Up* and Winchell's *Guide to Reference Books*.

The general collection of any library is where most of its books are kept. To use a library's general collection, you turn first to the card catalog, where the collection is indexed (usually by author, title, and subject). The call number at the upper left-hand corner of a catalog card is your key to locating a book.

Periodicals, the third type of library holding, are the best source of current information, information that hasn't had time to find its way into books. Here are just a few of the many indexes for finding articles published in periodicals:

1. *General indexes*—the *Reader's Guide to Periodical Literature* indexes periodical articles by author, title, and subject. The *International Index to Periodicals* indexes articles from more scholarly periodicals than does the *Reader's Guide*.
2. *Specialized indexes*—the *Agricultural Index*, the *Engineering Index*, the *Index to Legal Periodicals*, and the *Business Periodicals Index*.
3. *Indexes to pamphlets and bulletins*—the *United States Government Publications Monthly Catalog*, the *Public Affairs Information Service Index* (PAIS), and the *Supplements to the Vertical File Service Catalog*.

In addition to general libraries there are many special libraries maintained by trade associations, professional schools, chambers of commerce, foundations, labor unions, and companies themselves. Access to these libraries is not always general, but permission to use these special collections can often be obtained upon request. The better special libraries around the country are listed in the guidebook *Special Library Resources*.

Once you have found a source of information you need, you must extract and record that information for use in your report. As you gather your information, keep the following guidelines in mind.

GUIDELINES—NOTETAKING

1. Try to divide the subject into main headings. Investigate these main headings first.
2. When you locate a promising source, search out the information you need by consulting the table of contents and then the index. If the source has neither, you must skim it very carefully.
3. Take notes on material you need. The following tips are useful in taking notes.

a. *Follow major topics.* Take only notes that come under one of your major topics. You may, of course, decide that you need to add one or two topics to your list, but don't let your list get too long. Avoid irrelevant and unreliable information.

b. *Use note cards.* Take notes on cards (usually 4 x 6) labeled with the major topic at the top of each card. By using note cards, you can easily add new material, throw out useless material, and reorganize what you have collected.

c. *List the source.* At the bottom of a note card identify the source from which the notes are taken. This can be done by a number system or by writing the name of the author.

d. *Give page number.* If there is material on the card—quotations, exact figures, or information or ideas not widely known among educated people—that will require a footnote, be sure to write the page number where this material is found. You will need the page number or numbers for writing the footnotes.

e. *Separate your topics.* Notes for different major topics should always be put on different cards.

f. *Separate your topics.* Notes for different major topics should always be put on different cards.

g. *Identify the kind of note.* Distinguish on the card just what kind of note it is—how close it is to a complete passage or an exact quotation. You will need to know this when you work the note into the paper. Usually there are four kinds of notes:

(1) Direct quotation (must be exact)—use quotation marks.
(2) Paraphrase—can be labeled "par."
(3) Summary—can be labeled "sum."
(4) Your own comment—brackets are useful.

PRIMARY RESEARCH—OBSERVE, EXPERIMENT, INTERROGATE. In *observational research* you systematically witness a situation and record the significant facts about it. Observation will probably be one of your sources of information in writing reports such as one on what effects the noise in the shop has on the attitudes and efficiency of workers.

In *experimental research* you set up test cases under uniform conditions, add a variable, and note the results. Any change is assumed to be due to the new factor. If your project is to study the effects of incentive pay on clerk-typists, you may wish to set up an experiment. You separate the clerk-typists into two groups that are about equal in experience, skill, and production rates. Then you place one group on an incentive-pay basis for a time and note the difference in production of the two groups. If the incentive pay is the only variable, it has caused the difference.

Experimentation, if well controlled, produces highly accurate and reliable results. The method is useful, however, only where the object or the condition under study is susceptible to manipulation and control by the researcher. Such conditions do not often prevail in business-report problems.

In *interrogational research* you ask people questions. In method, interrogational research can range from an informal chat over coffee to the formal interviewing of a department store manager, to a survey of 10,000 car drivers. The techniques of interrogation vary with the method used. Preparation for effective questioning, however, remains the same.

First, you should determine that interrogation will be an effective way to get the information you need. The complexities of the interrogational process make it, on the whole, the least reliable kind of research. While it is not unreliable, it is more susceptible to error and distortion. Usually, however, interrogation is the necessary method for ascertaining motives, intentions, preferences, and reasons. Report writers in search of this kind of information, therefore, sharpen their interrogational techniques and proceed the only way they can—by asking questions.

Before asking questions, you must carefully determine whom to ask, how to phrase your questions, and how to transmit those questions to your respondents. If you need only one person's answers, or those of a small group, whom to ask becomes self-evident; but if you want to measure the buying motives of 50,000 consumers, whom to ask becomes a complex problem. Because you can't ask them all, you have to take a sample that will still be typical. You have to phrase your questions to allow for differences in interests, background, and ability to understand. How to transmit your questions is essentially a problem of accessibility. Can you get to see all your respondents face to face? Or must you use a less direct means of communication, like the telephone or the mail? You must use the most practicable method.

As you carry out your research, regardless of the research techniques you use, keep complete and accurate reference notations. If you use printed materials, keep a bibliography. If you conduct interviews, be sure to be consistent and careful in identifying who said what. Even though careful documentation may seem to take extra time, it will save time in the long run. Since the report must include any sources used in its preparation, an accurate list is essential.

Organize the Findings

You have collected the information you expect to use in your report. You have a small stack of cards on which you have made notes from reading, a stack on which you jotted down notes from interviews, and perhaps a batch of questionnaires that were completed by interviewers. Now there are two immediate steps ahead of you: (1) to analyze the material and (2) to prepare a working outline to write from.

Analyze the information collected. Which parts of the information are most significant to developing the stated purpose of the report? How are these parts significant? Select only the information pertinent to the specific purpose under consideration. Eliminate any information that is, upon closer analysis, clearly irrelevant. You might file less significant information for future reference. The selected information will compose the body of the report, and the other parts will be taken from the body of the report.

Prepare a working outline to write from. Adjust the outline you developed in analyzing the problem prior to research. Each of the questions raised in that outline has been answered now. You may find that your outline, as you fit your findings into it, needs some revision to allow those findings to relate more logically to one another. This is nothing to be concerned about; a working outline should not be rigid. During research you may have found information you didn't anticipate earlier; it must now be worked into the outline. Perhaps some information you anticipated and found proves to be unnecessary; it must be trimmed. The process of fitting your findings into the working outline will also reveal any contradictions or inconsistencies that need to be resolved. Gaps in your information may also be revealed, pointing to the need for further research.

Draw Conclusions and Make Recommendations

Often a report requires conclusions and recommendations. On the basis of the information collected, the writer draws conclusions and formulates recommendations. Generally any investigation will result in a conclusion, which may be nothing more than the recognition of a need for further investigation. Conclusions reached should be arranged in order from the most important to the least important. If an investigation reveals a need for recommendations, the writer formulates these recommendations and includes them within the report. Conclusions and recommendations should be presented at the same point within a report and identified by a heading: "Conclusions" or "Recommendations." For an example, see the report on p. 296 to Thomas Munson of the Ohio Department of Highways. Any conclusion reached and any recommendation suggested should be based solely on the evidence offered in the report.

Write a First Draft

Report writing is divided into these steps: getting ideas on paper, writing headings, writing introductory material, writing a title, and supplying identifying information.

GET YOUR IDEAS ON PAPER.   In writing a report, follow the outline prepared during the planning stage. Write as rapidly as you can. Get your ideas on paper; a blank sheet of paper is frustrating. At this stage don't worry too much about spelling a certain word correctly, writing a sentence in a special way, punctuation, mechanics, or organizing the material in any final order. All these things can be corrected during revision. Right now the big issue is to get the ideas on paper.

Develop each point of the outline enough to supply evidence, explanation, and justification for any conclusions and recommendations you make. The writer who has a reputation for knowledge in a certain field may not need to include as much supporting material as the unknown writer. It is a good idea, however, to give adequate support for conclusions and recommendations, regardless of your status.

Include only material relevant to the specific subject of the report. Sometimes you may be tempted to bring in side issues discovered during investigation and research. Put the temptation aside. If you have uncovered some information of value to your employer or the company, present it in a separate report.

WRITE HEADINGS.   Once the body of the report is written, you can analyze the content and write final headings to identify various parts of the material. If you divided the report subject into headings during research you may use these headings, or a modification of them, in the final report. The outline, whether formal or informal, should also aid you to determine headings for parts of the report.

Headings are perhaps the major difference between reports and other compositions. They help to subdivide the material for a comprehensive listing in the table of contents and thus provide a quick reference to specific sections of the report. A reader interested in only one or two sections of the report can rapidly locate these sections.

WRITE INTRODUCTORY MATERIAL.   After writing the body of the report, you will be thoroughly familiar with its actual content and better able to write an adequate introductory section. Include a brief statement of the main purpose, the main points of the body of the report, and conclusions and recommendations. In a longer report the conclusions and recommendations may also make up the final portion of the report.

WRITE A TITLE.   Perhaps the last step will be to write a title. You may wish to write a possible title at an earlier stage, especially if such a title will help you keep on the subject as you write. Evaluate that title carefully in view of what the report actually says. If necessary, change the title so that it clearly identifies the report so that a person could retrieve it at a later date from files. Most reports are kept on file, by title, for future reference; thus it is essential that the title clearly identify the report.

SUPPLY IDENTIFYING INFORMATION.   Any report should include identifying information. While there is no standard list of needed identification, there are identifying facts that should always be included, such as the name of the person or persons writing the report and the date. Often the name of the person or group to whom the report is directed are included. You should supply any identifying information you think is necessary, depending on the purpose of the report.

Use Illustrative Aids

The picture that is worth a thousand words can certainly help make your report clear, interesting, and significant. Preparation for writing may have taken several months, but your aim when writing is to communicate your material completely and quickly. When you can report material in a graph, a chart, or a table, do so. Give the reader the best help you can. Imagine trying to report in sentence form all the detail that is included in a balance sheet or a profit-and-loss statement. Or imagine the problems of a designer in using only words to describe a new emission control system. Graphs, tables, charts, photographs, diagrams, and maps can all serve to illustrate a report.

Graphs are presentations of data in diagram form. They can give the reader sharp pictures of significant statistical relationships and comparative values. The *line graph*, the *pie graph*, and the *bar graph* are the most common types of graphs used.

Line graphs are especially useful in representing changes over a series of short time intervals (such as monthly sales figures for a year or the turnover in personnel over several years). The line graph in Figure 12-2 shows the fluctuations in the Consumer Price Index from January 1977 to January 1978. The January 1978 figure of 187.2 means that products that consumers bought for $100 in 1967 now cost $187.20.

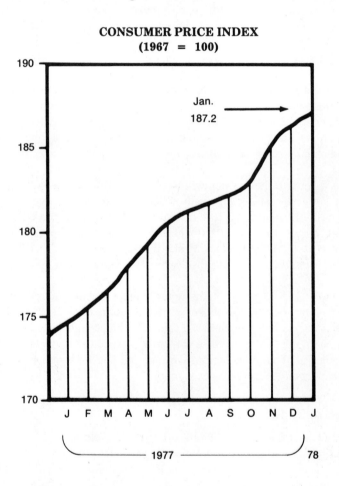

CONSUMER PRICE INDEX
(1967 = 100)

Figure 12-2   Sample Line Graph

Pie graphs are used to display the distribution of parts of a whole. Each slice of the pie constitutes a percentage or part. As in Figure 12-3, the pie must total 100% of something, and the caption tells what that something is. The first slice of the pie starts at 12:00 and the graph is read clockwise. The first slice is the largest slice, the second slice is second largest, and so forth.

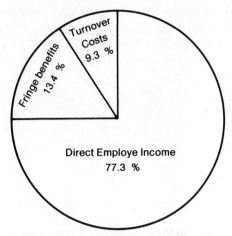

Distribution of Office Payroll Dollar

Figure 12-3   Sample Pie Graph

The *bar graph* is probably the most effective device for comparing quantities (such as total oil production for each of three states in a previous year or the characteristics of residents in an area). Figure 12-4 illustrates a simple bar graph.

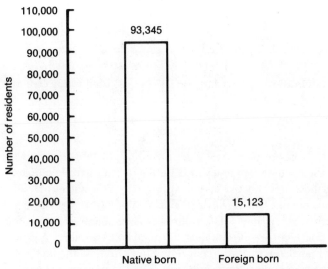

Number of residents in Plainfield on January 1, 1978, classified by nativity.

Figure 12-4   Sample Bar Graph

Many variations of graphs are possible. For instance, a frequency curve of weekly earnings is illustrated by a line graph in Figure 12-5. In Figure 12-6 the same frequency distribution is shown by a bar graph. The line graph in Figure 12-7 includes a trend line with a comparison of output of services over a ten-year period.

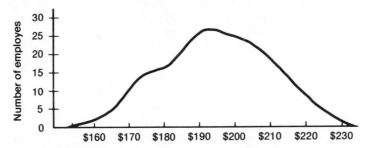

Frequency curve for the distribution of earnings of 100 semiskilled employes of Fleming Industries for one week in 1977.

Figure 12-5   Line Graph

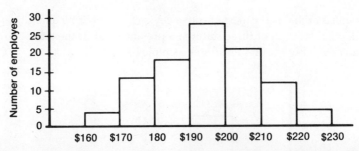

Frequency distribution of earnings of 100 semiskilled employes of Fleming Industries for one week in 1977.

Figure 12-6   Bar Graph

A *table* is a display of numerical data in columns. A table can be very effective in laying before the reader a frequency distribution or a statistical comparison. The table in Figure 12-8 illustrates effective layout, appropriate title, and clearly labeled headings for the vertical columns and the horizontal rows of items.

Charts can be used to show relationships between nonquantitative items. The *static chart* and the *flow chart* are the two most common kinds of charts. A typical static chart is a diagram of labeled boxes with connecting lines to show the hierarchy of authority within a company. A typical flow chart would trace a piece of raw material through a manufacturing process—from chunk of metal through milling, trepanning, lathing, and drilling to hydraulic landing gear tube.

Diagrams, photographs, and *maps* are other possible ways of illustrating data. Just keep several principles in mind concerning all illustrative aids. Don't use an illustration for its own sake; its purpose is to clarify and enhance. Make any illustration as simple as it can be and still serve its purpose. Label all relevant parts clearly, and use a precise caption. Tie the illustration into your written text.

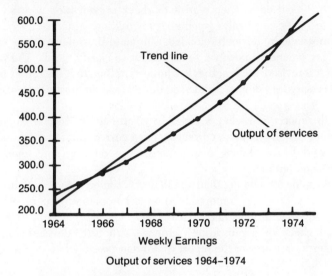

Figure 12-7   Line Graph with Trend Line

TABLE 8

A Comparison of Annual Cost per Employe of Medical Insurance Policies Submitted by Seven Companies May 1, 1978

Company	Plan 1 $10,000 Maximum Annual Coverage	Plan 2 $15,000 Maximum Annual Coverage
Allegheny	$325.00	$450.00
ATA Life	350.00	475.00
Cleveland Mutual	375.00	492.50
Great Lakes General	315.50	445.50
Midwest Life	380.50	480.60
National Security	415.00	503.00
Surety, Inc.	308.40	403.28

Figure 12-8   Sample Table

Revise the Report

The report should be revised. Read it through several times, looking each time for specific needed corrections. For example, read the report one time to check the correctness of technical data. Then read it to check organization and development. Read it again to check mechanics (spelling, punctuation, grammar). Conciseness is important but meaning should not be clouded. Eliminate all irrelevant data. Use graphs, charts, and tables, whenever possible, to replace or to clarify words. The report may grow shorter as it is revised, but length is less important than that the report includes all information necessary for complete understanding. Meaning must not be sacrificed for brevity.

In writing all reports, use what is generally identified as "formal language." Use complete sentences, good grammar, correct spelling, correct punctuation, and effective word choice. Avoid the use of slang, contractions, clipped terms (*auto, phone, TV*), and colloquial words and phrases.

Put the report aside for a while; then reread it. Ask someone to read it and comment on its effectiveness. Read the report aloud or ask someone else to do so. These techniques may reveal additional needed revisions.

Make a final check of organization, sentence structure, development of ideas, spelling, mechanics—any area of the report that might possibly have a flaw that would reduce clearness.

Proper Format

Write the final draft of the report. All technical reports should be typewritten. Be sure to proofread the copy that is to be submitted to an instructor or employer to catch any typographical or other errors you might have overlooked. Correct any errors and, if necessary, retype the report; the final draft should contain no errors.

Numerous forms may be used to organize and present the information in a report. Some companies require certain forms for reports and an employee of that company would be expected to use the appropriate form. If no form is specified, choose the one that seems best suited to a clear presentation of the material in a given report. Any report must have a logical organization if it is to achieve its basic reason for being: to communicate.

The basic plan of a report will usually include the following parts in the order listed.

Title or subject
Summary—gives the main points of the report
Introduction or background—explains briefly any information needed to understand the report
Body—presents all the facts of the report in detail
Conclusions
Recommendations
Appendix—when applicable
Bibliography—when applicable

Let's look at each of these parts in more detail.

TITLE.   The title of a report must give an accurate and comprehensive identification of the subject or content of the report. Since the title is the first thing a reader sees and it is the clue to finding a specific report after it has been filed, great care should be taken in titling a report. Usually the title should be the last step in writing the report.

SUMMARY.   The summary is a concise presentation of the main points of the report, conclusions, and recommendations. If the information is not included elsewhere, the summary may include the date when the information of the report was requested and the name of the person requesting the report, although this material usually appears on a page with the report title.

INTRODUCTION.   The introduction of a brief report may be used for various purposes. It should include any background information needed to explain the discussion. It may list the main topics of the discussion to follow, it may list references, or it may mention any assistance received in preparing the report. The intended reader should be a major consideration in determining the extent of the introduction. Include the problem and the purpose here.

BODY.   The discussion is the detailed presentation of all the facts and details of the investigation. Therefore, it is most important that this section be organized clearly and logically. It is the heart, or core, of the report. Paragraphs should be well developed. Transition between ideas, in both sentences and paragraphs, should show clearly the relationship of these ideas. Meaning can be made clearer by dividing the content into such major areas as theory, procedure, history of the subject, apparatus, or others. It is also good practice to use subject headings to identify the areas of discussion. Put footnoted material into proper form.

FOOTNOTES.   Footnotes are used in business reports for either of two reasons: (1) to elaborate on something in the text if that elaboration in the text would be digressive, or (2) to give the source of a piece of information in the text. Footnotes should be numbered consecutively throughout the paper and placed at the bottom of the page on which the cited material occurs (or, if your reader prefers, in one list at the end of the paper). The first footnote for a source must be complete with author, title, and all facts of publication. Later references to that footnote can be abbreviated. Follow these rules for the format of footnotes:

FOOTNOTES—GUIDELINES

1.   Set the footnotes off from the rest of the page by typing a 1½-inch dash at the left margin, single spaced after the last line on the page. Double-space after typing this line.

2. Indent five spaces, and number each footnote consecutively by typing a superior figure at the beginning of the footnote.
3. Single-space each footnote, but double-space between footnotes.
4. Type the name of the author, if any, in a first name, last name sequence.
5. Indicate the complete title of the cited reference. Put quotation marks around the titles of magazine articles, sections of books, and newspaper columns. Underline the titles of books, magazines, and newspapers.
6. After the complete title of the book, put the city where it was published, the name of the publisher, and the date of publication. Indicate the edition, if other than the first.
7. After the complete title of magazines and newspapers, put the date of publication.
8. End each footnote with the page number of the cited material.

The following sample footnotes illustrate common forms.

Book with one author:

   [1] Charles P. Blankenship, *History of Industry in Kentucky* (Chicago: Palmer Publishers, 1974), p. 78.

Book with more than one author:

   [2] E. Bryant Phillips and Sylvia Lane, *Personal Finance*, 2nd ed. (New York: John Wiley & Sons, Inc., 1969), p. 234.

Magazine or periodical:

   [3] Henry Roberts, "Univac Flies with United," *Business Week*, December 25, 1970, p. 34.
   [4] Carol J. Loomis, "For the Utilities, It's a Fight for Survival," *Fortune*, Vol. XCI, No. 3 (March, 1975), p. 98.

Newspaper:

   [5] Dana L. Spitzer, "Negro Teachers Tell of Job Losses," St. Louis *Post-Dispatch*, July 1, 1970, Sec. D, p. 1.
   [6] "Wall Street Slippage," *Christian Science Monitor*, April 28, 1978, p. 2.

Explanatory material:

   [7] You can place the credit terms either before or after the resale or promotion. If before, the reader is more likely to notice them; if after, you seem to be stressing the you attitude rather than "what's in it for me."

Bulletin, Pamphlet:

   [8] U. S. Bureau of the Census. *Statistical Abstract of the United States*, 1975, 96th ed. (Washington, D. C., U. S. Government Printing Office, 1975), p. 345.

Interview:

[9] John Jeffries, Executive of Regional Division of Continental Hotels, November 2, 1977.

Second References: Use a shortened form, usually the author's last name and the page number.

[10] Roberts, p. 35.

CONCLUSIONS AND RECOMMENDATIONS.   In a brief report the conclusions and the recommendations, if any, are given in the summary only. In a longer report the main conclusions and the recommendations are given in the summary, and the detailed explanation of conclusions and recommendations is given as the last section of the report.

APPENDIX.   Often even a relatively brief report will include an appendix and a bibliography. The appendix includes items such as detailed graphs, charts, or maps that are necessary for a complete understanding of a report. The information from these items may be summarized within the body of the report. Generally, all illustrative material is placed in the appendix except for material needed to make a point immediately clear, which should be placed within the body of the report.

BIBLIOGRAPHY.   If a report includes many references to sources, a bibliographical list of these references is usually included as a separate part of the report. If a report includes only a few references, these can be identified in a footnote or within the text of the report. In a single report the method used should be consistent. If a footnote is used for the first reference, use footnotes for all references in the report. A list of sources, such as the one shown in Figure 12-13, should be added as a back section to any report for which you needed to consult at least several published sources. Your reader will probably be interested in these sources too. The following rules and examples should be followed in preparing a report bibliography.

BIBLIOGRAPHY—GUIDELINES

1. List the items in the bibliography alphabetically by the author's last name.
2. Type the heading "Bibliography" or "List of Sources."
3. Triple-space between the heading and the first reference. Single-space each reference, and double-space between references. If a reference requires more than one line, indent the second line (and each succeeding line) five spaces.
4. If an author has written more than one of your sources, type a five-space line in place of his or her name for each item after the first.
5. When the author is unknown, alphabetize the reference by its title.
6. End each reference to a magazine, journal, or other multi-articled source with page indicators.

The parts of this basic plan can be adapted to most reports—whether the brief informal report or the longer formal report. The longer report will usually require additional parts to the basic plan.

TYPICAL REPORTS

Short Informal Report

A short informal report usually deals with a very limited subject. It is generally written as a reply to a specific request. Periodic reports and progress reports often are presented as informal reports. They may use the form of a letter or an interoffice memorandum.

LETTER FORM.   An informal report in letter form is addressed to a specific person who usually is not a part of the writer's own company. (See Figure 12-9.) The letter includes the standard parts of a business letter: heading, date, inside address, salutation, body, complimentary close, and signature. The letter also may include an attention line, a reference line, a subject line, typist's initials, and notice of enclosures and carbon copies mailed to others.

The body of the letter includes the content of the report, and it follows the basic plan outlined:

> Summary
> Introduction
> Details of the investigation
> Conclusions
> Recommendations

It may also include an appendix and a list of references.

INTEROFFICE MEMORANDUM.   The brief informal report may also be presented in the form of a memorandum. (See Figure 12-10.) The report memo includes the standard parts of a memo plus the elements in the basic plan for a report. You will use a heading for "To," "From," "Subject," "Date," possibly the "Name of the Company," and perhaps "Reference."

The body of the memo contains the details of the report and adapts the parts of the basic plan:

> Summary
> Introduction
> Details of the investigation
> Conclusion
> Recommendations

An appendix and list of references may be included.

AM-TEX PLUMBING AND HEATING, INC.

28 Semour Circle

Louisville, Kentucky 40208

July 20, 1978

Reference: Your letter,
            July 10, 1978

Drake Development Corp.
3912 Park Road
Louisville, Kentucky 40208

Attention: Mr. Stephen Smith

Title   Subject: Installing central heat and air systems

Gentlemen:

Summary   You will be pleased to know that Am-Tex Plumbing and Heating can
                      install central air conditioning in any Drake home at a cost of
                      $1530.00. This price includes duct work, a Fedders furnace model
                      290X636211, a condensing unit model 207X636211, and installation.

Introduction-   After examining the blueprints for the model you are currently
Background   building, we have drawn the following conclusions as to how it will
                      need to be centrally air-conditioned.

Body   A vertical unit will be installed in the closet space between kitchen
                      and living room. A plenum built to the specifications of the unit
                      will be installed on the unit. Twelve-inch round duct will be used
                      to run the trunk line from the plenum. Eight-inch round vents will
                      be placed in each room of the house except the baths, which are small
                      and will take only a six-inch vent. All ducts will be covered with
                      one-inch fiberglass vapor barrier insulation. Both inside and
                      outside units will be Fedders equipment. A return air duct will be
                      run in the wall under the staircase.

Recommendation   We believe that the system described above will offer the best
                      possible heat and cooling for the house under construction at the
                      most reasonable price.

                              Sincerely yours,

                              AM-TEX PLUMBING AND HEATING, INC.

                              John Silver
                              Estimate Department

JS:bs

Figure 12-9   Informal report in letter form

OHIO DEPARTMENT OF HIGHWAYS

Lancaster, Ohio

<u>To</u>: Mr. Thomas Munson   <u>Date</u>: September 11, 1978
      Chief Engineer
      Safety Division

<u>From</u>: P.D. Goler
       Survey Division

Title   <u>Subject</u>: Curve on Highway 23, 2 3/10 miles north of Logan

Background   At the request of the Safety Division, the Survey Division

Summary   has investigated the curve on Highway 23, 2 3/10 miles north of

                   Logan. Without question it is unsafe for motorists. On the

                   basis of the conclusions reached, the following recommendations

                   are made.

Conclusions   Conclusions

                          1.   It is a 30° curve, unbanked.

                          2.   A downward slope begins 10 feet from the

                               edge of the shoulder.

Details   3.   The slope descends at a 49° angle for 63 feet.

                          4.   There are no warning signs.

Recommendations   Recommendations

                          1.   That a metal guardrail be installed on the

                               east side along the length of the curve.

                          2.   That the road be banked.

                          3.   That warning signs be installed at both

                               approaches to the curve.

Figure 12-10   Interoffice memorandum

Longer Formal Report

With a complex subject the report becomes longer and more formal. It may range in length from several pages to several volumes. It may present materials on which a decision will be made to open a branch store, to launch a new product on the market, to change the system of paying employees. It may deal with the development of new products or techniques that may involve huge sums of money. Any large-scale investigation of any problem, situation, or condition provides material for a formal report. Listed below are the items included in the longer formal report. Again, these parts are adapted to a specific report depending on its purpose. Only a very long, elaborate report would include all these items.

    Cover
    Title page
    Letter of transmittal
    Table of contents
    Introduction, foreword, or summary
        Results
        Conclusions
        Recommendations
    Body
        History of subject
        Explanation of study
        Results
        Conclusions (with detailed discussion)
        Recommendations
    Appendix
        Bibliography
        Supplemental material
        Index

Let's describe in detail the composition of the major parts of the formal report.

TITLE PAGE.   The title page includes the following information, usually the same as the headings for a memo: the subject of the report; the name of the person, company, or organization to whom the report is submitted; the name of the person, company, or organization submitting the report; and the date. A sample title page is shown in Figure 12-11.

LETTER OF TRANSMITTAL.   A transmittal is used to forward the report to a person, a company, or an organization. It actually introduces the report and can take the place of the summary (see Figure 12-12). Most often it simply introduces the report, sometimes saying little more than "Attached is the report you asked for about customer complaints at the Southland Store."

TABLE OF CONTENTS.   The table of contents lists the divisions of the report and the page on which each division begins. If a report uses several graphs, charts, pictures, or other illustrations, there is a separate list of these. The table of contents helps the reader to select and locate parts of the report he or she may want to read (see Figure 12-13).

INTRODUCTION, FOREWARD, OR SUMMARY.   The introduction usually tells who requested the report (especially if the letter of transmittal has not included this information) and clearly presents the purpose of the report. It then goes on to state the main points included and gives reasons why certain points have not been included, or simply lists these points. The introduction explains something of the procedure followed in gathering the information and mentions any persons who may have helped with the investigation and preparation of the report. Also, this section includes the significant findings, major conclusions, and recommendations. Detailed explanation of results, conclusions, and recommendations will be given in the body of the report.

The abstract, or summary, may be the most important part of the report. It provides a concise presentation of the main points in the report. The abstract may well be the only part of the report read by busy executives, board members, or engineers. The summary should include a statement of the main purpose of the report, the main points of the investigation, and the main conclusions and recommendations (see Figure 12-14). It is a separate and complete part of the whole, depending on no other parts for meaning.

BODY.   The body of the report contains the complete, detailed discussion of the report. It develops the main points mentioned in the summary or introduction. It provides evidence or support for conclusions and recommendations. No specific listing of parts of the body will be usable in all types of report.

The body may give historical background needed for complete understanding of the report. It may describe the procedure used in carrying out the study; for example, in an experimental report the body might include a description of the devices and techniques used in the experiment. The body may explain what the writer did in carrying out the experiment. The explanation of procedure leads directly into a detailed discussion of the results mentioned briefly in the summary. Then follows a detailed presentation of conclusions and recommendations, also included briefly in the summary. The presentation of conclusions and recommendations should be clear and logical because they are the parts that are of major significance to the reader.

APPENDIX.   The appendix contains illustrative material, such as graphs, charts, diagrams, and pictures. It may also contain nonpictorial material such as additional reports, glossaries of terms, and bibliographies. In effect, the appendix contains any supplementary material that may be useful to the reader in attempting to understand the report. A sample bibliography is shown in Figure 12-15.

INDUSTRY AND THE ECONOMIC FUTURE

A Study of the Potential for Industrial

Growth in Springfield, Kentucky

presented to

The Springfield Chamber of Commerce

by

Perkins-Jones and Associates

Cincinnati, Ohio

May 18, 1978

Figure 12-11   Sample title page from a business report

PERKINS-JONES AND ASSOCIATES

Industrial Consultants

298 Lakewood Blvd.

Cincinnati, Ohio

Milton Thomas, Director

May 18, 1978

The Chamber of Commerce
Springfield, Kentucky 40208

Gentlemen:

We are pleased to submit to the Chamber of Commerce this report
on "Industry and the Economic Future of Springfield."

Perkins-Jones and Associates has analyzed the factors it believes
pertinent to the potential for industrial expansion in the city.
Definite conclusions came from this study, conclusions that we
believe speak well for the future of Springfield.

Please call upon us for any further service we can give you on
this matter.

Sincerely,

Milton Thomas

Milton Thomas

MT:lg

Figure 12-12   Sample transmittal letter for a business report

Table of Contents

Figure 12-13   Sample table of contents for a business report

Abstract

    After careful analysis of pertinent factors, Perkins-Jones and
Associates conclude (1) that Springfield's most likely sources of
industrial growth are (a) diversification of present industries
to open new markets and (b) attraction of new industry; (2) that
the industries most likely to be attracted are certain light
industries not requiring huge movements of heavy materials; and
(3) that as a result of diversification and new industry the
economic conditions in Springfield will improve greatly.

    We recommend (1) that the data and conclusions of this
report on diversification be made available to appropriate area
industries and (2) that a public relations firm, one specializing
in industrial relocations, be retained by the Chamber of Commerce
to devise plans for attracting new industries.

Figure 12-14 Sample abstract for a business report

Bibliography

Blankenship, Charles P. <u>History of Industry in Kentucky</u>. Chicago:
    Palmer Publishers, 1974.

Dalton, Paul. <u>Midwest Markets</u>. New York: Hutton and Co., 1976.

Hempleman, Gerald. <u>Guide to City and State Taxes</u>. Louisville,
    Kentucky: Hill Press, 1974.

Roberts, Henry. "Univac Flies with United." <u>Business Week</u>, December 25,
    1970, pp. 33-39.

U.S. Bureau of the Census. <u>Statistical Abstract of the United
    States</u>. 1975. 96th ed. Washington, D.C.: U.S. Government
    Printing Office, 1975.

Figure 12-15 Sample bibliography for a business report

CHECKLIST: PARTS AND GUIDELINES FOR REPORTS

I. *Letter of Transmittal*
   A. Let the letter of transmittal carry your cordial greeting to the reader.
   B. Open quickly with a "Here is the report you requested" tone.
   C. Establish the subject in the first sentence.
   D. Follow the opening with a brief summary of the study. Expand the discussion if a separate summary is not to be included in the report.
   E. Acknowledge the assistance of those who helped with the study.
   F. Close the letter with a "thank you" and a forward look.

II. *Title Page*
   A. Include the following on the title page:
      1. The title of the report.
      2. Full identification of the authority for the report (the party for whom the report is prepared).
      3. Full identification of the one who prepared the report.
      4. The date of completion of the report.
   B. Use attractive layout. If the items are to be centered, leave an extra ½ inch on the left for binding.

III. *Contents Page*
   A. Use either "Contents" or "Table of Contents" as the title.
   B. Use a tabular arrangement to indicate the heading degrees used in the report.
   C. All headings used in the report should be included in the content outline.
   D. If many graphs or tables are used, list them in a separate "List of Figures." Otherwise, the graphs or tables should not be listed, because they are not separate sections of your outline but only supporting data within a section of the report.
   E. Center the content outline horizontally and vertically on the page.

IV. *Abstract*
   A. Center the word "Abstract" at the top of the page, or use some other one-word title such as "synopsis," "summary," "brief," or "précis."
   B. Prepare the synopsis from condensed statements of your purpose, methods, findings, and conclusions sections of the report body.
   C. Concentrate on writing effective, generalized statements that avoid detail available in the report itself.

V. *The Body of the Report*
   A. Physical layout
      1. Use headings to assist the reader by making them descriptive of the contents of the section. Verbal headings are preferred.
      2. Maintain consistency in the mechanical placement of headings of the same degree.

3. Use parallel construction in headings of the same degree in the same section of the report.
4. Use the picture-frame layout for all pages. The margins should be: top—1 inch, right—1 inch, bottom—1½ inches, left—1½ inches. (The extra inch is for binding.)
5. Number all pages, with the first page of the body of the report being page one. For pages such as page one, having a major title at the top, omit the number or place it in the center of a line a double space below the last line on the page. For all other pages place the number in the center of the line or in the upper-right corner a double space above the first line on the page, or center the number a double space below the last line on the page.

B. Graphics or tabular data:
1. Number consecutively the graphs and tables used in the report.
2. Give each graph or table a descriptive title.
3. Refer to the graph or table within the text discussion.
4. Place the graph or table as close to the textual reference as possible.
5. Use effective layout, appropriate captions and legends, and realistic vertical and horizontal scales that help the table or graph stand clearly by itself.

C. Reporting your analysis:
1. Question each statement for its contribution to the solution of the problem. Is each statement either descriptive or evaluative?
2. Reduce large, unwieldy numbers to understandable ones through a common language, such as units of production, percentage, or ratios.
3. Use an objective reporting style rather than persuasive language; avoid emotional terms. Identify assumptions and opinions. Avoid unwarranted judgments and inferences.
4. Document your report wherever necessary.
5. Tabulate or enumerate items when it will simplify the reading.

D. Drawing conclusions:
1. State the conclusions carefully and clearly, and make sure they grow out of your findings.
2. If you believe it necessary, repeat the major supporting findings for each conclusion.
3. If recommendations are called for, make them grow naturally from the conclusions.

VI. *The Addenda:*
A. Prepare the bibliography in alphabetic sequence by author from index cards.
B. If the bibliography is lengthy, include separate sections for books, articles, governmental publications, and unpublished references.
C. Use an alphabetic sequence, such as *A, B, C,* and so on, for each exhibit in the appendix.

EXERCISES

1. In preparation for a Chamber of Commerce brochure to attract new industry to your city, you are requested to write a report on the quality of medical facilities of the city.

2. As department head supervising eight typists, you believe that all eight typewriters should be replaced. According to your records, three are four years old, three are two years old, and one was purchased eight months ago. Write a report to your boss describing the condition of the typewriters, drawing conclusions, and making recommendations.

3. The boss has approved your request to purchase eight new typewriters for your department. Obtain information about three makes of typewriters from your local office machines distributors. Then prepare a report to your boss, justifying your recommendation of one make of typewriter. Include sales or advertising materials in the appendix of your report.

4. Select some major company of interest to you, and investigate its methods of recruiting employees. When you have concluded your study, write a report revealing your findings. If your instructor requests it, submit first a detailed pre-project report describing your plan of research.

5. Select an interesting article or report from a business journal and, after reading it carefully, prepare a 150-to-200-word abstract of it.

6. Write a report entitled "Billboards in [your city]: well used or ill used." Make use of observational research to gather your data, and use library research and inter-rogational research to establish criteria.

7. The Atlas Home and Auto Supply Company plans to open a new branch in one of three locations—urban, suburban, or rural. About $500,000 is available for con-struction of the store and purchase of the land. As an independent marketing consultant, plan a study to determine where the store should be located.

8. You are to report on a study of the comparative qualities of three compact cars—C, P, and F. Prepare an outline of the entire problem. Show a clear statement of the problem, the qualities to be evaluated in selecting one of the cars as most desirable for a company using 20 cars a year, and the sources of information available to you. Prepare a possible Table of Contents page for the report. Also prepare a letter of transmittal.

9. Write a report on vehicle accidents in your state during the last 20 years. Use library research to obtain your facts and interrogational research to find out what is being done about the accident rate. You may wish to use charts, tables, and graphs.

10. Write a formal report with a body of about 15–25 double-spaced pages. Choose a topic broad enough to justify the length but one not so large that it requires volumes. Find a topic that involves a business problem. For example, you may know there is too great a turnover of employees in a certain store or shop. Or you may know of a shopping center that is losing its business to another area of town.

Define your problem, clarify your purpose, and begin your research. Here are some other ideas you can use as a springboard for a topic:

a. Opening of a restaurant or doughnut shop

b. Development of a marina

c. A program for hiring and training minority groups in a certain company

d. Explanation for a certain policy or procedure—such as methods of communication used by a certain department store in collecting retail accounts

e. Evaluation of two or three career areas. You might make use of this in your own specific career selection.

f. A study, report, and recommendation on attitudes toward a certain troublesome problem, such as the opinions of a certain company's employees about wages, working hours, food services, or promotion plan

Part 3

Strategies Of Oral Communication

13

Strategies of Oral Communication

Listening
Nonverbal Communication
Face-to-Face Speaking
The Interview
The Formal Talk
Telephone Communication

This book has been emphasizing the principles and strategies of effective business writing, but much of one's communication in business is done not on paper but through the spoken word. A sales talk, a telephone conversation, a speech, or an interview may support a written message. A letter may be a follow-up to face-to-face negotiations. Some business situations are handled almost entirely by oral communication, with only the formal details left to writing.

To make the best of your business communications, you need to give some attention to oral communication—to the strategies of speaking and to the modes that affect the oral situation, such as listening and body language.

In many ways, talking is much easier than writing a letter, a memo, or a report. In the first place, you have had more practice in speaking and tend to be more at ease. Furthermore, you don't need to bother with troublesome mechanics such as spelling and punctuation. And you have the aid of facial expressions, tone of voice, and gestures to make meaning clear. Finally, you have immediate feedback from the audience. If you notice raised eyebrows, excessive coughing, blank expressions, or other signs that indicate boredom or lack of understanding, you can clarify your point by restating or using an illustration, or you can simply ask if the listeners understand.

Yet the easy spontaneity of talking may mask some of the pitfalls, as well as some of the possibilities of improvement. So we will look at some of the modes of nonwritten communication used in speaking situations: at the strategies of *listening*, at the devices of *nonverbal communication* (such as body movements and tones of voice), at *face-to-face speaking situations* themselves (such as the conversation, the interview, and the formal talk), and, finally, at the *telephone message*, a speaking situation not face-to-face.

LISTENING

The businessperson who listens effectively will be ahead of the game. To steer your own communication so that it will get across to the other person just as you want it to, you must listen sharply to see just what is on his mind. Here are some guidelines to being an effective listener.

LISTEN FOR INFORMATION.   Just what is the person saying—does it involve facts, ideas, details? You may have to respond to them immediately or store them in the mind for future reference.

DETERMINE THE SPEAKER'S PURPOSE.   Where is the speaker going? What does he want out of you? He may state his purpose clearly and openly, but not always. He may be confused or assume you can see his purpose. Or he may even try to hide his real purpose from you.

    As soon as you are sure what the purpose is, you are in a position to help or hinder him in achieving it (whichever you wish) by how you respond. And you know how long to let him speak before you offer a reply. Knowing his purpose, you not only hear the details, but you are able to weigh those details as relevant to the speaker's purpose. You can also see what kinds of details, if any, he is leaving out or ignoring.

DISCERN BIAS.   Listen for connotations and emotional meanings of words as well as for literal sense. The words a speaker chooses to transmit his information will very quickly reveal any biases he feels about that information. This is probably even truer for speakers than writers, for writers have a chance to reconsider their words in a rough draft, while speakers (at least those who are speaking extemporaneously) generally use the first words that come to mind. Or they will fumble around for substitute words. In either case, their bias shows. Evaluate also the speaker's selection or omission of certain details as showing his bias or attitude toward the subject at hand.

ENCOURAGE THE SPEAKER TO OPEN UP.   The good listener catches more than details, purposes, and biases. He also encourages a speaker to express himself or herself more freely and more fully, thereby learning as much as possible from the speaker. When someone is talking to you, give him or her your complete attention. That is what the speaker wants, and he will be flattered to have it. Establish eye contact with the speaker, and maintain it as best you can. Be sure that your posture and facial expression imply that what you are hearing is important to you. You may, in fact, be able to listen very well from a slouch or with a blank look on your face, but the speaker will feel that such a manner betrays a lack of interest on your part—and will be more likely to "clam up" than "open up." The more he talks the more you will learn and the better you will be able to communicate to him to get exactly the response you want.

CHECK YOUR OWN BIASES.   You may have some preconceived opinions or prejudices about what the speaker is talking about. Your opinions may even be more valid than the speaker's. However, keep open the possibility that the speaker has a new slant on the matter or some new information you can use. If your mind is already made up, of course, you cannot learn something new.

CONTROL YOUR BOREDOM.   Many people listen carefully for a minute; then, if the subject seems dry or the speaker clumsy, they lose interest. They continue listening, if at all, grudgingly. Under such a cloud they don't hear very well. Good listeners, when they find themselves trapped by dry subjects or dull speakers, remind themselves that even the driest presentations can yield some fertile facts or ideas. They also remember that there is little relationship between the quality of a person's mind and the fluency of his tongue; the most tongue-tied of speakers can put forth valuable information and insight.

DON'T BECOME DISTRACTED.   Because the mind is faster than the voice, we can receive information at a much faster rate than a speaker can give it to us. There is, thus, always a risk that the mind will drift from what the speaker is saying. You must keep a tight rein on your attention. Concentrate, shut the door or the window if necessary. Turn off the radio or the intercom. Move closer to the speaker. Use that faster thinking rate to anticipate where the speaker is going, to mentally summarize where he has been, to assess his nonverbal signals, and to measure his motives and purposes.

TAKE NOTES SPARINGLY.   You may need to take some notes in certain business situations, such as conferences, interviews, and formal talks. If so, remember that though you can think more quickly than a speaker can speak, you cannot (unless you're a master of shorthand) write as fast. As a consequence, listeners who try to get down everything the speaker says usually fall behind and lose track of the central idea being developed. Tests have shown that only one out of four people listening to formal speeches are able to grasp the central idea. People speaking extemporaneously are usually even less organized than formal speakers. In spite of good intentions, therefore, the copious note taker often distracts himself more than he helps himself by trying to get everything down on paper. If you do take notes, put down only major ideas and direction signals. Listen carefully, and jot down statements of purpose, patterns of idea development, and recapitulations. Let the rest sink in without the distracting effort of a pencil losing its race for time against a speaker's words.

NONVERBAL COMMUNICATION

An important companion to effective listening is careful observation, for people communicate many things nonverbally. Speaking or not speaking, people are always sending out signals about themselves—many of these signals they are not even aware of. These nonverbal signals sometimes reinforce, often add to or modify, and even at times contradict what the words are saying. If you are sensitive to these nonverbal components of a person's speech, you will receive the "complete" communication—at times more complete than the speaker intends.

Here are some of the nonverbal messages you must be alert for, perceive, and interpret.

HANDSHAKE.   One of the most common nonverbal signals is the handshake. The person who extends a limp or weak hand to another businessperson usually conveys a sense of weakness or untrustworthiness. The bone-crushing handshake is usually taken as a sign of an overbearing or a dominating personality. A golden mean, therefore, is advisable for those in business: make the handshake firm, but only as strong as necessary to reciprocate the firmness of the other person's grasp.

VOICE.   The character of the voice—the pitch, the volume, and the speed—often indicates the speaker's state of mind. Varied voice pitch (a natural mixture of high and low tones) implies genuine interest and spontaneity—although too much obvious alteration in high and low tones will convey a sense of well-oiled artificiality. An unvaried monotone implies a lack of interest, or, if accompanied by body tenseness, a sense of nervousness. The volume of one's voice will also reveal state of mind: a loud talker conveys a sense of either annoyance or bluster, depending on other signals that accompany the loudness; the too-soft speaker implies either nervousness or a desire to establish confidentiality. The speed of oral delivery also reflects a speaker's attitude toward listeners: unvarying rapidity suggests that the speaker is more interested in getting done than in transmitting information; frequent pauses or a halting hesitancy often signify indecision, resistance, or some other tension.

BODY MOVEMENTS.   Body movements also provide significant signs that can reinforce or contradict a verbal message. The study of this relationship between words and body ments is known as *kinesics*. Posture or gestures that close off part of the body—arms folded across the chest, legs tightly crossed, a fist clenched—usually betray some defensiveness in a person. Sustained eye contact conveys a sense of self-assuredness. While we are still a long way from an exact science of kinesics, an awareness of the more obvious relationships between body and speech will undoubtedly increase your ability to communicate.

SPACE AND DISTANCE.   Space and distance are also nonverbal factors that communicate meaning. The distance around or across a conference table, even the shape of the table, have been shown to affect dramatically the amount of personal interaction at business meetings. The interviewer who pulls a chair up alongside you conveys a different attitude toward you than the interviewer who stays behind a desk. The size of that desk and the presence or absence of paperwork on it also convey meaning, as does the size of the interviewer's office and the vista out the window.

TOTAL BEHAVIOR.   Although we can't go very deeply into it here, everything we do sends a message to other people. As the philosopher Ralph Waldo Emerson said, "Character teaches over our head." If the other person perceives and interprets, he or she has received an advantageous communication. Certainly we convey a sense of businesslike efficiency by being punctual for appointments; lateness implies carelessness, and arriving too early can imply that you haven't much else to occupy your time. The clothes you wear, the car you drive, the home you live in, the address of the place you work—all, for better or worse, are felt to say something relevant about your success or your temperment and hence about your business ability.

The time you spend hanging around the water fountain or coffee shop, the things you smoke or drink, the way you scratch your mustache, the way your rouge or mascara is applied—these are a few of the kinds of behavior that tell on you and become part of a business situation.

Even many things you don't do convey messages to other people. Your failure to acknowledge the presence of another person in a business or a social situation, your failure to be at your desk or work station at starting time, your forgetting to express thanks when the situation calls for it, your silence when someone expects or hopes to hear from you—all these, too, are signals that convey messages to people about you. Of course, other people send messages to you in the same ways.

FACE-TO-FACE SPEAKING

Keeping in mind listening and nonverbal communication as underlying factors, let's turn to the most obvious form of nonwritten communication—face-to-face speaking. Three kinds are most common—conversation, interview, and formal presentation.

CONVERSATION

Whether it is a sales talk to a customer, a strategy session with a fellow worker, a planning conference with a supervisor, or negotiations with a business associate, the conversation is almost an instant process. Some words and phrases may have been somewhat previewed, but mostly we think and plan on the spot. There is no way of knowing precisely where a conversation is going—even though we try to control it. There is almost no opportunity to ponder the best way of saying something or to reconsider something already said. Unlike writers, speakers are on the firing line the moment they open their mouths. What writers can carefully plan to do, speakers must condition themselves to do reflexively—that is, say the right things in the right way to achieve the reactions they seek.

What should you do to condition yourself to become a better on-the-spot speaker? Here are a few guidelines.

KEEP YOUR PURPOSE CLEARLY IN MIND.   You usually speak in business for the same reasons you write—to initiate routine contact with someone, make a routine reply, create goodwill, transmit good news or bad news, make demands, alleviate bruised feelings, or persuade people to do things they weren't planning to do. In short, to do all those things we examined in chapters 8 through 11. To achieve each of those functions, a writer has to take the reader through a series of mental phases. Remember the recommended strategy patterns for each of those purposes. The speaker must also take the listener's mind and feelings through those same phases. The difference, of course, is that the speaker has the listener in front of him. The speaker gets verbal and nonverbal feedback from a listener and can tell—if sensitive to that feedback—when each phase of the strategy is completed and when it is not.

STAY ON THE SUBJECT.   Avoid tangents. If you have a specific purpose in mind in a face-to-face discussion, don't let the discussion get off on a tangent. Tangents develop when one idea reminds you of another, then that other reminds you of a third, and so on. You can't stop yourself from thinking tangentially, but you *can* resist expressing those tangents when they do come to mind. When the person you are speaking to goes off on a tangent, pursue it only as far as courtesy dictates, then graciously guide the discussion back on the track.

CONTROL YOUR INTENSITY.   Be sure that your conversational speech shows a balanced enthusiasm. Avoid, on the one hand, any tendency to become too intense—to speak too loudly or too fast, to use heavily connotative language, or to "talk with your hands." These traits will actually distract your listener and cause him or her to focus on your intensity rather than on your message. On the other hand, if you fail to show *some* feeling for what you are saying, you can hardly expect your listener to develop any feeling for it. It is a matter of balance.

USE APPROPRIATE LANGUAGE.   In speaking as well as in writing, the language and mood appropriate to one situation may not be appropriate to another. Informal diction, joking, some four-letter expletive—all of these can be helpful in some conversations but destructive in others. When a listener, whether because of upbringing, sex, professional position, or self-assumed status, construes what you have said, or how you have said it, as inappropriate, you have not communicated, but rather built a barrier against communication.

USE A PLEASING VOICE.   Whenever you can find the chance, listen to your own voice on a tape recorder. Speak extemporaneously into it, talk with someone while the microphone is on, read a page of your favorite book into it. If you don't have a recorder available, another way to objectively hear the sound of your own voice is to cup your hands in front of your ears with the palms backward. As you speak, your voice will seem to come from a distance, from somebody else.

The chances are that if the voice you hear coming back at you is pleasing to you, it will be pleasing to other people. If it isn't, you have some self-improvement ahead. Try to rid your voice of any inclination toward harsh or nasal tones. You should also overcome any tendency to fragment your speech with meaningless "uhs," "likes," and "you knows." If you have a strong regional or cultural accent, don't try to purge it entirely, but work on softening it; make it less pronounced. Make sure you pronounce all your words and syllables clearly, but without assuming a clipped or overly formal tone. (Again, it is a matter of balance.) Work on building as resonant a quality as possible into your voice. There is no escaping the fact that people are moved not only by what you say, but by how you say it—and that "how" includes the quality of your voice.

THE INTERVIEW

An interview is a formalized conversation, usually conducted for some specific purpose—to get answers from someone who has them, to probe for the reasons behind a situation, to brief someone in preparation for a task, or to measure a person's qualifications for a job opening. All the qualities of extemporaneous speaking (which we have just discussed) come into play, plus some additional preparations and strategies that we ought to consider.

As an example, we will examine the strategies of the interview from the standpoint of one of the most common and important of all—the job interview.

Both the interviewer and interviewee must prepare for an upcoming interview. Too many interviews bog down—to the disadvantage of both parties—because neither participant had a clear idea of how the interview should proceed. They knew what they wanted from the interview, but didn't know precisely how to get it. Let's consider first the interviewer's role and then shift our focus to the interviewee.

Strategies for the Interviewer

Experienced interviewers, those who know how to get the most from their time, will carefully define what they hope to achieve in an interview and prepare their questions directly toward that end; this keeps the interview from straying once it starts. They plan a brief several minutes to establish a friendly atmosphere: both to get the interviewee talking freely and to assess the interviewee's personality, his nervousness, and the like. Skillful interviewers do all the homework necessary to have pertinent data at their fingertips during the interview. They prepare their questions in the way most likely to evoke full responses from the interviewee—usually by asking easier, less open-ended questions like, "How then would you increase sales?" or "What specific abilities can you bring to the firm?"

The interviewer's objective is not to dominate the interview, but to have the interviewee make responses and reveal himself. Though perhaps doing most of the talking in the early stages, the interviewer should become primarily a listener once the interview is in full swing. When all has been learned that the interviewer wishes to learn, he or she graciously brings the interview to an end—never letting it just dwindle off or end with some outside intrusion like a telephone call or a secretary's interruption. If a resolution is possible at the end of an interview—that is, if the interviewer has decided what action to take or what the next step should be—the interviewee should not be kept in suspense, but should be told where things stand.

GUIDELINES FOR THE INTERVIEWER

1. *Plan the interview.*   Know clearly the purpose of the interview, know the candidate's credentials, and have questions in mind.
2. *Let the applicant do most of the talking.*   If you talk more than half the time, you are likely not interviewing, but giving an oration about yourself.
3. *Keep the applicant talking.*   Prod with brief responses like "That's interesting," "How did that work out?" and "What happened then?"
4. *Use encouraging body language.*   Use facial expressions, movement and expression of the eyes, and nods of the head.
5. *Observe the nonverbal messages.*   If the candidate blushes, begins to stammer, casts his eyes downward, or barks out an angry reply, he is telling far more than anything he or she might put into words. You can partially but reliably judge any statement from the tone and inflection of the person's voice, gestures, hesitations, and general conduct. One's behavior tells much about personality and social skills.
6. *Allow pauses.*   Let the interviewee think and reveal important information. But avoid long pauses when he has definitely finished a topic.
7. *Be sympathetic and understanding.*   Respect the applicant's opinions even though you consider them wrong.
8. *Always accept what he says.*   Never frown, show surprise, or show disapproval.
9. *Don't cut the applicant off or change the subject abruptly.*
10. *Never argue.*
11. *Be informal and friendly.*   Sit on the same side of the desk as the applicant and use plain language.
12. *Avoid bias and prejudice.*   Here are some of the common ones:
    a.   Stereotype error trap is a tendency to categorize the applicant on the basis of a few surface clues. For instance, some people foolishly think all redheads are hot tempered, fat people are jovial, swarthy complexions reveal dishonest tendencies, short people are domineering, people with close-set eyes are unintelligent or stubborn.
    b.   Halo effect describes a tendency of the interviewer to form an overall opinion about the applicant on the basis of a single aspect of his makeup.
    c.   Expectancy error is a tendency of the applicant to anticipate the needs and preferences of the interviewer and to respond accordingly.
    d.   Ideal image error is one in which the interviewer's mental picture of the ideal man may not necessarily coincide with the man who can actually be most effective on the job.

Strategies for the Interviewee

Things look a little different from the other side of the desk, from the viewpoint of the interviewee. But careful planning and preparation are just as necessary. Let's consider the interviewee's role in the job interview. If you can handle this interview successfully, you won't have many problems with other kinds.

The most important item you are taking to the interview is you. Make sure it is properly packaged, with shined shoes, neat haircut or attractive hairdo, conservative (not dull or outdated) dress or suit, and firm handshake. Then know enough about the employer's business to ask intelligent and specific questions.

Take one more look at yourself from the employer's point of view. Presumably you've been doing this all along or you'd never have gotten to the interview; so don't stop now. When an employer hires you, he or she will be making an investment that can run into the hundreds of thousands of dollars, considering salary, fringes, taxes, and training costs. Can you blame the employer for wanting a quality product? Therefore, look and act the part, because you are really worth it.

Keep in mind that the employment interview is a two-way freeway. Its primary purpose, from your standpoint, is to get you the best job available to suit your capabilities. From an employer's standpoint it is to get the company the best person available for the job. For both goals to be met, each of you must learn as much as possible about the other.

You must be prepared. All your planning, resumé preparation, letter writing, and pavement pounding have led you to this crucial meeting. It is really too late now to think. You must know. Advance preparation is the only way you can carry if off successfully. How do you prepare? First by knowing your product (yourself), and second by knowing your customer (the company you are interviewing for).

GUIDELINES FOR THE INTERVIEWEE

1. *Be alert and interested,* and show it in the way you sit and look, in eye contact, and in the questions you ask.
2. *Be courteous.* Don't chew gum, and don't smoke unless the interviewer invites you to do so, and he himself smokes.
3. *Be honest and straightforward.* If you begin to exaggerate or fabricate details —and the interviewer catches you—you will lose status as a favorable candidate for the job.
4. *Be yourself.* Don't try to put on airs. By being yourself, you will be on familiar ground, seem more comfortable, and be more at ease.
5. *Be a good listener.* By doing so, you will be ready to reply to a question the interviewer asks, seem interested, and also receive valuable clues from his actions.
6. *Avoid the following negative attitudes or actions:*
   a. Poor personal appearance
   b. Overbearing or conceited attitude
   c. Evasiveness or hedging on unfavorable factors in your record
   d. Lack of confidence and poise
   e. Overemphasis on money and job security
   f. Lack of knowledge of the company

The following list of questions can serve as training ground for both interviewer and interviewee. They represent questions frequently asked during an employment interview. The interviewer may usefully draw from the list. The interviewee could well prepare himself by practicing answers.

You might try to answer these questions—about five or ten each day—and to really make the assignment challenging, try to answer "why" to the questions that permit you to do so. Some you can answer without too much effort. Answers to others, however, might be so difficult (and important) that you want to actually write them out after long and serious thought. If you know the answers to these questions, you will be well prepared to answer almost any question the interviewer might ask you.

QUESTIONS FREQUENTLY ASKED DURING INTERVIEWS

The questions below are adapted from a compilation by Frank S. Endicott, Director of Placement, Northwestern University, from a survey of 92 companies. The questions are also available in the New York Life Insurance Company's booklet, *Making the Most of Your Job Interview.*

1. What are your future vocational plans?
2. In what school activities have you participated? Why? Which did you enjoy the most?
3. How do you spend your spare time? What are your hobbies?
4. In what type of position are you most interested?
5. Why do you think you might like to work for our company?
6. What jobs have you held? How were they obtained, and why did you leave?
7. What courses did you like best? Least? Why?
8. Why did you choose your particular field of work?
9. What percentage of your college expenses did you earn? How?
10. How did you spend your vacations while in school?
11. What do you think about our company?
12. Do you feel that you have received a good general training?
13. What qualifications do you have that make you feel you will be successful in your field?
14. What extracurricular offices have you held?
15. What are your ideas on salary?
16. How do you feel about your family?
17. How interested are you in sports?
18. If you were starting college all over again, what courses would you take?
19. Can you forget your education and start from scratch?
20. Do you prefer any specific geographic location? Why?
21. Are you romantically involved with anyone? Is it serious?
22. How much money do you hope to earn at age 30? 35?

23. Why did you decide to go to this particular school?
24. How did you rank in your graduating class in high school? Where will you probably rank in college?
25. Do you think that your extracurricular activities were worth the time you devoted to them? Why?
26. What do you think determines a person's progress in a good company?
27. What personal characteristics are necessary for success in your chosen field?
28. Why do you think you would like this particular type of job?
29. What are your parents' occupations?
30. Tell me about your home life during the time you were growing up.
31. Are you looking for a permanent or temporary job?
32. Do you prefer working with others or by yourself?
33. Who are your best friends?
34. What kind of boss do you prefer?
35. Are you primarily interested in making money, or do you feel that service to society is a satisfactory accomplishment?
36. Can you take instructions without feeling upset?
37. Tell me a story!
38. Do you live with your parents? Which of your parents has had the most profound influence on you?
39. How did previous employers treat you?
40. What have you learned from some of the jobs you have held?
41. Can you get recommendations from previous employers?
42. What interests you about our product or service?
43. What was your record in military service?
44. Have you ever changed your major field of interest while in college? Why?
45. When did you choose your college major?
46. How do your college grades after military service compare with those previously earned?
47. Do you feel you have done the best scholastic work of which you are capable?
48. How did you happen to go to college?
49. What do you know about opportunities in the field in which you are trained?
50. How long do you expect to work?
51. Have you ever had any difficulty getting along with fellow students and faculty.
52. Which of your college years was the most difficult?
53. What is the source of your spending money?
54. Do you own any life insurance?
55. Have you saved any money?
56. Do you have any debts?
57. How old were you when you became self-supporting?
58. Do you attend church?
59. Did you enjoy your four years at this university?
60. Do you like routine work?

61. Do you like regular hours?
62. What size city do you prefer?
63. When did you first contribute to family income?
64. What is your major weakness?
65. Define cooperation.
66. Will you fight to get ahead?
67. Do you demand attention?
68. Do you have an analytical mind?
69. Are you eager to please?
70. What do you do to keep in good physical condition?
71. How do you usually spend Sunday?
72. Have you had any serious illness or injury?
73. Are you willing to go where the company sends you?
74. What job in our company would you choose if you were entirely free to do so?
75. Is it an effort for you to be tolerant of persons with a background and interests different from your own?
76. What types of books have you read?
77. Have you plans for graduate work?
78. What types of people seem to "rub you the wrong way"?
79. Do you enjoy sports as a participant? As an observer?
88. Have you ever tutored an underclassman?
81. What jobs have you enjoyed the most? The least? Why?
82. What are your own special abilities?
83. What job in our company do you want to work toward?
84. Would you prefer a large or a small company? Why?
85. What is your idea of how industry operates today?
86. Do you like to travel?
87. How about overtime work?
88. What kind of work interests you?
89. What are the disadvantages of your chosen field?
90. Do you think that grades should be considered by employers? Why or why not?
91. Are you interested in research?
92. How often do you entertain at home?
93. To what extent do you use liquor?
94. What have you done that shows initiative and willingness to work?

THE FORMAL TALK

Not all businesspeople have to stand up before an audience and give a specially prepared speech. But as one advances in knowledge and authority, he or she is quite likely to be called upon for a formal talk before a group. The principles of effective face-to-face speaking apply to the formal talk—except that there is less audience feedback to guide you as you talk, and your talk must be more formally planned. Follow these principles in preparing and giving your talk.

USE EFFECTIVE VOICE AND BODY MOVEMENT.   Your quality of voice, your controlled enthusiasm, your eye contact, your gestures and facial expressions must come into play. But they do need some amplifying to reach the back row.

KNOW YOUR SUBJECT.   Business audiences do not demand dramatic, spellbinding presentations. What they do expect is a speaker who knows his subject. Nothing turns off audience members more than to feel thes are spending time listening to someone who knows less about the subject than they do. It is sound advice never to accept an offer to speak on a subject with which you are not entirely familiar. If circumstances compel you to, then immerse yourself in the subject as thoroughly as you can, and do not pretend to expertness once you get before the audience.

HAVE EMPATHY FOR THE AUDIENCE.   Your speech is for them. Check the chapter on the you attitude. An audience expects a speaker to address himself or herself to their particular problems and interests. Empathy also requires that you carefully adapt your presentation to your audience's ability to understand it completely. Your choice of words must be tailored, your visual aids designed, and your handouts written directly for their level of understanding. That does not mean you should underestimate an audience; simply realize that they want to hear something for their own benefit—that's why they invited you.

HAVE A WELL-ORGANIZED SPEECH.   Your purpose, your central ideas and your main points should be made clear to the listeners. Sometimes it is helpful to hand out a written outline of your preparation.

PLAN YOUR OPENING AND CLOSING.   Skillful speakers usually plan their openings and closings. Sometimes the opening is a light remark, even a joke; but it should always have obvious bearing on the subject to be discussed. If it doesn't, it will seem but an empty device to capture attention. Closings too can be clever and witty—but unless they are also highly appropriate to the subject, it is better to end with a simple and clear summary of what has been presented.

SPEAK FROM NOTES.   Some formal speakers can work well from written text; they can go before an audience and read a completely written speech with enough vitality and seeming spontaneity to keep it from being boring. But not many speakers can do this; you almost have to be a trained actor. Most formal presentations are better done when the speaker works from an outline and note cards. They keep the presentation on track, yet allow the speaker's personality and obvious grasp of the subject to come through. By speaking from notes, you can keep eye contact with the audience.

PREPARE FOR A QUESTION PERIOD.   In all but the most formal situations, audiences expect to ask questions of the speaker when the presentation is over. If you are well prepared, you will anticipate the questions most likely to be asked and have answers for them. If you do not have the answer to a question, admit it honestly and move on to the next one.

TELEPHONE COMMUNICATION

The telephone has become so vital in business that we almost instinctively reach for the telephone instead of the pencil, the dictating machine, or the car key. We take the telephone so much for granted that we sometimes neglect to consider what its real advantages and disadvantages are. Let's look at the two sides.

Advantages

The most obvious of the telephone's advantages are its convenience and its efficiency. By using the phone, you can reach many people during a working day, with little time wasted in moving from conversation to conversation. Under time-pressure, the telephone can also save you the day or two it takes to get a letter through the mails.

The telephone is also economical. Telephone costs are rising less rapidly than the total costs (including secretarial time) of preparing a business letter. Only when long-distance calls become lengthy do telephone charges exceed those of letters—and even then, sometimes, the speed and direct voice contact are worth the added cost.

A telephone call—especially a long-distance call—can also help give a sense of urgency to your message. In addition to its actual speed, the call implies that you couldn't wait for any of the slower means of communication. The telephone is a relatively inexpensive way to express frequent concern. The salesperson who follows up a sale with several calls to the customer probably could not afford to make several follow-up visits, but the calls help to generate the same goodwill.

With the telephone you can combine the spontaneity and personableness of direct voice-to-voice contact with the wisdom of having an outline or even written remarks or questions in front of you to make sure that you say everything you have to and say it in precisely the right way. You can also arrange conference calls, linking three or more parties at different places—even different cities—into the same conversation.

Disadvantages

The kinds of communications you can handle by phone are the same as those examined in Chapters 8–11. But with these written messages we examined the strategies of carefully shaping your communication to achieve a specific reaction. Some of these situations are very touchy—such as conciliating anger, collecting an overdue account, or dealing with other bad news. If the recipient of such a message had gotten it by phone instead of in a letter or a memo, he or she would undoubtedly have interrupted the message a number of times to ask questions, raise objections, or offer a different viewpoint. The carefully structured message would have been forced into tangents and sudden quarrels, and its structure would have broken down. This is why business people often decide against the phone and instead write or dictate sensitive communications.

The telephone is also a less personal means of communicating. The importance of some communications—presentations, proposals, interviews—demands that they be made face to face. The telephone can be used to schedule them, but not to conduct the actual conversation. Your insistence on doing it all over the phone will strike some business people as self-serving expediency and not as the right way to do business. The telephone also does not allow visual feedback from the person you are talking to. And it is easier for someone to break off a phone conversation than a face-to-face conversation.

Unless a person has secretarial protection to help fend off telephone calls when he or she is busy, your call may interrupt at a busy time. If it does, the recipient will surely be less receptive to your message, especially if it seems self-interested. Many people dislike—even detest—unexpected sales calls, especially when the caller phones at dinner time.

These many disadvantages certainly do not diminish the value of the telephone as a business tool, but they do warn you to think twice about the nature of your message before you pick up the telephone to convey it.

EXERCISES

1. In one of your other classes, a lecture-discussion class, play the role of listener and observer of nonwritten communication. Listen for facts, purposes (obvious and hidden), and biases. Note body movements, such as slouches, nail biting, scratching, smiles, and frowns.

    Make brief notes of your observations, and interpret their significance as communication. Prepare a brief memo-report, and submit it to your instructor.

2. Prepare to deliver a short, formal talk to your class. The following are among the topics you may use.

    Services performed by travel agents
    Difficulties with computers
    Teenagers as consumers
    Who patronizes motels?
    Who travels by bus?
    Should our company do something for the arts?
    Why don't shoppers buy unknown brands?
    College extracurricular activities that will have later value.

3. Imagine yourself Thom Atkinson, the sales manager who wrote the letter on p. 229. You have received the stinging letter from Donald Keeter on p. 228, and you must respond with conciliation and the same adjustment offer that Atkinson makes in his letter. However, instead of writing, you decide to phone Keeter because it is quicker. Will your effort be just as satisfactory? More so? Less so? More importantly, why?

    As you think through this problem, play out the telephone situation in your mind. What will Keeter's response to you be when you identify yourself? Will you have the opportunity to apologize as effectively? To explain as fully? To offer your adjustment as clearly and persuasively?

Some people feel the telephone is the best way to handle a problem like this one. What do you think?

4. Assume you are Burton Langstrom, the customer service manager who wrote the letter to Outdoors, Inc., on p. 239. You have to turn down the request for credit; yet you want to gain their patronage on a cash basis. However, instead of writing Outdoors a letter, you decide to do it by phone. Carefully plan your call. Then, with a classmate, simulate the phone call, achieving the same results the problem asks you to achieve.

After the call discuss (or write a memo regarding) the advantages and the disadvantages of using the telephone to convey this bad-news message.

5. With a classmate, prepare for a job interview—you as interviewer and the other as interviewee. Be prepared to switch roles. Study the guidelines and typical questions, and be prepared to conduct a sample interview before the class.

Appendix A

FORMS OF ADDRESS AND SALUTATION

The following forms of address and salutation are among those accepted and commonly used. The salutations shown after each address are listed in decreasing order of formality.

Note: Only the masculine forms of address have been used in order to save space and avoid the repetition of Miss, Mrs., or Ms. Whenever an office is held by a woman, substitute the appropriate feminine form, as follows:

FOR	USE
Mr.	Miss, Mrs., or Ms.
Sir:	Madam:
Dear Sir:	Dear Madam:
My dear Mr. (surname):	My dear Miss, Mrs., or Ms. (surname):
My dear Mr. Secretary:	My dear Madam Secretary:
My dear Mr. Mayor:	My dear Madam Mayor:

ENVELOPE AND INSIDE ADDRESS: SALUTATION

Public Officials

The President of the United States
    The President
    The White House
    Washington, D.C. 20500

Sir:
My dear Mr. President:
Dear Mr. President:

Wife of the President
    Mrs. (full name)
    The White House
    Washington, D.C. 20500

Dear Mrs. (surname):

Vice-President of the United States
    The Vice-President
    The United States Senate
    Washington, D.C. 20510

Sir:
Dear Sir:
My dear Mr. Vice-President:
Dear Mr. Vice-President:

Senator
    The Honorable (name in full)   Sir:
    The United States Senate   Dear Sir:
    Washington, D.C. 20510   My dear Senator:
                                     Dear Senator (surname):

Speaker of the House of Representatives
    The Honorable (name in full)   Sir:
    Speaker of the House of Representatives   Dear Sir:
    Washington, D.C. 20515   Dear Mr. Speaker:
                                     Dear Mr. (surname):

Member of Congress
    The Honorable (name in full)   Sir:
    The House of Representatives   Dear Sir:
    Washington, D.C. 20515   My dear Congressman:
                                   Dear Mr. (surname):

Cabinet Member
    The Honorable (name in full)   Sir:
    Secretary of (department)   Dear Sir:
    Washington, D.C. (ZIP code number)   Dear Mr. Secretary:
                                   Dear Mr. (surname):

Chief Justice of the United States
    The Honorable (name in full)   Sir:
    Chief Justice of the United States   My dear Mr. Chief Justice:
    Washington, D.C. 20543   Dear Mr. Chief Justice:

Associate Justice of the United States
    Supreme Court
    The Honorable (name in full)   Sir:
    Justice of the Supreme Court
      of the United States
    Washington, D.C. 20543   My dear Mr. Justice:

Governor of the State
    The Honorable (name in full)   Sir :
    Governor of (name of state)   Dear Sir:
    (state capital), State (ZIP code number)   Dear Governor (surname):

Lieutenant Governor of State
 The Honorable (name in full)   Sir:
 Lieutenant Governor of (name of state) Dear Sir:
 (state capital), State (ZIP code number) Dear Mr. (surname):

State Senator
 The Honorable (name in full)   Dear Sir:
 The State Senate   Dear Senator (surname):
 (state capital), State (ZIP code Number)

State Assemblyman or Representative
 The Honorable (name in full)   Dear Sir:
 House of Representatives or
  The State Assembly   Dear Mr. (surname):
 (state capital), State (ZIP code number)

Secretary of State
 The Honorable (name in full)   Dear Sir:
 Secretary of State of (name of state)   Dear Mr. (surname):
 (state capital), State (ZIP code number)

Mayor
 The Honorable (name in full)   Dear Sir:
 Mayor of (name of city)   Dear Mr. Mayor:
 (name of city), State (ZIP code number) Dear Mr. (surname):

City Councilman
 Councilman (name in full)   Dear Sir:
 City Hall   Dear Mr. (surname):
 (name of city), State (ZIP code number)

Commissioner of a City Department
 The Honorable (name in full)   Dear Sir:
 Commissioner of (name of department) Dear Commissioner (surname):
 (street address)
              Dear Mr. (surname):
 (name of city), State (ZIP code number)

Education Officials

President
    Dr. (name in full)   Dear Sir:
    President of (name of school)   Dear Dr. (surname):

    (street address)   My dear President:
    (name of city), State (ZIP code number)

Dean
    Dean (name in full)   Dear Sir:
    (name of school)   Dear Dean (surname):

    (name of university)   Dear Dr. (surname):

    (postal address)   Dear Mr. (surname):

Professor
    Professor (name in full)   Dear Sir:
    (name of department)   Dear Professor (surname):

    (name of university)   Dear Dr. (surname):

    (postal address)

Instructor
    Dr. (name in full)   Dear Sir:
            or   Dear Dr. (surname):
    Mr. (name in full)   Dear Mr. (surname):
    (name of department)
    (name of university)
    (postal address)

Superintendent of Schools
    Dr. (name in full)   Dear Sir:
            or   My dear Dr. (surname):
    Mr. (name in full)   My dear Mr. (surname):
    Superintendent of Schools   Dear Dr. (surname):
    (name of school system)   Dear Mr. (surname):
    (postal address)

School Principal
    Dr. (name in full)   Dear Sir:
            or   My dear Dr. (surname):
    Mr. (name in full)   My dear Mr. (surname):
    Principal of (name of school)   Dear Dr. (surname):
    (postal address)   Dear Mr. (surname):

Schoolteacher
    Dr. (name in full)   Dear Sir:
        or   Dear Dr. (surname):
    Mr. (name in full)   Dear Mr. (surname):
    (name of school)
    (postal address)

Members of the Clergy—Catholic

The Pope
    His Holiness, the Pope   Your Holiness:
        or   Most Holy Father:
    His Holiness, Pope (name)
    Vatican City
    Italy

Cardinal
    His Eminence (first name),   Your Eminence:
        Cardinal (surname)   Dear Cardinal (surname):
    (postal address)

Archbishop
    The Most Reverend (name in full)   Your Excellency:
    Archbishop of (locality)   Dear Archbishop (surname):
    (postal address)

Bishop
    The Most Reverend (name in full)   Your Excellency:
    Bishop of (locality)   Dear Bishop (surname):
    (postal address)

Monsignor
    The Right Reverend Monsignor   Right Reverend Monsignor:
        (name in full)   Dear Monsignor (surname):
    (postal address)

Priest
    The Reverend (name in full)   Reverend Father:
    (postal address)   Dear Father (surname):

Mother Superior
    The Reverend Mother (name in full)   Reverend Mother:
    (postal address)   Dear Reverend Mother:
                          Dear Mother (name):

Sister
> Sister (name in full),   My dear Sister:
> (initials of order)   Dear Sister (name):
> (postal address)

MEMBERS OF THE CLERGY—PROTESTANT

Protestant Episcopal Bishop
> The Right Reverend (name in full)   Right Reverend Sir:
> Bishop of (locality)   Dear Bishop (surname):
> (postal address)

Protestant Episcopal Dean
> The Very Reverend (name in full)   Very Reverend Sir:
> Dean of (locality)   Dear Dean (surname):
> (postal address)

Methodist Bishop
> The Reverend (name in full)   Dear Sir:
> Bishop of (locality)   Dear Bishop (surname):
> (postal address)

Protestant Minister
> The Reverend (name in full)   Dear Sir:
>   or   Dear Dr. (surname):
> Reverend (name in full), D.D.   Dear Reverend (surname):
> (postal address)

MEMBERS OF THE CLERGY—JEWISH

Rabbi
> Rabbi (name in full)   Dear Sir:
>   or   My dear Rabbi (surname):
> Dr. (name in full)   Dear Rabbi (surname):
> (postal address)

Members of the Armed Forces

Correspondence to members of the armed forces must contain the complete address, including the exact title or rank, full name, and complete military or naval address (branch of service, unit, and station or ship).

Rank or Rating	*Salutation*
General	Dear General (surname):
Lieutenant General	
Major General	
Brigadier General	
Colonel	Dear Colonel (surname):
Lieutenant Colonel	
Major	Dear Major (surname):
Captain	Dear Captain (surname):
1st Lieutenant	Dear Lieutenant (surname):
2nd Lieutenant	
Warrant Officers	Dear Mr. (surname):
Noncommissioned Officers	Dear Sergeant (surname):
	Dear Corporal (surname):
Fleet Admiral	Dear Admiral (surname):
Admiral	
Vice Admiral	
Rear Admiral	
Commodore	Dear Commodore (surname):
Captain (Navy)	Dear Captain (surname):
Commander	Dear Commander (surname):
Lieutenant Commander	Dear Mr. (surname):
Lieutenant	
Lieutenant Junior Grade	
Ensign	
Petty Officers	Dear Mr. (surname):

PROPER SPACING

Horizontal Spacing

1. *After a comma or a semicolon*—one space.

> We sold all 24 units, however, at a discount.
> The driver left at one o'clock; he was ill.

2. *After a period, a question mark, or a colon at the end of a sentence*—two spaces.

> All 24 units have been sold. Therefore. . .
> When can you make shipment? We must. . .
> There are three alternatives: (1) We can. . .

3. *After a period following an initial*—one space.

> Dr. Dennis C. Gerlach   Dr. D. C. Gerlach

4. *After a period following abbreviations that are part of a unit, such as "No.," "Co.," and "Corp."*—one space.

> Send a dozen of the No. 4 maps to the Speirman Co. of Urbana.

5. *Title or company name requiring two lines*—indent second line two spaces.

> Mr. Ralph Cannon
> Tri-State Farm Equipment
>   Company, Inc.
> 278 River Drive
> Shreveport, Louisiana 71104

6. *Between state and ZIP code*—one or two spaces.

> Shreveport, Louisiana 71104
> Shreveport, Louisiana 71104

7. *Between a hyphen and letters before and after*—no space.

> self-conscious

8. *Between a dash and words before and after*—no space.

> He was alert—that is, not asleep—on the job.

Vertical Spacing

Some spacings are invariable and should be exactly as indicated. Others, where indicated below, may vary.

1. Attention line—double space above and below.
2. Body (individual lines)—single space.

3. Carbon copies and identification-enclosure block—either single space or double space.
4. Complimentary close and last paragraph—double space.
5. Complimentary close and name of firm—double space.
6. Complimentary close and typewritten signature—at least quadruple space.
7. Date and reference line—at least quadruple space.
8. Heading (individual lines)—single space.
9. Identification and enclosure block—single space or double space.
10. Inside address (individual lines)—single space.
11. Inside address and salutation—double space.
12. Letter head and date—double space or more.
13. Mailing notation—double space above and below.
14. Paragraphs—double space.
15. Personal notation and inside address—at least quadruple space.
16. Postscript—at least double space below all other notations.
17. Salutation and first paragraph—double space.
18. Signature (typed) and title (if on different line)—single space.
19. Subject line—double space above and below.

Appendix B

ABBREVIATIONS

In general, don't abbreviate much. Spell out words in standard English. Keep the following rule in mind: "When in doubt, spell out."

Standard Abbreviations

1. Titles before and after proper names: Dr., Mrs., Jr., Sr., M.D., B.A., C.P.A.

   Dr. Wilson examined me.

   These titles are normally spelled out: president, superintendent, honorable, professor, manager, principal, vice-president.

2. Signs for hours, numbers, dollars, and "and"

   Abbreviations and signs are correct only with numerals.

   8:30 A.M.   at Gate No. 2   about $750

   The ampersand (&) is correct only when it is part of a title.

   T & G Company   Benson & Hedges

3. Names of organizations and agencies usually referred to by initials:

   YMCA   NAM   FBI   UN   FDIC   FCC   FHA

4. Names of businesses when their letterheads contain abbreviations:

   The James T. Drew Co.
   Frey and Styler, Ltd.
   Multiplex Developments, Inc.

5. The terms St. (Saint), Mt. (Mount), and D.C. (District of Columbia):

    Mt. Wilson Observatory   St. Paul   Washington, D.C.

6. Compound directions:

    NW.   NW   N.W.   (Northwest)

7. Commonly used business expressions: C.O.D.   amt.   advt.

Words to Spell Out

1. Names of persons, countries, states, courses of study, months, days of the week:

    Friday   (not *Fri.*)
    Los Angeles   (not *L.A.*)
    Fifth Street   (not *Fifth St.*)
    Charles   (not *Chas.*)
    Corporation finance   (not *corp. fin.*)
    West Virginia   (not *WV* or *W. Va.*)

The U.S. Post Office Department two-letter abbreviations may be used on envelopes, but the letter itself achieves a higher tone when words are spelled out.

2. The words "avenue," "road," "street," "boulevard," "park," "company," "high school," "university," "department"

Other Commonly Used Abbreviations

You will not want to use many of these abbreviations in your own serious business letters. You may, however, use them in various memos, statements, or records, and you will want to identify their meaning when you see them in other documents. Note that some abbreviations have almost lost their identity as abbreviations, have become words in themselves, and have dropped the usual period that follows an abbreviation (*doz, FBI, IOU, IQ*).

abbr.	abbreviation
a.c.	alternating current
actg.	acting
A.D.	in the year of our Lord
ad, advt.	advertisement
Adm.	Admiral
ADP	Automatic Data Processing

AFL-CIO	American Federation of Labor and Congress of Industrial Organizations
Aly.	Alley
A.M.	before noon
Am.	American
amt.	amount
anon.	anonymous
approx.	approximately
Apr.	April
apt.	apartment
Arc.	Arcade
assn.	association
asst.	assistant
Atty.	Attorney
Aug.	August
Ave., Av.	Avenue
bbl.	barrel
B.C.	before Christ
B/E	bill of exchange
B/L	bill of lading
bldg.	building
Blvd.	Boulevard
Brig. Gen.	Brigadier General
Bro(s).	Brother(s)
B/S	bill of sale
bu	bushel
bx.	box, boxes
c,C	centigrade, centimeter, Celsius
Capt.	Captain
cc.	carbon copy
cc, c.c.	cubic centimeter(s)
cf.	compare
ch., chap.	chapter
Cir.	Circle
cm.	centimeter
cml.	commercial
Co.	Company
c/o	care of
C.O.D.	cash on delivery
Col.	Colonel
Comdr.	Commander

Corp.	Corporation
C.P.A.	Certified Public Accountant
Cpl.	Corporal
cr.	credit, creditor
C.S.T.	Central Standard Time
Ctr.	Center
cwt	hundredweight
d.c.	direct current
D.D.	Doctor of Divinity
D.D.S.	Doctor of Dental Surgery
Dec.	December
deg.	degree, degrees
Dem.	Democrat
dept.	department
dia., diam.	diameter
dol	dollar
doz	dozen
dr.	debit, debtor
Dr.	Doctor, Drive
D.S.T.	Daylight Saving Time
E.	East
ea.	each
ed.	edition, editor
e.g.	for example
enc., encl.	enclosure
Eng.	English
Ens.	Ensign
e.o.m.	end of month
Esq.	Esquire
E.S.T.	Eastern Standard Time
et al.	and others
et seq.	and the following
etc.	and so forth
Expy.	Expressway
Ext.	Extended, Extension
F	Fahrenheit
FBI	Federal Bureau of Investigation
fbm	board foot
Feb.	February
Fed.	Federal

fig.	figure
fl. oz.	fluid ounce, fluid ounces
F.O.B.	free on board
Fri.	Friday
frt.	freight
ft	feet, foot
Frwy.	Freeway
G., g.	grain, gram(s)
gal	gallon, gallons
Gdns.	Gardens
Gen.	General
gi.	gill, gills
gm	gram(s)
Gov.	Governor
govt.	government
gr	grain(s), gram(s)
gr. wt.	gross weight
Hon.	Honorable
hosp.	hospital
h.p., hp	horsepower
hr.	hour
Hts.	Heights
Hwy.	Highway
Ibid.	in the same place
id.	the same
i.e.	that is
in	inch, inches
Inc.	Incorporated
Inst.	Institute
IOU	I owe you
IQ	intelligence quotient
ital.	italic, italics
Jan.	January
Jct.	Junction
J.D.	Doctor of Laws
jour.	journal
Jr.	Junior
kc	kilocycle, kilocycles

kt.	carat, kiloton
kw	kilowatt
l	liter
La.	Lane
lat.	latitude
lb	pound
Lt.	Lieutenant
LL.D.	Doctor of Laws
long.	longitude
Ltd.	Limited
m.	meter, noon
Maj.	Major
M.D.	Doctor of Medicine
mdse.	merchandise
memo	memorandum
Messrs.	plural for Mr.
mfg.	manufacturing
mfr.	manufacturer
Mgr.	Manager, Monsignor
mi	mile, miles
min	minute, minutes
misc.	miscellaneous
Mlle.	Mademoiselle
Mme.	Madame
mo.	month
Mon.	Monday
mpg	miles per gallon
m.p.h.	miles per hour
Mr.	Mister
Mrs.	Mistress, title used before the name of a married woman
Ms.	feminine equivalent of Mr.—does not denote marital status
M.S.T.	Mountain Standard Time
Mt.	Mount, Mountain
mtge.	mortgage
mun.	municipal
N.	North
Natl.	National
N.B.	note carefully

N.D., n.d.	no date
No.	number
Nov.	November
nt. wt.	net weight
Oct.	October
O.K.	all correct, approved
o.s.	out of stock
oz	ounce
p., pp.	page, pages
par.	paragraph
pd.	paid
Ph.D.	Doctor of Philosophy
Pk.	Park
pkg.	package
Pkway.	Parkway
Pl.	Place
Plz.	Plaza
p.m.	afternoon
P.O.	post office
ppd.	prepaid
pr.	pair
Pres.	President
pro tem	temporarily
Prof.	Professor
P.S.	postscript
P.S.T.	Pacific Standard Time
pt.	part, point
pt	pint
q.	question, quire
qt	quart
quot.	quotation
Rd.	Road
recd.	received
Rep.	Republican
Rev.	Reverend
R.F.D.	Rural Free Delivery
rm.	ream, room
rms.	reams, rooms
R.N.	registered nurse

r/min.	revolutions per minute
r.p.m., rpm	revolutions per minute
R.R.	Railroad, Right Reverend
R.S.V.P., r.s.v.p.	please reply
Ry.	Railway
S	South
Sat.	Saturday
sec.	second
secy.	secretary
Sept.	September
Sgt.	Sergeant
SOS	radio distress signal
Sq.	Square
Sr.	Senior
S.S.	Steamship
St.	Saint, Street
subj.	subject
Sun.	Sunday
Supt.	Superintendent
tbsp	tablespoonful
tel.	telegram, telephone
temp.	temperature
Ter.	Terrace
terr.	territory
Thurs.	Thursday
Trl.	Trail
Treas.	Treasurer
tsp	teaspoonful
Tues.	Tuesday
Tpke.	Turnpike
U.N., UN	United Nations
U.S.A.	United States of America
Via.	Viaduct
vid.	see
viz.	namely
vol.	volume
V.P.	Vice-President
vs.	versus

W.	West
Wed.	Wednesday
wk.	week
wkly.	weekly
wt.	weight
yd	yard
yr	year
ZIP	Zone Improvement Plan

CAPITALIZATION

The most common uses of the capital present no problems. We capitalize proper nouns and their derivatives (France, French), first words in sentences, first words in items in outlines, the pronoun "I" the interjection "Oh," and abbreviations for degrees and names of organizations (M.D., CIO). In addition, use capitals in the following situations.

1. First word of a direct quotation:

   The salesperson said, "We leave tomorrow."

2. First word of a title (book, magazine, article, report) and all other words of a title except coordinate conjunctions, articles, and prepositions:

   Theory of the Leisure Class (a book)
   "The Worth of My Customer" (an article)

3. First word following a colon when a formal statement or question follows:

   Here is an important rule for report writers: Plan your work and work your plan. Each salesperson should ask himself this question: Do I really believe in my product?

4. Religious names such as God, Allah, Virgin Mary, Jehovah, Holy Ghost, Son of Man. Capitalize pronouns such as He, Him, and His when they refer to God only when it eliminates confusion in meaning. Capitalize "Bible," but not "biblical."

   The minister prayed for His guidance.

5. Names of planes, ships, and trains (these should also be italicized or underscored):

   The Spirit of St. Louis   Williamsburg   El Capitan

6. First and last words in salutations only and the first word in complimentary closes only:

   My dear Mr. President:
   Respectfully yours,

7. Names of documents and historical events:

   Missouri Constitution   Battle of Bunker Hill

8. Titles that come before or after a name:

   Editor Smith   Mr. John Smith, Editor
   President King   Dr. John King, President

   Do not capitalize titles used without names unless they are titles of exalted rank:

   I met Judge Smith. He is one of our judges.
   The President and the Vice-President of our country will decide.
   The president of our company is here. The mayor of our town will speak.

9. Proper nouns and proper adjectives:

   Ireland
   Harvard
   George Washington
   They were shipped on a Liberian freighter.
   We sell all the Italian shoes we can buy.
   How about putting in a line of French perfumes?

   Do not capitalize words that were originally proper nouns or proper adjectives but have now become common nouns or common adjectives:

   watt   ampere
   manila paper   derby hat

10. Names of persons, organizations, institutions, places, streets, avenues, buildings, parks:

Lewis Ward   Mississippi River   Pine Street
Maine   NAM   Central Park
Boston   Empire State Building   FBI
American Red Cross   Eastman Kodak Company

11. Names that indicate family relationships if they are used as part of a name or as a substitute for a name—but do not capitalize them if they are preceded by a possessive noun or pronoun:

I spoke to Cousin Joe.   I spoke to Father.
I spoke to Joe, my cousin.   I spoke to my father.

12. Names of school courses only if they are names of languages or numbered courses:

I am taking mathematics, ethics, French, and History 47.

13. Points of the compass only when they refer to a section of a country:

I lived in the South.
I drove south for five miles.

PUNCTUATION

To End Sentences

1. *Statements:* Use a period.

A storm broke three windows in the warehouse.
The glasses you sent were defective.

2. *Questions:* Use a question mark.

Does the radio operate on direct current?
He asked, "When will you ship the suits?"

3. *Questions in a series:* Use a question mark after each question in a series that has the same beginning.

What is the horsepower of the Watercraft Model? of the Sportsman Model? of the Ranger?

4. *Indirect Questions:* Use a period. These are not actually questions, but statements about questions.

> INDIRECT QUESTION: The driver asked where we wanted him to put the drums.
>
> DIRECT QUESTION: The driver asked, "Where do you want me to put the drums?"

5. *Commands and Requests:* Use a period for a standard directive and an exclamation point for an emotional statement.

> STANDARD DIRECTIVE: Stop by and pick up your free gift.
>
> EMOTIONAL STATEMENT: Don't park there!

6. *Courtesy Requests:* Use a period or question mark. Courtesy questions, often used in business letters, may end with either a question mark or a period. They are not really questions, which require a verbal answer, but imperatives that suggest an action answer. A phrase like "Will you" is often equivalent to "Please."

> May I have your answer this week.
>
> May I have your answer this week?

7. *Exclamations:* Use an exclamation point after words of emotional intent and after an ironical or emphatic expression:

> What an exciting project!
>
> How many times I have heard that excuse!
>
> Wow!
>
> Watch out!
>
> Congratulations!

Except in sales messages, the words themselves must convey the emotion. The exclamation point will not create the emotion; it will only signal the intent.

> "Look out!" Ann yelled. "Are you trying to spill the coffee?"

If the words themselves do not convey the emotion, the exclamation point is a poor crutch. Use a period, or revise the sentence.

> QUESTIONABLE: It was hard to believe! "Honest John" was actually trying to cheat!
>
> IMPROVED: It was hard to believe that "Honest John" was actually trying to cheat.

REVISED: What a shock! "Honest John"—I could hardly believe it—old
                  "Honest" himself was actually trying to cheat!

To Separate Pairs of Main Statements

1. *Full break, stressing equal importance:* Use a period.

    She nodded and smiled all the time I talked. I could not, however, get her to buy
    the TV set.

2. *Separate statements, but two parts of one idea:* Use a comma with coordinating
    conjunction ("and," "but," "or," "nor," "for").

    She smiled and nodded all the time I talked, but still I could not get her to buy
    the TV set.

If one of the main statements contains a comma, you may for clarity put a semicolon
at the major break between the two statements.

    We would like delivery on Friday morning at eight o'clock, but Thursday night
    at nine o'clock will be satisfactory.
    As we have told you, we would like delivery on Friday morning at eight o'clock;
    but Thursday night at nine o'clock will be satisfactory.
    We would like delivery on Friday morning at eight o'clock; but, if it is more
    convenient for you, Thursday night at nine o'clock will be satisfactory.

No comma is necessary when both clauses are short—usually no more than five
words each.

    I like the company and the company likes me.

You may use a comma to separate very short main clauses that are not joined by one
of the five conjunctions ("and," "but," "or," "nor," "for").

    They came, they saw, they bought.

3. *A semibreak, with close relationship:* Use a semicolon.

    He prefers a person with college training; I prefer a person with field experience.
    She nodded and smiled all the time I talked; however, I could not get her to buy
    the TV set.

The word "however" is a connective adverb, not a conjunction. It is preceded by a semicolon when used between main statements. Other connective adverbs include "still," "therefore," "also," "accordingly," "furthermore," "otherwise," "likewise," "yet," "so," "for example," "that is," "namely."

> The clocks arrived too late for our weekend sale; therefore, we are returning them to you.
> We have plans for expansion; for example, in January we will open a new store in Southmoore.

4. *Suspense or abrupt break:* Use a dash.

> She nodded and smiled all the time I talked—still I could not get her to buy the TV set.

5. *Balance —the second statement echoes or amplifies the first:* Use a colon.

> To make a sale adds to your commission: to make a customer adds to your future.

To Separate Introductory Elements

1. *To avoid confusion:* Use a comma. The subject begins the main idea of the sentence. Unless the subject of your sentence stands out clearly, put a comma after introductory elements to mark where the subject begins.

> Yes, people of ability will get ahead in this company.
> As long as I remained, the cashier watched me suspiciously.
> Although the car was actually a wreck, the eager young man thought it was a bargain.
> Having many people to see, the women canvassed the neighborhood ten hours a day.
> To get the full benefit of our insurance plan, fill out and return the enclosed card.

The following sentences are clear without a comma.

> In the show window stood three naked mannequins.
> On Sunday he rests.

2. *For a double start:* Use a dash. Use a dash to separate a beginning list from a summary word.

> Suits, sportcoats, shoes—these are on sale.
> Oil, wheat, cattle—these are the state's main products.

When a list is not followed by a summary word but by the verb, a dash is not necessary:

Suits, sportcoats, shoes, and many other items are on sale.

3. *After the salutation in business letters:* Use a colon, unless open punctuation is used.

Dear Sir: Gentlemen: Dear Mrs. Eidelstein:

4. *To introduce an item or a list of items:* Use a colon.

Success in business requires these qualities: hard work, intelligence, personality, and imagination.
This is what he said: "Choose a profession that you can give your heart to as well as your ability."

To Set Off Parenthetical Items

1. *Slight interruption:* Use a comma. The parenthetical material can be removed from the sentence without changing the meaning of what remains.

John Vielkind, who is head of the credit department, will get in touch with you.
Mrs. Thomas, speaking on behalf of the entire department, chose her words carefully.

A word or a group of words necessary to identify or distinguish the word they refer to are part of the main thought, not an interruption. Therefore, no punctuation is used.

The person who is head of the credit department will get in touch with you.
Any man speaking on behalf of the entire department must choose his words carefully.

Here are some typical slight interruptions:

DIRECT ADDRESS:	Joe, I believe you can handle the territory.
APPOSITIVE:	(A term restated in another way) James Henson, the new district manager, will arrive Tuesday.
SPEAKER IN DIRECT QUOTATION:	"This engine," said the salesperson, "is the largest we build."

LOOSELY CONNECTED	It was, to be sure, his first day on the job.
TRANSITIONAL EXPRESSION:	You will agree, however, that the merchandise was defective.
	We will begin our sale, therefore, on July 12.

A tightly connected expression is not set off by commas.

We will therefore begin our sale on July 12.

2. *Abrupt or violent interruption:* Use dashes.

Then Vic—good old high-pressure Vic—had not a word to say.

An interruption in full statement form, unless it is an idiom ("it seems to me"), takes dashes, not commas.

The committee decided—you may think it's a joke, but it isn't—that the resolution should be adopted.
Shall we—can we—increase our sales quotas?

3. *Nonemphatic, supplementary material:* Use parentheses. Some examples are explanations, restatements in different form, and letters in enumeration.

Three of our typists (Jean Stacey, John Terrell, and Mary Saunders) are demanding new typewriters.
Not one of our employees (you'll not believe this, I'm sure) was absent during July.
Please send your check for fifteen dollars ($15.00) immediately.

4. *Incidental remarks made by someone who is quoting someone else:* Use brackets.

Johnson said: "Jake Benson, our company's founder, used to say 'Full steam ahead' [he meant "speed"] whenever the problems got heavy."

Lists and Series

1. *Any three or more items in a series:* Use a comma.

The engine is powerful, it is well built, and it is economical.
She grabbed her purse, jumped from her seat, and marched from the store.
Ted Smith, Bill Avery, and Mary Olson will make the trip to St. Louis with me.

For clarity, separate each item with a comma, including one before "and." In the example below, without the comma after the word "green," no one can tell for sure whether there are four choices, the last of which is white; or whether there are three choices, the last of which is a combination of green and white.

You have a choice of red, yellow, green, and white.

Commas are not needed for separation if all items are joined by *and.*

He worked and fought and cheated his way to the top.

2. *Two equal adjectives:* Use a comma. Equal adjectives modify the noun separately. Two adjectives are equal if their order can be reversed or they can be connected by *and.* They are not equal if each adjective in turn modifies the total idea that follows it.

    EQUAL :   We need an experienced, intelligent salesperson.
    NOT EQUAL :   We need an experienced car salesperson.

3. *Commas within items:* Use a semicolon at the major breaks in a series that contains commas.

    The planning team is made up of Janet Wilson, a market research specialist; Thomas Crampton, an industrialist; and Jack Billings, a city councilman.
    Some of our employees have worked overtime this week: Greene, 7 hours; Howard, 6 hours; Collins, 10; and Mitler, 4.
    We sent reports to shareholders in Akron, Ohio; Baltimore, Maryland; Dallas, Texas; Richmond, Virginia; San Francisco, California; and Seattle, Washington.

4. *A series as a parenthetical group containing commas:* Use dashes.

    Three problems—loafing, absenteeism, and theft—are costing us heavily.
    Their scores—Mary, 21; Sally, 20; and Jo, 19—were the highest in a group of 300.

5. *A formally announced list:* Use a colon. Such words as "these," "those," and "the following" are signals. Use a colon only after a grammatically complete statement—with subject-verb-direct object or predicate noun.

    The manager listed our problems as these: loafing, absenteeism, and theft.

To Set Off Final Items

Items tacked on to the end of your main statement can be separated from it by a comma, a colon, or a dash.

1. *Parenthetical items:* Use a comma. Final parenthetical items are not necessary to the direct line of thought and are often afterthoughts, such as modifiers and tag questions.

   > Jay Johnson was manager then, if I am not mistaken.
   > The police arrested Tim Riley, whom they charged with breaking and entering.
   > It's a great bargain, isn't it?

2. *Complimentary closing of a letter:* Use a comma, unless you are using open punctuation.

   > Sincerely yours,

3. *Formal announcement of something to follow:* Use a colon. The colon signals "Watch this space: special information to follow." Such words as "this," "these," "one," and "the following" are signals. In sentences, the colon is normally used after a full subject-verb-complement statement. Here are some typical patterns.

   To announce that a word or a list will follow:

   > I am enclosing copies of the following: your original letter, our return letter, and your answer.
   > No Parking: Reserved for Vice-President
   > For Sale: Three-Bedroom House

   To stress an appositive or restatement of a term:

   > The success of the V-20 is due to the efforts of one man: Henry Hatton.
   > His eye is fixed on one thing: promotion.

   To introduce a long quotation:

   > This is what he advised us: "Choose a company with a ground floor—you can build the top floor yourself."

   After the salutation of a letter:

   > Dear Miss Torrence:

4. *Informal introduction of summarizing word or emphatic words:* Use a dash.

> He wanted to sit in the show window—a ridiculous notion.
> She wanted only one thing out of her staff—hard work.

To Separate Parts

Parts of items must be separated by commas or a colon to prevent misreading and to give clarity.

1. *Dates:*   Use two commas.

> On June 6, 1976, we opened the new store.
> On Thursday, June 6, 1976, we opened the new store.
> At 1 A.M., Thursday, June 6, 1976, we opened the new store.

If no day of the month is given, the comma may be omitted.

> In June 1968 he joined the company.

2. *Addresses:*   Use two commas.

> She lived in Oran, New Jersey, for two years.
> She lived at 138 Main Street, Oran, New Jersey, for two years.

3. *Titles and Names:*   Use two commas.

> Ralph James, M.D., was appointed to the Advisory Commission.
> Ralph James, Jr., was appointed to the Advisory Commission.
> Ralph James, Jr., M.D., was appointed.
> Ted Emmons, Credit Manager, will answer your letter.
> American Dye Co., Inc.,got the contract.
> London Mills, Ltd., bid too high.

4. *Statistical material:* Use one comma to separate the hundreds from the thousands, the thousands from the millions, and so on, in numbers of more than four digits:

> 1,845,223   57,828   3200

5. *To express "to" in ratios:*   Use a colon.

> 7:5   3:1

6. *To separate hours from minutes:*   Use a colon.

      9:45 A.M.   4:30 P.M.

7. *To separate the initials of the typist from those of the person who dictated a letter:*   Use a colon or slash.

      HBM:tb   HBM/tb

Ambiguous Meanings

1. *To prevent two words or figures from being read together:* Use a comma.

    AMBIGUOUS: Inside business went on as usual.
    CLEAR: Inside, business went on as usual.
                Whatever happens, happens.
                In 1975, 235 employees took vacations in August.

2. *To indicate when two words are connected:* Use a hyphen.

    MEANING 1:   guaranteed used cars (used cars that are guaranteed)
    MEANING 2:   guaranteed-used cars (cars that are guaranteed to have been used)

    MEANING 1:   6 foot-soldiers (6 soldiers who travel by walking)
    MEANING 2:   6-foot soldiers (soldiers 6 feet tall)

    MEANING 1:   9 inch blades (9 blades each of which is an inch long)
    MEANING 2:   9-inch blades (blades 9 inches long)

    MEANING 1:   recover a couch (to obtain possession of a couch once more)
    MEANING 2:   re-cover a couch (to cover a couch again)

Quotations

1. *To indicate direct quotations from a written or spoken source:* Use a pair of double quotation marks around the quoted parts.

    She asked, "What special items are on sale?"
    "What special items," she asked, "are on sale?"
    The dictionary says, "*Ain't* should be shunned by all who prefer to avoid being considered illiterate."

Note that the parenthetical, unquoted part is left out of the quotation marks.

"That's the price," he said, "such as it is."
"That's the price," he said. "Take it or leave it."

2. *Quotations within quotations:* Use single quotation marks.

The business manager said, "Believe me when I say 'A penny saved is a penny earned' is the best advice I ever had."

Except in journalistic and British English, single quotation marks are never correct alone. Use them only within double quotation marks.

INCORRECT: The customer thought 'darn' was a swearword.
CORRECT: The customer thought "darn" was a swearword.

3. A *series of sentences by one speaker:* one set of quotation marks.

The manager said, "Sit down, gentlemen. I'm dictating a letter. I should be finished in about four minutes. Please wait."

4. *More than one quoted paragraph:* Use quotation marks before each paragraph and only at the close of the last paragraph.

A pertinent section of *The Communist Manifesto* reads as follows:
"Centralization of credit in the hands of the State, by means of a national bank with State capital and an exclusive monopoly.
"Centralization of the means of communication and transport in the hands of the State.
"Extension of factories and instruments of production owned by the State; the bringing into cultivation of waste lands, and the improvement of the soil generally in accordance with a common plan."

5. *Other punctuation with quotation marks.*
Periods and commas go inside quotation marks.

He called the Spring Sale a "flop."
The common expression, "dog eat dog," refers to Darwin's theory.

Semicolons and colons go outside quotation marks.

He came to the door and said only one thing: "She quit"; then he left.

Dashes, question marks, and exclamation points go inside quotation marks when they are part of the quote and outside when they are not part of the quote.

> He asked, "Would you buy another one?"
> Didn't General Smiley say, "I'll keep us out of war"?
> We heard him cry "Fire!"

If the mark applies to both the quotation and the whole sentence, use it only once.

> Did she ask, "How many accidents can we afford?"

Titles

In handwritten and typed letters and papers, underlining takes the place of italics.

1. *Publications and works of art.* In works issued separately, use italics for titles of books, plays, magazines, newspapers, bulletins, pamphlets, paintings, musical compositions, and movies.

Theory of the Leisure Class	the *New York Times*
Beethoven's *Fifth Symphony*	*Playboy* magazine
The *Sound of Music*	the *Mona Lisa*

   For parts of other works, use quotation marks for titles of short stories, poems, essays, subdivisions of books, articles in a magazine, songs in musicals, and movements of symphonies.

   > Hawthorne's short story "Dr. Heidigger's Experiment" from *Twice-Told Tales* contains a lesson for the businessperson.

   > The article "Priorities for the Eighties" appeared in the *Businessman's Weekly*.

2. *Ships, trains, aircraft:* Use italics.

   > the *Queen Elizabeth*   the *Santa Fe Flyer*   the United Airlines' *Sky King*

3. *The.* Do not underline the word "the" unless it is part of the title.

   > *The Red Badge of Courage*   the *Saturday Review*

4. *Historical documents and events, books of the Bible:* no italics or quotation marks.

   > He memorized The Sermon on the Mount from the book of Matthew.

He quoted from The Declaration of Independence, which is a Revolutionary War document.

Possessives

1. *Singular nouns*: Add an apostrophe and an *s*.

    the driver's side   a day's wait   a woman's rights

2. *Plurals ending in s*: Add only an apostrophe.

    the clerks' coffee break   three days' wait
    the Joneses' house   two dollars' worth

3. *Singular nouns ending in s or z sound*: Add an apostrophe and an *s* or only an apostrophe, whichever form you prefer.

    the boss's desk   James' hat   James's hat

4. *Indefinite pronouns*: Add apostrophe and *s*.

    anybody's guess   everybody's responsibility

5. *Plurals that do not end in s:* Add apostrophe and *s*.

    men's suits   children's dresses

6. *Compound expressions used as a single noun:* Add apostrophe and *s*.

    his brother-in-law's car
    the Director of Budget's parking space
    Thomas and Hedges' sale
    somebody else's seat
    Jack and Bill's customers (same customers)

Special Words

1. *Words used as words:* Use italics (underline) or quotation marks. You have a choice. However, be consistent in using the method you choose in a single piece of writing.

    The word *receive* is often misspelled.

2. *Letters and numbers used as words:* Use italics.

> The *a* and the *o* in the sign looked alike.
> He doesn't dot his *i's* or cross his *t's*.

3. *Foreign words that are not commonly used in English:* Use italics. Check the dictionary for confirmation.

> *femme fatale, tempus fugit*
> menu, rodeo, blitz

4. *Words used in special context:* Use quotation marks. These words include definitions, single quoted words, words out of normal context (such as slang in standard writing), and nicknames.

> He defined "ego" as "awareness of one's self."
> Mr. Jackson did not appreciate having his Jaguar referred to as a "hot rod."
> His favorite customer is John "Tiny" Benson.

5. *In spelling out compound numbers from twenty-one to ninety-nine:* Use a hyphen.

> one hundred and twenty-eight   thirty-one   ninety-seven

6. *To express fractions that precede a noun:* Use a hyphen.

> a two-thirds interest   a three-fourths majority

Fractions not followed by nouns are not hyphenated: two thirds of the numbers.

7. *To avoid an awkward union between the prefix or suffix and the root of the word:* Use a hyphen.

re-enter	un-American	shell-like
semi-invalid	bell-like	de-emphasize
re-address	pre-inventory	

8. *With the prefixes all-, ex-, half-, quarter-, self-, and the suffix -elect:* Use a hyphen.

all-American	quarter-turn	half-awake
ex-soldier	self-sufficient	President-elect

9. *To connect two or more words used as a single adjective preceding a noun:* Use a hyphen.

    a blue-green sweater   an up-to-date record

    a well-balanced diet   a do-it-yourself kit

    an attention-getting device

The hyphen is omitted, however, when the first word of the modifier is an adverb that ends in *ly* or when the qualifying words follow a noun:

    a freshly prepared solution
    the diet is well balanced
    a record that is up to date

10. *With compound words or expressions:* Use a hyphen. Check the dictionary to see if words should be written solid (*blackberry*), hyphenated (*tough-minded*), or open (*high school*).

    jack-of-all-trades
    a middle-of-the-roader
    brother-in-law

11. *The past tense of coined words:* Use an apostrophe and *d*.

    O.K.'d   X'd out

12. *Plural of numbers, letters, and words used as words:* Add an apostrophe and *s*.

    7's   Q's   1960's   C.O.D.'s
    11's   T's   &'s   IOU's
    He used too many *but's* and *if's*.
    The 1930's were the Depression years.

Omission of Words

1. *Omission of words from a quotation:* Use an ellipsis (three spaced periods).

    Mr. Akins said, "We are sure . . . that the building will be ready by July 1 for a grand opening."

For an ellipsis at the end of a quotation use four periods, one to indicate the end of the sentence.

> Mr. Akins said, "We are sure, with good evidence, that the building will be ready by July 1 . . . ."

If the omission overlaps beyond one sentence, use four periods, one for the period between the sentences.

> Mr. Akins said, "We are sure . . . that the building will be ready by July 1 for a grand opening . . . . or a sale."

2. *Omission of words in a patterned series:* Use a comma.

> One of the men who was injured is a lathe operator; the other, a toolmaker.
> Nancy scored 98 on the speech test; Sally, 110.

3. *To avoid repetition of a root word:* Use a hyphen.

> short- and long-run objectives
> first-, second-, and third-class mail

Special Emphasis

1. *Emphatic pause before an important word or phrase:* Use a dash.

> The secret of his success is —hard work.
> We can't say Edwards is not an effective salesman—he is the second highest in sales.

2. *To indicate emotional force for a phrase or statement:* Use an exclamation point.

> Make your reservations now!

3. *Emphatic restatement:* Use dashes.

> His decision—the best decision—was based on years of experience.
> Compare the price—$159—with the cost of rental.
> We are concerned with one thing—satisfied customers.

4. *To pinpoint specific words:* Use italics.

> She couldn't understand that *to want* is not *to get.*

5. *To hint at a double meaning:* Use quotation marks.

    our "happy" office force   (Hints that the force is not happy)
    out for "lunch"   (Suggests that the reason for being out is something other than lunch)

NUMBERS AS FIGURES OR WORDS

In general, use the figure instead of the word because the reader can more easily read the figure and grasp its meaning. With invoices, tabular materials, purchase orders, and the like, always use figures. In letters and reports, use the rule of 10: spell out the numbers one through nine; use figures for numbers 10 and above except for amounts of money and for isolated cases, as shown below.

1. *Dates* are expressed as figures. Avoid the bureaucratic form of writing (13 May, 1974) and all number forms (8–20–77; 8/20/77).

    May 13, 1974
    Your letter of May 13 was appreciated.
    The shipment arrived the 3rd of June.

2. *Numbered names of streets:* Write names of streets over 10 that require two words as figures.

    328 42 Street
    329-42 Street

    Names of streets under 10 or that require only one word can be expressed as either words or figures.

    780 Sixth Street   780 6 Street
    1128 40 Street   1128 Fortieth Street

    Separate the place number and the street number by a double space or by a hyphen.
    Do not use number indicators (*st, nd, d, rd,* or *th*) with figures for numbered streets.

3. *House or room numbers* (except the number one) are expressed as figures.

    328 48 Street
    One Adams Avenue

4. *Decimals* are expressed in figures.

      12.25   2.1612   .3333

5. *Dimensions* are expressed in figures.

    .32 calibre   9½ × 12 feet
    2 × 4 inches   9½ by 12 feet
    2 by 4 inches

6. *Numbered items*—such as page numbers, chapter numbers, table numbers, figure numbers, and telephone numbers—are expressed as figures.

    page 2   Serial No. 1092372
    chapter 5   Policy #289783
    chapter V   Policy 289783
    table 10   Claim No. 374829
    figure 7   Telephone 692-6611
    chart 12   Telephone NW-2-6611
    chart XII

7. *Time:* The hour of the day when followed by A.M. or P.M. is expressed as a figure.

    The doors open at 8:30 A.M.
    The doors open at eight-thirty.
    The doors close at 5:00 P.M.
    The doors close at five o'clock.
    The doors close at five in the afternoon.

8. *Percentages* are expressed as figures.

    27%   6.5 percent
    6%   6.5%
    6 percent   6½ percent

9. *Fractions* are expressed as figures.

    1/12   1/3
    3/32   5 3/4
    27/64   5.75

Fractions used as modifiers in standard sentence structure are spelled out.

The new policy passed by a three-fourths vote. [not 3/4]
Sam is about one third [not 1/3] as efficient as Bill.

10. *Isolated numbers below ten* are expressed in words. This rule does not apply to exact dimensions or amounts of money.

Jeb sold eight sets last month. He plans to sell 24 this month.
The desk is about 342 feet wide.
The machine uses 3-inch tape.

11. *Numbers that begin a sentence* are expressed in words.

Fifteen people complained.
Five hundred and twenty businesses answered the request.

It is often best to revise the sentence so that you can use figures.

The request was answered by 520 businesses.

12. *One number immediately preceding another number of different context:* Express one number in words; the other, in figures.

There were only twenty-one 5's in the cash drawer.
There were only 21 five's in the cash drawer.
You ordered 144 four-foot lines.
The plans call for fifty-two 2 × 4's.

13. *Amounts of money* are normally expressed in figures. Additionally, the following practices are recommended.

a. *Dollars and cents:* Use dollar sign and decimal point.

The invoice was $25.96
The truck was sold for $875.75

b. *Dollars only:* Omit the decimal point and the double zero.

The invoice was $25.

c. *Tabulated column with both dollars and cents:* Use the double zero.

$$
\begin{array}{r}
\$ \quad 25.96 \\
875.75 \\
400.00 \\
\underline{29.25} \\
\$1,330.96
\end{array}
$$

d. *A series of money amounts with mixed figures:* Use double zero for all figures.

On three successive days Betson took in exactly $428.25, $33.00, and $275.47.

e. *Cents only:* Use any of the following forms.

The amount to be returned is $.68.
The amount to be returned is 68 cents.
The amount to be returned is 68¢.

f. *Repeated amounts in parentheses:* Use both words and figures only in legal and financial documents.

STANDARD: The cost of replacement is $87.
                      The total investment is $35,478.50.

FINANCIAL PAPERS: eighty-seven dollars ($87.00)
                      eight dollars ($8.00)
                      twenty-four and 57/100 ($24.57)
                      twenty-four dollars and fifty-seven cents
                      ($24.57)

14. *A sentence containing one series of numbers:* Express all the numbers as figures.

We have 12 salespeople in Illinois, 11 in Indiana, and 5 in Iowa.

15. *A sentence containing two series of numbers:* Express one set in words and the other in figures.

Twelve salespeople reached 15 customers each; eleven reached 9 each; and five reached 4 each.

16.   *More than two series of numbers:* Tabulate.

Name of Salesperson	Number of Contacts	Number of Sales	% of Sales
Hill, Barton	15	11	.73
Darter, Carla	15	8	.53
Smith, Leon	15	4	.26

SYLLABICATION—DIVIDING WORDS

1.   Do not divide words of one syllable.

   planned   friend   length   guessed

2.   Divide words between syllables only.

   pro-duct   mix-ture   prob-ably   knowl-edge

3.   Do not divide words at the ends of more than two consecutive lines of typing.

4.   Do not divide words containing fewer than six letters.

   final   upon   idea   index

5.   Do not separate a one-vowel syllable at the beginning or end of a word.

   *a*mount   bacteri*a*   *e*nough

6.   Two-letter prefixes such as *de, en, ex, it, im, in, ir, re,* and *un* may be separated from the rest of the word.

   il-legal   im-possible   ex-pensive

7.   Other two-letter beginning syllables and ending syllables should not be separated.

   new*ly*   *de*mocracy   *po*litical   wast*ed*

8.   As a rule, divide between a prefix and the rest of the word.

   trans-fer   con-sign   dis-tribute

9. In words of three or more syllables, a one-letter syllable should be typed on the first rather than on the second line.

    sepa-rate   (not *sep-arate*)   presi-dent   regu-lar   compari-son

10. When two consecutive vowels are pronounced separately, divide between them.

    radi-ator   cre-ated   gradu-ated   idi-omatic

11. Double consonants can usually be divided.

    shut-ter   drug-gist   mil-lion   tal-low

12. When the root word ends with a double consonant, separate the ending from the root word.

    full-est   guess-ing   tell-ing

13. In words ending with *able* and *ible*, the "ble" is considered to be the ending and the "a" or "i" is considered part of the preceding syllable.

    feasi-ble   defensi-ble   amena-ble

14. These endings are kept as syllables: *cian, cion, gion, sion,* and *tion.*

    expres-sion   physi-cian   conta-gion

15. As a rule, divide between the root and the ending of a word.

    quick-ness   announce-ment   depart-ment

16. Divide compound words between the major parts.

    business-man   text-book

17. Divide hyphenated words only at the hyphen.

    ex-president   self-control   court-martial

18. Do not divide abbreviations, contractions, figures, or proper names.

    FBI   o'clock   they've $159,628   Denver

19. Do not divide the last word in a paragraph or on a page.

ABBREVIATIONS OF STATES

The following special two-letter abbreviations have been devised by the U.S. Postal Service for use with the ZIP Code. You may use any one of the following three forms in the address on the envelope: the full name of the state, the abbreviation in parentheses, or the two-letter abbreviation. Most writers of serious letters do not use the abbreviated forms in the heading and inside address of the letter itself. For a more dignified tone, it is preferable to spell out the full name of the state, except D.C. which is always substituted for District of Columbia.

Alabama	(Ala.)	AL
Alaska		AK
Arizona	(Ariz.)	AZ
Arkansas	(Ark.)	AR
California	(Calif.)	CA
Colorado	(Colo.)	CO
Connecticut	(Conn.)	CT
Delaware	(Del.)	DE
Florida	(Fla.)	FL
Georgia	(Ga.)	GA
Hawaii		HI
Idaho		ID
Illinois	(Ill.)	IL
Indiana	(Ind.)	IN
Iowa		IA
Kansas	(Kans.)	KS
Kentucky	(Ky.)	KY
Louisiana	(La.)	LA
Maine		ME
Maryland	(Md.)	MD
Massachusetts	(Mass.)	MA
Michigan	(Mich.)	MI
Minnesota	(Minn.)	MN
Mississippi	(Miss.)	MS
Missouri	(Mo.)	MO
Montana	(Mont.)	MT
Nebraska	(Nebr.)	NB
Nevada	(Nev.)	NV
New Hampshire	(N.H.)	NH
New Jersey	(N.J.)	NJ
New Mexico	(N. Mex.)	NM
New York	(N.Y.)	NY
North Carolina	(N.C.)	NC

North Dakota	(N. Dak.)	ND
Ohio		OH
Oklahoma	(Okla.)	OK
Oregon	(Oreg.)	OR
Pennsylvania	(Pa.)	PA
Rhode Island	(R.I.)	RI
South Carolina	(S.C.)	SC
South Dakota	(S. Dak.)	SD
Tennessee	(Tenn.)	TN
Texas	(Tex.)	TX
Utah		UT
Vermont	(Vt.)	VT
Virginia	(Va.)	VA
Washington	(Wash.)	WA
West Virginia	(W. Va.)	WV
Wisconsin	(Wis.)	WI
Wyoming	(Wyo.)	WY
Canal Zone	(C.Z.)	CZ
Guam		GU
Puerto Rico	(P.R.)	PR
Virgin Islands	(V.I.)	VI
District of Columbia	(D.C.)	DC

Appendix C

GLOSSARY OF USAGE

As an educated user of English, you will be called upon to use different kinds of language at different times. Sometimes you may say, "It is I"; other times you may say, "It's I"; and still other times "It's me." All are proper if they fit the speaking or writing situation. The following table will help you to classify and select certain words and phrases according to the occasion.

Standard English

GENERAL ENGLISH.   General English is the central language, suitable for all occasions. It is also called *standard* and *informal*. This is the language spoken and written by educated people in their everyday communications. It includes all-purpose words such as "go," "look," "into," "the," "radio." It excludes nonstandard terms of slang, illiteracy, and extreme formality.

> As the first of the women's death sentences was read, two women jurors appeared to be blinking back tears. One wiped her eyes. However, when each was polled as to whether the verdicts were theirs, all clearly announced "Yes."
> —The Associated Press, March 30, 1971

FORMAL.   Formal English is the language of serious articles, reports, books, and addresses. It is usually written.

> The computer makes possible a phenomenal leap in human proficiency; it demolishes the fences around the practical and even the theoretical intelligence. But the question persists and indeed grows whether the computer will make it easier or harder for human beings to know who they really are.
> —Norman Cousins

COLLOQUIAL.   Colloquial English is used in familiar and conversational writing and is not acceptable in most serious business letters. Examples of colloquial usage are: "Mrs. Higgins was mad" instead of "Mrs. Higgins was angry"; and "That was a funny thing to say" instead of "That was a strange thing to say." Most of the words labeled colloquial in this glossary should be avoided in business letters, except those that demand a familiar, personal tone.

Nonstandard English

SLANG.   Slang is a special type of group language that uses coined terms, new and unusual combinations, and metaphors. It is generally unacceptable outside the group. Examples of slang are "lousy" for "unpleasing" and "make a crack about" for "insult."

Beverly decided to split before that screwball customer freaked out.

DIALECT.   A dialect is a special type of group language confined to a locality or ethnic group. An example is the word "fetch" for "Go get and bring back."

I reckon you all better mosey along.

ILLITERATE.   Words and expressions not consistent with the grammatical patterns of General English are considered illiterate. Obscenity, profanity, poor grammar, and misspellings are included here. Examples are "ain't" for "is not" and "he don't" for "he doesn't."

This glossary discusses a number of words and phrases that present usage problems. The list is not complete, but it includes the most common troublemakers. A dictionary will give detailed information on words and expressions not included here.

a, an	Use "a" before a consonant sound and "an" before a vowel sound.

a tree, a book, an oak,
a history book, an honest man,
a European, an American

aggravate	General meaning is "to make worse." Colloquial for "annoy" or "irritate."

GENERAL:	The wet climate will *aggravate* his illness.
COLLOQUIAL:	Don't *aggravate* Mr. Henson with your questions.

ain't, aren't I, amn't	Illiterate for "am not," "isn't," and "am I not."
alibi	Colloquial for "excuse"

COLLOQUIAL:	He had no *alibi* for his impolite actions.

GENERAL:	He had no *excuse* for his impolite actions.
GENERAL:	The police accepted his *alibi* that he had been at home when the store was robbed.

almost, most   "Most" is a colloquial substitution for "almost."

COLLOQUIAL:	*Most* everything was sold by noon.
GENERAL:	*Almost* everything was sold by noon.

a lot, lots   Colloquial for "much," or "many." "Alot" is a misspelling of "a lot."

COLLOQUIAL:	I have thought *a lot* about your suggestion.
GENERAL:	I have thought *much* about your suggestion.

alright   "Alright" is a misspelling of "all right."

a.m., p.m. (A.M.,P.M.)   Correct only with figures. Lowercase letters are more commonly used.

The guests arrived at 2:00 p.m. (not "in the p.m.")
The guests arrived in the afternoon.

among, between   "Among" implies more than two. "Between" implies only two. "Between" may be used with more than two when each is regarded individually.

He divided his fortune *among* his three sons.
He divided his fortune *between* his two sons.
Agreement was finally reached *between* the five contending countries.

amount, number   "Amount" refers to bulk or mass. "Number" refers to things that can be counted.

A large *amount* of clothing was left over.
A large *number* of garments were left over.

and etc.

Illiterate and redundant for "etc." "Etc." is an abbreviation of "et cetera" ("and" plus "other" things.)

anyone, any one

"Anyone" is a pronoun meaning "anybody." "Any one" is an adjective-pronoun combination that singles out one of a group. Use "anyone" if "any" is to be accented; use "any one" if the "one" is to be emphasized. "Any one" will usually be followed by "of."

He talks to *anyone* who will listen.
Any one of these errors is cause for dismissal.

anyplace

Colloquial for "anywhere."

COLLOQUIAL: We couldn't find a taxi *anyplace*.
GENERAL: We couldn't find a taxi *anywhere*.

any ways

Dialect for "*anyway*."

GENERAL: We did not believe him *anyway*.

anywheres

Dialect for *anywhere*.

He couldn't find the invoice *anywhere*.

apt, likely

"Apt" means "having a natural ability or tendency." "Likely" means "a probability."

Ted was *apt* at learning to type.
He is *likely* to become a good typist.

as

Dialect for "that." Vague for " because," "for," "since," "while," "why," or "whether."

DIALECT: I don't know *as* I believe his story.
GENERAL: I don't know *that* I believe his story.
VAGUE: *As* the store was not busy, we played cards.
IMPROVED: *Because* the store was not busy, we played cards.
IMPROVED: *While* the store was not busy, we played cards.

as to   Vague for "about."

He questioned us *about* (not "as to") his share in the profits.

at about   Contradictory. Use one or the other, not both.

The ship will dock *at* noon.
The ship will dock *about* noon.

awful, awfully   Colloquial and vague for "very," or "unattractive."

COLLOQUIAL: His new clothes look *awful*.
GENERAL: His new clothes are *unattractive*.
COLLOQUIAL: He seems *awfully* sure of himself.
GENERAL: He seems *very* sure of himself.

bad, badly   "Bad" is an adjective. "Badly" is an adverb.

He feels *bad* about his mistake.
He behaved *badly* at the party.

Colloquial in the sense of "very much."

The man needed a new suit *badly*.

being as, being that   Illiterate for "since" or "because."

NONSTANDARD: *Being as* he had already read the book, he let me borrow it for a week.
GENERAL: *Since* he had already read the book, he let me borrow it for a week.

bursted, bust, busted   Corruptions of " burst."

The dam *burst* and flooded the town.

As slang "bust" and "busted" have several meanings, such as "dismissed," "without money," "party," "arrested."

but that, but what Colloquial for "that" in negative expressions.

> COLLOQUIAL: I do not doubt *but what* he can sell the piano.
>
> GENERAL: I do not doubt *that* he can sell the piano.

calculate Dialect for "guess," "suppose," "think."

can, may Interchangeable in colloquial questions and negations.

> *Can* I go with you?
> *May* I go with you?

In General English "can" denotes ability; "may" denotes permission or possibility.

> *May* I go with you? It *may* rain on Friday.

> *Can* you operate the 3D Copier?

can't hardly,
couldn't hardly,
won't hardly,
wouldn't hardly Double negatives are illiterate.

> ILLITERATE: It was so dark I *couldn't hardly* see.
> STANDARD: It was so dark I *could hardly* see.
> STANDARD: It was so dark I *couldn't* see.

complected Dialect for "complexioned."

> DIALECT: He was dark *complected*.
> STANDARD: He was dark *complexioned*.

complete This adjective has no comparative or superlative form. A thing is either complete or not.

> The list of names is *complete* (not "more complete").

consensus of opinion "Consensus" means "general opinion"; therefore, "of opinion" is redundant.

considerable   Illiterate when used as an adverb.

                       ILLITERATE: The temperature dropped *con-siderable.*

                       STANDARD: The temperature dropped *con-siderably.*

could of   Illiterate for "could have."

        They *could have* (not "of ") left earlier.

criteria   Plural of "criterion."

        He uses one *criterion* for judging credit customers.
        We will have to form some *criteria* for giving pay raises.

data   The singular form, "datum," is not often used. "Data," the plural form, is often considered as a singular collective noun.

        The *data* have not all been assembled yet.
        The *data* has not all been assembled yet.

deal   Colloquial for "business," "transaction," "agreement," "plan."

        Hillside Hotel offers a good *deal* for conventions.

differ from, differ with   "Differ from" means "to be unlike." "Differ with" means "disagree."

        South American cowboys *differ from* those in North America.
        I *differ with* him about politics.

different from,   "Different from" is correct. Avoid "different than."
different than

        His machine is *different from* mine.

don't   Illiterate as a contraction for "does not."

                       ILLITERATE: He *don't* mean any harm.
                       STANDARD: He *doesn't* mean any harm.

due to	Colloquial as a preposition for " because of " in an adverb phrase. General English when "due" is a predicate adjective.

> COLLOQUIAL: *Due to* the rain the picnic was postponed.
>
> GENERAL: *Because of* the rain the picnic was postponed.
>
> GENERAL: The postponement of the picnic was *due to* the rain.

each other, one another	Interchangeable, although some writers prefer "each other" when referring to two and "one another" when referring to more than two.

> Joe and Jim praised *each other*.
>
> The members of the accounting department praised *one another*.

enthuse	Colloquial for "become enthusiastic."

> COLLOQUIAL: Everybody was *enthused* about the holiday.
>
> GENERAL: Everybody was *enthusiastic* about the holiday.

equally as	Redundant. Omit "as."

> The two machines seemed *equally* efficient.

etc.	See "and etc."
everyone, every one	See "anyone."
everyplace	Colloquial for "everywhere."

> COLLOQUIAL: He looked *everyplace* for his wallet.
>
> GENERAL: He looked *everywhere* for his wallet.

exam	Colloquial shortening for "examination."

expect   Colloquial for "suppose," "think."

        COLLOQUIAL: I *expect* the shipment will arrive tomorrow.

        GENERAL: I *suppose* the shipment will arrive tomorrow.

extra   Colloquial for "very," "unusually."

        COLLOQUIAL: He seems *extra* happy today.

        GENERAL: He seems *unusually* happy today.

farther, further   "Farther" usually applies to geographical distance, "further" to degree.

        The town was *farther* than we had thought.
        He refused to discuss it *further*.

female   Do not use as a synonym for "girl," "lady," or "woman."

figure   Colloquial for " believe," "think."

        COLLOQUIAL: I *figure* that is too big a job for him.

        GENERAL: I *believe* that is too big a job for him.

fine   Colloquial for "well" as an adverb. Vague as an adjective of approval.

        COLLOQUIAL: The computer works *fine* since the technician checked it.

        GENERAL: The computer works *well* since the technician checked it.

        VAGUE: He is a *fine* person.

        MORE SPECIFIC: He is a *likeable* person.

flunk   Colloquial for "fail."

folks   Colloquial or dialect for "relatives."

funny   Colloquial for "peculiar" or "odd." In General English, "funny" applies to the laughable.

gentleman, lady   Stilted for "man," "woman." Appropriate in the salutation to a letter.

get   Nonstandard for "understand" or "move emotionally."

> I couldn't *get* what he was saying.
> Music like that always *gets* me.

It is General English in idioms like *to get the better of, to get along with* (a person), *to get over* (an illness).

good   Illiterate as an adverb. Vague as an adjective of general approval.

ILLITERATE:	He surely types *good.*
STANDARD:	He surely types *skillfully.*
VAGUE:	The movie was *good.*
IMPROVED:	The movie was *interesting.*

good and   Colloquial as an intensive.

COLLOQUIAL:	Jensen became *good and* tired of her complaining.
GENERAL:	Jensen became *very tired* of her complaining.

guess   Colloquial for "suppose," "think."

COLLOQUIAL:	I *guess* production was delayed by the strike.
GENERAL:	I *believe* production was delayed by the strike.

gym   Colloquial shortening of "gymnasium."

had of   Illiterate for " had."

> If he *had gone* (not " had of gone") he would have liked the demonstration.

had ought   Illiterate for "ought."

> He ought (not " had ought") to have gone to the demonstration.

hanged, hung	"Hanged" applies to executions; "hung" to other situations. The murderer was *hanged*. The pictures were *hung* immediately. In British English "hung" also applies to executions.
hardly	See "can't hardly."
herself, himself myself, yourself	Intensive or reflexive pronouns. Substandard when used for "she," "her," "he," "him," "I," "me," "you."

SUBSTANDARD: John and *myself* were selected.
GENERAL: I *myself* wrote the memo.

hisself	Illiterate for "himself."
in, into	"In" implies location within. "Into" applies to movement from without to within. He is *in* the store. He walks *in* the store. He walked from the street *into* the store.
individual, party	"Individual" is stilted for "person." The word refers to a single thing, animal or person. "Party" is illiterate for "person" or "individual" except in legal language.

STANDARD: We must respect the rights of the *individual*.
STILTED: I've seen that *individual* somewhere before.
STANDARD: I've seen that *person* somewhere before.
ILLITERATE: I know the *party* you are talking about.
STANDARD: I know the *person* you are talking about.

in regards to	Illiterate for "in regard to" or "as regards."
invite	Illiterate when used as a noun for "invitation."
irregardless	Illiterate for "regardless."

is when, is where   Illiterate in definitions.

ILLITERATE:	The bull market *is when* prices are rising.
STANDARD:	The bull market is the stock market when prices are rising.

just   Colloquial as an intensive.

COLLOQUIAL:	The fire in the paint department was *just* terrible.
GENERAL:	The fire in the paint department was terrible.

kind, sort   Singular words that can be modified only by "that" or "this," not "these" or "those."

CORRECT:	I prefer *this kind* of tennis racket.
INCORRECT:	I prefer *these kinds* of tennis rackets.

kindly   Avoid "kindly" for "please."

Please (not "kindly") fill out the attached form.

kind of, sort of   Colloquial as an adverb of degree, as "somewhat."

COLLOQUIAL:	He was *kind of* displeased.
GENERAL:	He was *somewhat* displeased.

kind of a   Nonstandard for "kind of."

What *kind of* flower is that?

lady, gentleman   See "gentleman, lady."

lay, lie   "Lay," "laid," "laid" are transitive verbs and take a direct object.

Lay the *book* down.
He *laid* the *book* down.

"Lie," "lay," "lain" do not take an object.

> He *lies* down.
> He *lay* there yesterday.
> He *has lain* there often.

learn, teach "Learn" means to get knowledge. "Teach" means to give knowledge.

> A good student *learns* more than a teacher is able to *teach* him.

leave, let "Leave" is illiterate for "allow." "Leave" means to "depart from" or "cause to remain."

> Don't *let* (not *leave*) him have his way.
> He will *leave* town tomorrow.
> *Leave* the book on the table.
> *Let* me alone.

like Colloquial for "as if," "as though."

> COLLOQUIAL: He looks *like* he's angry.
> GENERAL: He looks *as if* he were angry.

likely See "apt."

locate Colloquial for "settle."

> COLLOQUIAL: He finally *located* in Montana.
> GENERAL: He finally *settled* in Montana.
> GENERAL: He *located* his business in Montana.

lots See "a lot."

mad Colloquial for "angry."

> COLLOQUIAL: He was *mad* at me for spilling ink on his suit.
> GENERAL: He was *angry* with me for spilling ink on his suit.

math Colloquial shortening for "mathematics."

may be, maybe   "May be" is a verb phrase. "Maybe" is an adverb.

       He *may be* the winner.
       Maybe he will be the winner.

might of   Illiterate for "might have."

       They *might have* (not *of*) had car trouble.

mighty   Colloquial for "very."

COLLOQUIAL:	Jack is a *mighty* good salesperson.
GENERAL:	Jack is a *very* good salesperson.
GENERAL:	A *mighty* smokestack towers over the power plant.

moral, morale   "Moral" as a noun means "lesson." *Moral* as an adjective means "right conduct." The noun "morale" refers to a state of mind.

       What was the *moral* of the story?

       Stealing is a *moral* situation.

       Morale has been high since Tim Conners left the department.

nice   Vague word of approval. Use a more precise word.

VAGUE:	He did a *nice* job of cleaning the supply room.
PRECISE:	He did a *thorough* job of cleaning the supply room.

no account   Colloquial for "worthless."

no place   Colloquial for "nowhere."

COLLOQUIAL:	That lazy salesclerk was *no place* around.
GENERAL:	That lazy salesclerk was *nowhere* around.

nowhere near   Colloquial for "not nearly."

                                GENERAL: His report is *not nearly* finished.

number   See "amount."

off of   Colloquial for "off."

                                GENERAL: The boy fell *off* the counter.

OK, O.K., okay   Colloquial for "all right."

one another   See "each other."

ought   See "had ought."

party   See "individual."

perfect   This adjective has no comparative or superlative form. Anything is either perfect or it is not.

                                His score is perfect (not "more perfect" or "most perfect").

phenomena   Plural of "phenomenon."

piece   Colloquial for "a short distance."

                                COLLOQUIAL: She drove down the road a *piece*.
                                GENERAL: She drove down the road a *short distance*.

plenty   Illiterate as an adverb meaning "very."

                                ILLITERATE: I was *plenty* tired after taking inventory.
                                STANDARD: I was *very* tired after taking inventory.

p.m.   See "a.m."

prof   Colloquial for "professor."

raise, rise   "Raise," "raised," "raised" are transitive verbs, requiring a direct object.

> He wanted to *raise* the window.

"Rise," "rose," "risen" never take an object.

> He tried to *rise* from his seat to raise a window.

real   Colloquial as an adverb for *"very"* or other intensives.

COLLOQUIAL: He seemed *real* sure of himself.
GENERAL: He seemed *very* sure of himself.

said   Substandard for "previously mentioned."

SUBSTANDARD: He got in *said* car and drove away.
STANDARD: He got into the car I mentioned before and drove away.

same   Substandard as a pronoun except in legal language. The word "it" is preferable.

SUBSTANDARD: So I paid him the money and got a receipt for *same*.
STANDARD: So I paid him the money and got a receipt for *it*.

seldom ever,   Illiterate for "seldom," "seldom if ever," or "hardly
seldom or ever   ever."

INCORRECT: He *seldom ever* watches TV.
CORRECT: He *seldom* watches TV.

set, sit   "Set" is illiterate when used to mean "occupy a seat." "Set" means "place something in position."

CORRECT: They *set* the box on the floor.

"Sit" and "sat" mean "occupy a seat."

ILLITERATE: They *set* in the lounge most of the day.
STANDARD: They *sit* in the lounge most of the day.

shall, will   Interchangeable as auxiliary verbs to form the simple future.

                                               I will (shall) go.
                                               You will (shall) go.
                                               She will (shall) go.

should, would   "Should" is used as an auxiliary verb to indicate condition or obligation.

      If they *should* arrive early, we will have to be ready.
      I *should* have gathered more facts.

"Would" is used to indicate wish or customary action.

      Mr. Jackson *would* always be at his desk early.
      Would you please send a diagram?

should of   Illiterate for "should have."

      He should *have* (not *of*) checked the order.

sit   See "set."

so   Vague as a conjunction or a transitional adverb. "Because," "since," or "so that" are more exact.

FAULTY: I smelled smoke, *so* I looked in the lounge.

EXACT: *Because* I smelled smoke, I looked in the lounge.

FAULTY: We arrived early *so* we could be ready for the crowd.

EXACT: We arrived early *so that* we could be ready for the crowd.

"So" as an intensive must be followed by a qualifying clause of result (a "that" clause).

INCOMPLETE: He was *so* angry.

COMPLETE: He was *so* angry *that* he could hardly talk.

some	Illiterate for "somewhat." Colloquial for "unusual" or "remarkable."

ILLITERATE:	The medicine made her feel *some* better.
STANDARD:	The medicine made her feel *somewhat* better.
COLLOQUIAL:	That police dog was *some* animal!
GENERAL:	That police dog was an *unusual* animal.

someone, some one	See "anyone."
someplace	Colloquial for "somewhere."

COLLOQUIAL:	Those lost keys just had to be *someplace*.
GENERAL:	Those lost keys just had to be *somewhere*.

someway	Colloquial for "somehow."

COLLOQUIAL:	He will raise the money *someway*.
GENERAL:	He will raise the money *somehow*.
GENERAL:	He will raise the money *in some way*.

somewheres	Dialect for "somewhere."
sort	See "kind."
sort of, sort of a	See "kind of."
strata	Plural of "stratum."
suspicion	Dialect when used as a verb meaning "suspect."

We suspected (not *suspicioned*) that he was lying to us.

teach	See "learn."
theirself, theirselves	Illiterate for "themselves."

these kind, these sort   See "kind."

they   Vague and colloquial as an indefinite pronoun to mean people in general.

> VAGUE: At the YMCA, *they* treat people of all backgrounds alike.
>
> EXACT: At the YMCA, the members (or, the supervisors) treat people of all backgrounds alike.

thusly   A pretentious form of "thus."

true facts   "True" is redundant. All facts are true.

> These are the *known* facts.
>
> I suspect that what he reports as facts are not *truly* facts.

try and   Colloquial for "try to."

> COLLOQUIAL: They will *try and* finish the job on time.
>
> GENERAL: They will *try to* finish the job on time.

type   Illiterate for "type of." "Type" is not an adjective, but a noun.

> ILLITERATE: He does not like that *type* person.
>
> STANDARD: He does not like that *type of* person.

unique   "Unique" means "only one of a kind" and therefore cannot be compared.

> INCORRECT: I have never known a more *unique* person.
>
> CORRECT: He is unique.

want that   Illiterate for "want".

> ILLITERATE: He *wanted that* I should lend him ten dollars.
>
> STANDARD: He *wanted* me to lend him ten dollars.

ways   Colloquial for *"way"* or *"distance."*

                                  COLLOQUIAL: It's a long *ways* to Omaha.
                                  GENERAL: It's a long *way* to Omaha.

when   Incorrectly used to introduce definitions. See "in when."

where   Illiterate for "that." See "is where."

                                  ILLITERATE: I read in the newspaper *where* there is a famine in India.
                                  STANDARD: I read in the newspaper *that* there is a famine in India.

where . . . at   Illiterate for "where." Omit "at."

                                  INCORRECT: *Where* is the service garage *at*?
                                  CORRECT: *Where* is the service garage?

which, who, that   "Which" and "that" apply to things. "Who" and "that" apply to people.

while   Illiterate for "and" or "but." Vague for "although."

                                  ILLITERATE: Ann is a ceaseless typist, *while* I prefer to rest occasionally.
                                  STANDARD: Ann is a ceaseless typist, *but* I prefer to rest occasionally.
                                  VAGUE: *While* I disapprove of your method, I approve of your motive.
                                  IMPROVED: *Although* I disapprove of your method, I approve of your motive.

who   "Who" is used as a subject, or its equivalent, in its own clause. If the verb needs a subject, use *who.*

                                  He asked *who* I thought owned the place.
                                  He asked me *who* I thought I was.

whom   "Whom" is used as an object in its own clause. It is usually a direct object or an object of a preposition.

I asked her *whom* she wanted to see.
He asked me to *whom* he should give the check.

will See "shall."

won't hardly See "can't hardly."

worst way "In the worst way" is nonstandard for "*very much.*"

NON-STANDARD:	Betty wanted a new job *in the worst way.*
STANDARD:	Betty wanted a new job *very much.*

would See "*should.*"

wouldn't hardly See "*can't hardly.*"
would of Illiterate for "would have."

I *would have* (not *of*) arrived earlier if I hadn't had car trouble.

you Vague and colloquial when used as an indefinite pronoun.

VAGUE:	A person should value his friends, for you never know when you will need them.
GENERAL:	A person should value his friends, for he never knows when he may need them.

yourself See "herself."

OUTDATED EXPRESSIONS—CHECKLIST

above mentioned	as a matter of fact
above numbered	as of this date
according to our records	as per (your account)
acknowledge receipt of	as per our (agreement, request, letter)
advise (when you mean "tell" or "inform")	as regards
allow me to	as stated above (below)
and oblige	assuring you of our prompt attention

as the case may be
at an early date
at hand
at the earliest possible moment
at the present writing
at this writing
at your convenience
at your earliest convenience
attached find, attached please find
attached hereto
avail yourself of this opportunity
awaiting your further orders
awaiting your further reply
bank on
be assured
be that as it may
beg to (state, advise, inform,
   acknowledge, differ)
bring to our attention
by return mail
come to hand
contents noted
date of July 1
Dear Mesdames
Dear Sirs
deem it advisable
don't hesitate to (call, write)
due course
duly (credited, entered, noted)
e. g. (avoid this Latin abbreviation)
enclosed herewith
enclosed please find
enclosed you will find
esteemed
favor (meaning letter)
feel free to (write, call)
for your information
gone forward
has come to hand
henceforth
herewith
hitherto
I am (hoping to hear from you, I am)

i. e. (avoid this Latin abbreviation)
I have your letter of (date)
in accordance with (your request)
in answer to your letter (reply,
   response, reference)
in re
in reply wish to state
in the amount of
in this connection
I remain (hoping to hear from you,
   I remain)
it has come to my attention
kindly (when you mean please)
let me call your attention to
may I call your attention to
our Mr. Smith
party (when you mean an individual)
per (your request)
permit me to say
please be advised that
pleased be assured (informed)
please do not hesitate to
please feel free to
please find enclosed
prior to
pursuant to (your request, inquiry)
re
receipt is hereby acknowledged
re your letter of
recent date
referenced loan number
referring to (your letter)
regarding the above matter
regret to advise
reply to yours of
replying to your letter of
respectfully submitted (requested)
said (the said individual)
same (as a pronoun—
   thank you for the same)
subject loan
take pleasure
take the liberty

take this opportunity
thank your for your attention
   in this matter
thank you in advance
thanking you, we remain
the writer
the undersigned
this is to advise you
this will acknowledge receipt
to date

under separate cover
undersigned
under the above subject
valued (letter, account)
we are in receipt of
we regret to inform you that
we transmit herewith
whole ball of wax
wise (cost wise, product wise,
   personality wise)
you are hereby advised

CHECKLIST OF CLICHÉS

abreast of the times
acid test
after all is said and done
agree to disagree
all work and no play
a long felt need
among those present
an uphill climb
artistic temperament
as cold as ice
as luck would have it
a sumptuous repast
at a loss for words
at cross purposes
beat a hasty retreat
better half
better late than never
bitter end
black as ink
blazing inferno
blighted romance
blissfully ignorant
blushing bride
bolt from the blue
bored to death
bow to the inevitable
breathless silence
brilliant performance
bring order out of chaos
budding genius
burn the midnight oil

busy as a bee
by leaps and bounds
by the sweat of his brow
call it quits
caught like rats in a trap
center of attraction
checkered career
classic performance
cold as ice
conspicuous by his absence
cool as a cucumber
crack of dawn
deep, dark secret
depths of despair
dire necessity, dire straits
do justice to a meal
doomed to disappointment
downy couch
drastic action
dull, sickening thud
each and every
easier said than done
equal to the occasion
fair sex
familiar landmark
festive occasion
few and far between
filthy lucre
financially embarrassed
finger of suspicion
for a considerable time

for better or worse
goes without saying
good personality
go to rack and ruin
green as grass
green with envy
heartfelt thanks
herculean efforts
holy matrimony
ignorance is bliss
in all its glory
in conclusion
in the final analysis
in the last analysis
in this day and age
irony of fate
irony of life
it stands to reason
last but not least
long arm of the law
make hay while the sun shines
memorable occasion
method in his madness
mine of information
mother nature
music hath charms
neat as a pin
needless to say
never put off till tomorrow
   what you can do today
nick of time
nip and tuck
nip in the bud
none the worse for wear
on the ball
on the beam
partake of refreshments
picture of health
point with pride
poor but honest
powers that be
preside at the piano
proud possessor of
psychological moment

put in an appearance
quick as a flash
reign supreme
rendered a selection
rich and varied experience
ripe old age
rotten to the core
rough-and-tumble struggle
sadder but wiser
slowly but surely
smell a rat
sober as a judge
speculation was rife
square meal
steady as a rock
stellar role
straight from the shoulder
table groaned
tall, dark, and handsome
this day and age
tide of battle
tiny tots
tired but happy
too funny for words
to the bitter end
traffic slowed to a snail's pace
traffic snarled
truth is stranger than fiction
undercurrent of excitement
untiring efforts
variety is the spice of life
venture a suggestion
view with alarm
watery grave
weaker sex
wee small hours
wend our way
wheel of fortune
white as snow
without further ado
words fail to describe
work like a horse
work like a Trojan
wreak havoc

Glossary of Terms Frequently Used in Business

account payable a debt that is owed by an enterprise to someone else, and which hasn't been paid yet

account receivable a debt that is owed to an enterprise, for which payment hasn't yet been received

actuary a mathematician who calculates insurance risks and the premiums based on those risks

ad valorem Latin phrase meaning "according to value"—that is, not according to weight or number of units

agent one who acts in another's behalf, such as an advertising agent or an independent sales representative

amortization   reduction in a debt by periodic payments of the principal and interest

arbitration a method of settling disputes by having them mediated by an impartial third party

attachment a legal document authorizing the sheriff to seize a debtor's property for nonpayment of a debt

balloon payment a lump sum, usually large, payable at the end of a loan period after the periodic payments have been made

bankruptcy a legal means by which a debtor relinquishes claim to his assets and relieves himself of his financial obligations

bear market the stock market when prices are falling

bid the price offered by a willing buyer

blue chip a stock-market term for a stock whose products and financial record are of a high quality

boycott a refusal to have commercial dealings with someone or some organization

bull market the stock market when prices are rising

cartel an agreement between companies of various countries to fix the world price on a commodity and thereby control the world market in that commodity

caveat emptor Latin phrase meaning "let the buyer beware"

chattel any property or right except real estate property

closed shop a business firm within which all wage-earning employees are required to be union members

compound interest interest that is due, calculated by adding to the principal the interest already earned

cooperative   a type of corporation set up to gain the benefits of large-scale operation, in which every member, regardless of the size of his or her investment, has a single vote

creditor   one to whom a debt is owed by another (by the debtor)

debtor   one who owes a debt to another (to the creditor)

demand   the amount of goods that buyers are ready to buy at a specified price at a given time

demography   the study of population and its characteristics—for example, age distribution, birth and death rates, and percentages of married/single, urban/suburban/rural

depletion   the decreasing value of an asset that is being reduced by being converted into a salable product—like oil in the ground

dividend   the earnings that a corporation pays out to its stockholders in cash, property, more securities, or any combination of these

domicile   in law, a person can have many residences, but only one domicile, the place he or she declares to be home

efficiency ratio   the ratio of ends produced (that is, output) to the means used to produce it (that is, input)

encumbrance   a claim—a mortgage, a lien, and so on—against a specific piece of property

entrepreneur   originally a French word, meaning "an enterpriser," or owner and operator of a business

equity   the amount of one's actual ownership in a piece of property—for example, one's equity in a $50,000 property may be $10,000

escalator clause   a provision in an agreement for adjusting a price if the cost of living or some other index rises

escrow   an arrangement by two parties to clear their transaction through a designated third party (the escrower) so that neither of the two can take unfair advantage of the other or jeopardize down-payment monies before the transaction clears

estate   the total of one's property left at death

exclusive agent   an agent who has sole rights to handle a product or service within a designated market area

extrapolation   estimation of a future value through projection of the curve of past and present values into the future

featherbedding   practices by labor unions to maintain or increase artificially the number of jobs at a company

Federal Reserve System   a system of twelve central banks, created in 1912 and controlled by a Board of Governors in Washington, to which national banks must belong and in which they must keep certain percentages of their assets to assure the security of their depositors

fiscal   adjective that means "pertaining to financial affairs"

fixed asset   any property used in operating a business, which won't be consumed or converted into cash during that business's operation

foreclosure   the legal procedure by which a mortgage holder forces the sale of property in order to recover the money owed him or her

franchise   a right granted by a corporation, or by the government, to someone to carry on a certain kind of business in a certain location—for example, utilities companies are public franchises; your local McDonald's is a corporate franchise

frequency distribution   a distribution determining how many of each item have the same value—for example, the frequency distribution of kinds of automobiles sold in a week may be twelve full-sized, fifteen compacts, three station wagons, and so on.

futures   contracts whose fulfillment by delivery of the goods is not required until a specified time in the future; most commodity exchanges—wheat, coffee, pork bellies, and others—work on the basis of "future delivery" contracts, or "futures"

gold standard   the monetary system under which money can be converted into gold, and gold into money, at specified, fixed rates

goon   slang term for a person hired by a company to intimidate its workers and hold their demands in check

Gresham's Law   "Bad money drives out good"—when two kinds of money circulate in the same economy, people hoard, melt down, or export the more valuable of the two, thereby keeping the less valuable money in circulation

gross national product (GNP)   money value of the total output of goods and services in a national economy during a given period of time, usually a year

head tax   a tax per person

hidden assets   assets carried on a company's books at less than their fair market value; the value of the "hidden asset" is the market value of the asset minus its book value

implied warranty   a warranty that a buyer can assume to exist when nothing to the contrary has been said by the seller

impounds   the money required to be put into an account to assure later payment (usually of taxes) when payment is due

inflation   a period when the purchasing power of one's money is falling

interest   the price paid for using someone else's money—usually stipulated as a percentage of the money being used (the principal)

interpolation   determination of an intermediate value by the plotting of a curve between two already determined points

inventory   all the salable goods on hand at a company or a list of those goods

jobber   same as "wholesaler" or one who buys in relatively small (that is, "job") lots for resale to a retailer

joint venture   a business transaction or project carried out by individuals who join together for that purpose

judgment   the decision a court makes in a lawsuit

Keynesian economics   a school of economics based on the thoughts of John Maynard Keynes (1883-1946); the school basically disagrees with classical economics in holding that an equilibrium (position of rest) can be reached even though some economic resources are unemployed; the remedy advocated is government intervention in one form or another

kickback   payment by someone of part of his or her earnings to assure himself or herself favorable treatment or to evade some requirement

lease or leasehold a contract to possess something for a fixed period of time in return for payment of a certain sum of money

letter of credit a letter authorizing that credit be extended to the bearer of the letter and assuring that the signer will pay the resulting debt

liability a valid claim by a creditor against one's assets

line position a line position in a company is any job—from president to laborer—that involves work on production, as distinguished from a staff position (see **staff position**)

liquidation turning one's assets into cash by selling them off

local option the right of local communities (as provided by state constitution or legislative act) to regulate certain activities as it sees fit

lockout the closing of a plant by an employer to enforce demands against employees or to avoid the employees' demands against him

margin in commercial transactions, the difference between the purchase price paid by someone and the price he or she gets for it when it's resold

mats short term for "matrices"—printing devices that serve as dies from which printing plates are made

maturity date the date on which an obligation is due

maturity value the amount that must be paid on the date the obligation is due

mean the "average" that is computed by adding all the pertinent numerical items and dividing by the number of items. If these are the following values in a group—3, 6, 6, 6, 7, 8, 8, 9, 10—the mean is 7, the median is 7, and the mode is 6. (See **median** and **mode.**)

median the "average" that is calculated by identifying the middle value in a group of numerical values—that is, there are the same number of items above the median as below it.

mediation the process by which a third party (the mediator) attempts to bring two disputing parties into agreement

mixed economy a national economy that has some characteristics of free enterprise and some of socialism (that is, governmental determination)

mode the "average" in a series of items that is determined by identifying the value that occurs most frequently

monopoly sufficient control of an industry or a commodity to be able to control or regulate its price

mortgage a legal claim on a property, derived from having loaned money to the purchaser of that property

mutual fund an investment trust whose managers decide which securities to buy and sell

nationalization the acquisition and operation by the government of a business that was previously owned and operated privately

net sales the total of all sales minus returned sales

nonprofit corporation a corporation organized for charitable, educational, humanitarian, or other purposes not primarily aimed at making a profit

notary public an official appointed by a state to administer oaths, certify documents, and perform similar functions

obsolescence   the decrease in value of something because of lessened demand or new invention, but not because of wear and tear

open-end contract   a contract that allows a buyer to order additional units, on the same terms, without additional consent by the seller

operations research (o.r.)   a term embracing all research that aims to quantify and analyze business data by scientific method and thereby guide the decision-making process

option   a contract that gives someone rights with respect to property, usually the right to buy it or sell it at a stipulated price

overdraft   a draft (or check) drawn in excess of the amount a person has on deposit in the bank

over-the-counter market   name applied to security transactions that take place outside an organized stock exchange, usually through local brokers

partition   in law, the division of property among co-owners; where division in kind is impractical, the whole is sold and the proceeds divided

par value   the value printed on the face of a stock or bond certificate, the stated value

patent   the exclusive right to an invention

peak load   in public utilities, refers to the time of the week during which the greatest consumption of electricity or gas occurs

per capita   Latin phrase meaning "by the heads" or "per individual"

perquisite   compensation or privileges over and above one's regular salary; now sometimes called "perks"

personal property or personalty   all one's property other than interests in real estate

petty cash   a cash fund kept on hand for small disbursements

piggyback service   the loading of motor-truck trailers onto railroad flat cars

portfolio   a term used to refer to all the securities held by one person or institution

power of attorney   a written instrument empowering someone else to act as your agent and signatory

prima facie   Latin phrase meaning "at first sight" or "on the face of it"—prima facie evidence will carry a legal verdict if nothing valid is presented in rebuttal

pro rata   Latin phrase meaning "in proportion"

proxy   a written authorization designating someone else to cast your vote

quick asset   assets that can be turned into cash immediately with a minium loss

quitclaim deed   a deed in which the grantor (the person giving the deed) signs away whatever rights he or she has in a property, but without guaranteeing what rights, if any, he or she has

quorum   the number of persons legally necessary (in person or by proxy) to conduct a valid business meeting

rationing   any arrangement, usually under governmental regulation, limiting the quantity of product that can be purchased by a given class of buyers

real estate   an interest in land or things attached to land

rebate   a return of some part of the charges that have been paid out for a service or commodity

receivership   the court's appointing a person to administer the affairs of a person or firm unable to meet its debts when they are due

registry   the flag a ship flies, designating the country whose laws the ship is governed by

rescind   in law, to revoke an action or an agreement

residence   see **domicile**

retainer   the fee charged by a professional person for services in a matter

right-to-work laws   laws that outlaw closed shops

riparian rights   the rights of an owner whose land abuts water to the land under the water

rolling stock   in transportation, movable property such as trucks, locomotives, freight and passenger cars, and so on

royalties   the money paid out per unit of goods sold to the person or company who owns or holds rights to the goods

salary   money paid to an employee at a fixed weekly or monthly rate

scab   derogatory slang term for a strikebreaker: someone who takes employment at a company when its regular employees are on strike

secondary boycott   a boycott of someone who uses or sells the product made by the company who is the primary object of the boycott—for example, a boycott against supermarkets who sell grapes in order to harm their suppliers, the grape growers

securities   collective term applying to all kinds of written instruments of investment value: mortgages, stocks, bonds, certificates of ownership, and so on

seniority   preference given solely on the basis of how long someone has been on the job

slowdown   a form of strike in which workers stay on the job but deliberately reduce their efficiency

solvency   a business is solvent when its assets exceed its liabilities, and it can pay its debts as they become due

staff position   a position in the company whose holder does not work directly in management, production, or distribution but gives specialized assistance to "line" employees

stock split   the issuance of a number of new shares to replace each share of stock now outstanding

subcontract   an agreement by which the party who has contracted to do a job gets someone else to do part or all of the work on that job

subsidy   money granted, usually by the state, to support an enterprise or a program felt to be in the public interest

subvention   a grant or subsidy

supply   the amount of a good that sellers are ready to sell at a specified price in a given market at a given time

surcharge   a charge imposed in addition to another charge

surtax   a tax levied in addition to another tax

syndicate   any combination of persons or corporations joined to achieve a common business purpose

tariff   a customs duty or tax levied on goods as they enter (or leave) a country

title   evidence of ownership in something of value

trading down   action by a merchandiser in buying and selling cheaper goods in an effort to increase sales volume

trading up   handling goods of higher price in an effort to increase the profit margin per item

underwriter   anyone who guarantees to furnish a definite sum of money by a definite date to a business or government in return for an issue of bonds or stock; in insurance, one who assumes somebody's risk in return for a premium payment

unlawful detainer   legal device by which a landlord can have a tenant evicted when the tenant has overstayed the tenancy or broken the terms of the lease

value added   the difference between the purchase price of raw materials and the sale price of the product; in some places, value added is now subject to taxation—a value-added tax

vendee   the buyer of something

vendor   the seller of something

vested   a legal term to identify a right of immediate enjoyment or future enjoyment that cannot be allotted without consent of the party having that right

wages   the money paid to those who render their work on an hourly or daily basis

waiver   voluntary abandonment by a person of some or all of his or her right to something

wildcat strike   a strike called suddenly without the preliminary procedures called for by the union's contract with the company

windfall gain   a gain that was not foreseen

writ   a written order by the court directing a court officer to perform an act—for example, seizing a property

Index

Index of Model Letters